A
LITERARY
HISTORY
OF
SPAIN

A LITERARY HISTORY OF SPAIN

General Editor: R. O. JONES
Cervantes Professor of Spanish, King's College, University of London

THE MIDDLE AGES
by A. D. DEYERMOND
Professor of Spanish, Westfield College, University of London

THE GOLDEN AGE: PROSE AND POETRY
by R. O. JONES

THE GOLDEN AGE: DRAMA
by EDWARD M. WILSON
Professor of Spanish, University of Cambridge

and DUNCAN MOIR
Lecturer in Spanish, University of Southampton

THE EIGHTEENTH CENTURY
by NIGEL GLENDINNING
Professor of Spanish, Trinity College, University of Dublin

THE NINETEENTH CENTURY
by DONALD L. SHAW
Senior Lecturer in Hispanic Studies, University of Edinburgh

THE TWENTIETH CENTURY
by G. G. BROWN
Lecturer in Spanish, Queen Mary College, University of London

SPANISH AMERICAN LITERATURE
SINCE INDEPENDENCE
by JEAN FRANCO
Professor of Latin American Literature, University of Essex

CATALAN LITERATURE
by ARTHUR TERRY
Professor of Spanish, The Queen's University, Belfast

THE GOLDEN AGE
DRAMA

1492–1700

A LITERARY
HISTORY OF SPAIN

THE GOLDEN AGE
DRAMA
1492–1700

EDWARD M. WILSON
Professor of Spanish, University of Cambridge

DUNCAN MOIR
Lecturer in Spanish, University of Southampton

LONDON · ERNEST BENN LIMITED

NEW YORK · BARNES & NOBLE INC

First published 1971 by Ernest Benn Limited

Bouverie House Fleet Street London EC4

and Barnes & Noble Inc. 105 Fifth Avenue New York 10003

Distributed in Canada by

The General Publishing Company Limited Toronto

© Edward M. Wilson and Duncan Moir 1971

Printed in Great Britain

ISBN *Library* 0 510-32263-8

0-389-04193-9 (USA)

Paperback 0 510-32264-6

Paperback 0-389-04194-7 (USA)

FOREWORD BY THE GENERAL EDITOR

SPANISH, the language of what was in its day the greatest of European powers, became the common tongue of the most far-flung Empire the world had until then seen. Today in number of speakers, Spanish is one of the world's major languages. The literature written in Spanish is correspondingly rich. The earliest European lyrics in a post-classical vernacular that we know of (if we except Welsh and Irish) were written in Spain; the modern novel was born there; there too was written some of the greatest European poetry and drama; and some of the most interesting works of our time are being written in Spanish.

Nevertheless, this new history may require some explanation and even justification. Our justification is that a new and up-to-date English-language history seemed called for to serve the increasing interest now being taken in Spanish. There have been other English-language histories in the past, some of them very good, but none on this scale.

Every history is a compromise between aims difficult or even impossible to reconcile. This one is no exception. While imaginative literature is our main concern, we have tried to relate that literature to the society in and for which it was written, but without subordinating criticism to amateur sociology. Since not everything could be given equal attention (even if it were desirable to do so) we have concentrated on those writers and works of manifestly outstanding artistic importance to us their modern readers, with the inevitable consequence that many interesting minor writers are reduced to names and dates, and the even lesser are often not mentioned at all. Though we have tried also to provide a usable work of general reference, we offer the history primarily as a guide to the understanding and appreciation of what we consider of greatest value in the literatures of Spain and Spanish America.

Beyond a necessary minimum, no attempt has been made to arrive at uniform criteria; the history displays therefore the variety of approach and opinion that is to be found in a good university department of literature, a variety which we hope will prove stimulating. Each section takes account of the accepted works of scholarship in its field, but we do not offer our history as a grey consensus of received opinion: each contributor has imposed his own interpretation to the extent that this could be supported with solid scholarship and argument.

Though the literature of Spanish America is not to be regarded simply as an offshoot of the literature of Spain, it seemed natural to link the two in our history since Spanish civilisation has left an indelible stamp on the Americas. Since Catalonia has been so long a part of Spain it seemed equally justified to include Catalan literature, an important influence on Spanish literature at certain times, and a highly interesting literature in its own right.

The bibliographies are not meant to be exhaustive. They are intended only as a guide to further reading. For more exhaustive inquiry recourse should be had to general bibliographies such as that by J. Simón Díaz.

R. O. J.

PREFACE

IN THIS VOLUME spelling has been generally modernised, except for certain phonetic features which it was desirable to retain.

This volume should be read in conjunction with the second volume in this Literary History: *The Golden Age: Prose and Poetry, the Sixteenth and Seventeenth Centuries,* which deals with the same period under another aspect.

Chapter 6, on Calderón, is the work of Edward M. Wilson. The rest of the volume has been written by Duncan Moir.

Cambridge,   E. M. W.
Southampton,   D. W. M.
March 1971

CONTENTS

LIST OF ABBREVIATIONS

Actas I	Actas del Primer Congreso Internacional de Hispanistas (Oxford, 1964)
Actas II	Actas del Segundo Congreso Internacional de Hispanistas (Nijmegen, 1967)
AIUN	Annali dell'Istituto Universitario Orientale, Naples
AUMad	Anales de la Universidad de Madrid
BAE	Biblioteca de Autores Españoles
BBMP	Boletín de la Biblioteca de Menéndez Pelayo
BH	Bulletin Hispanique
BHS	Bulletin of Hispanic Studies
BRABLB	Boletín de la Real Academia de Buenas Letras de Barcelona
BRAE	Boletín de la Real Academia Española
CC	Clásicos Castellanos
C Ca	Clásicos Castalia
CHA	Cuadernos Hispano-Americanos
FMLS	Forum for Modern Language Studies
H Balt	Hispania
Hisp	Hispanófila
HR	Hispanic Review
LR	Les Lettres Romanes
MLN	Modern Language Notes
MLR	Modern Language Review
MP	Modern Philology
MRAE	Memorias de la Real Academia Española
N	Neophilologus
NBAE	Nueva Biblioteca de Autores Españoles
NRFH	Nueva Revista de Filología Hispánica
PMLA	Publications of the Modern Language Association of America
PQ	Philological Quarterly
RABM	Revista de Archivos, Bibliotecas y Museos

RBAM	Revista de la Biblioteca, Archivo y Museo de Madrid
RdeL	Revista de Literatura
RF	Romanische Forschungen
RFE	Revista de Filología Española
RH	Revue Hispanique
RJahr	Romanistisches Jahrbuch
RN	Romanic Notes
RPhil	Romance Philology
RR	Romanic Review
Sef	Sefarad
Seg	Segismundo
SPh	Studies in Philology
Sym	Symposium
TCBS	Transactions of the Cambridge Bibliographical Society
TDR	Tulane Drama Review

INTRODUCTION

THE SPANISH DRAMA OF THE GOLDEN AGE was one of the most vigorous and glorious branches of the European theatre in the sixteenth and seventeenth centuries. It reflected the tastes, ideals, and preoccupations of a nation which rose swiftly to a position of immense power and wealth as the possessor of a vast empire in the Americas, the Low Countries, and Italy and to enjoy, for a spell, political primacy in Europe. The first plays of the Golden Age may have been written in Castile as early as 1492, the year in which Columbus discovered America and Ferdinand and Isabella recaptured the kingdom of Granada from the Moslems to complete the unification of Christian Spain. During the reigns of Charles V, Holy Roman Emperor from 1519 to 1558 and ruler of Spain and her empire as Charles I from 1516 to 1556, and of his son Philip II, who died in 1598, dramatists writing in Spanish gradually acquired new techniques and widened the range of subject-matter of their plays; and the two great Spanish dramatic art-forms, the *comedia* and the *auto sacramental*, emerged as results of continuous experimentation. The drama reached its greatest heights during the reigns of Philip III (1598-1621) and Philip IV (1621-1665), when Spain's strength and political influence as a nation were rapidly declining, but when Spanish literature and culture continued to flourish and to exert considerable influence in Europe. In the gloomy reign of Charles II (1665-1700), when the political, social, and economic decadence of Spain was marked, the output of new plays was much reduced, although a few playwrights still created works of merit, even after the death of the great Calderón in 1681.

Most Spanish dramatists wrote for a very wide range of society. From the middle of the sixteenth century companies of itinerant actors wandered from town to town and village to village, performing wherever an audience could be assembled. By the end of that century, all the main towns and cities of Spain had fixed playhouses, the *corrales*, with standing room for the poorest spectators, seats and gallery-boxes for the rich, and some stage-machinery. From the last years of the sixteenth century Madrid became the main centre of drama in Spain and the provincial centres tended to decline. There was some dramatic activity in the colonies which are now Mexico and Peru, mainly dependent on plays written in Spain. In the 1630s the long tradition of expensive spectacle at the Courts of Spanish monarchs and great nobles culminated in the construction of the most elaborate of Spanish theatres, the Italianate Coliseo in the royal family's pleasure-palace of the Buen Retiro, just outside Madrid, and in it complicated machine-plays were often performed. The royal palaces also had simpler stages for less complicated plays. A suitable play might pass from the Court to the public theatres or vice-versa. And the religious allegorical *autos sacramentales* for the celebration of the festival of Corpus Christi were performed in Madrid not only at the royal palace but also on stages in the streets for the populace. Thus the drama of the Golden Age tended to have a notable universality of appeal. It was, in fact, at its best a markedly didactic drama in which educated writers used plays to convey moral and political lessons to kings, nobles, and commoners alike, often with considerable subtlety. Pleasure was put to the service of doctrine, as Horace had prescribed.

The mature Spanish drama, because of its relative liberty of form, bore a closer resemblance to the English drama of the times than to the French. The Spanish playwrights of the seventeenth century, like the Elizabethans and Jacobeans, did not consider it essential to observe the neo-classical unities of time and place, although they did sometimes use these unities to increase dramatic tension, and they otherwise tended to follow several fundamental classical dramatic precepts, but not the five-act division, which in Spain was by their time reduced to the definitive three-act form of the *comedia*. The most striking aspect in which the Spanish drama stands apart from both the other great seventeenth-century national dramas is in its rich polymetric system, perfected by Lope de Vega. Within each play different metres and strophes were employed to express different types of dramatic scene, situation, or emotion. The system gave complex and melodious variations of tone in plays which might be comedies, tragedies, or a blend of serious and comic elements. Spain in this period produced many secular and religious plays which are intellectually stimulating, fine as poetry, and deeply moving, an important source of inspiration to playwrights in other countries up to the present day.

Chapter 1

FROM ENCINA TO THE MIDDLE OF THE SIXTEENTH CENTURY

THE INITIATOR AND PROGENITOR of the Renaissance drama in Spain was Juan del Encina (1468?-1530?). Son of a shoemaker in Salamanca, the future poet, musician, and playwright became a chorister in the Cathedral there, studied at the University of Salamanca, graduated as Bachelor of Law, and, after taking Minor Orders, perhaps as early as 1492 he entered the household of the duque de Alba, whom he served for several years as courtier, musician, poet, dramatist, and actor.[1] In 1498 he failed to obtain the vacant post of *cantor* at the Cathedral of Salamanca, which was given to his rival and dramatic disciple Lucas Fernández. Perhaps embittered by this frustration of his hopes, Encina left Spain for Rome, where his various talents would be better appreciated than at home. Indeed, he appears to have rapidly become a favourite, 'continus comensalis noster', of the Spanish Pope, Alexander VI. In 1500, Encina was granted benefices of several churches in the diocese of Salamanca, and two years later he contrived to be appointed *cantor* of the Cathedral, though Lucas Fernández, supported by the chapter, apparently continued to occupy the post. Encina did not leave Rome till 1509, when, under Pope Julius II, he was made archdeacon and canon of the Cathedral of Malaga, despite the fact that he had not been priested. Between 1512 and 1518 Encina returned three times more from Spain to Rome, where he obtained from Pope Leo X the position of prior of the Cathedral of León. In León he spent his last years and died at the end of 1529 or the beginning of 1530.

Encina's first eight dramatic *églogas* were printed in the first edition of his poetic works, the *Cancionero* (Salamanca, 1496), a collection which was to be issued in six more editions up to 1516 and exercise a considerable influence on the dramatists of the first half of the sixteenth century. To the editions of 1507 and 1509 were added the famous *Égloga de las grandes lluvias* and another play on the power of love which had been performed before Prince Juan of Castile, probably at

Alba de Tormes or in Salamanca; the eclogue of *Fileno, Zambardo y Cardonio*; and the *Auto del repelón*, a lively play whose authorship has been disputed (*Églogas* XII and XIII in the most recent modern editions by Humberto López Morales).[2] Two plays, the *Égloga de Cristino y Febea* (*Égloga* XI in Morales) and the *Égloga de Plácida y Vitoriano* (*Égloga* XIV in Morales), were printed separately during Encina's lifetime as *obras sueltas*.[3]

Encina's early playlets were probably all performed, sometimes in pairs, by the poet himself and other courtiers, in the ducal palace at Alba de Tormes. Most of them formed part of the court celebrations for Christmas, Shrovetide, and Holy Week. Except for the two *representaciones* for Easter, which have no rustic characters, they are all pastoral plays, simple in structure but cunning in artifice. They show no signs of Italian influence, although pastoral plays, likewise highly artificial and laden with flattering allusions to powerful patrons, were becoming fashionable in Italian Courts at the end of the fifteenth century. That the first modern Spanish court dramatist should conceive his plays as *églogas* is not surprising; there were several medieval traditions to guide him, apart from the bucolic poetry of Encina's beloved Virgil, from whom he derived the title of eclogues for his plays. Moreover, Encina was providing entertainment for a country aristocrat, and the great duke, with his family and noble guests, would be readily amused by deftly stylised rustic buffoonery and quaint language presented to them by servants who were themselves of peasant origin. Peasants have become courtiers who, on the stage, become peasants again and may even —in the course of a pair of playlets performed one after the other—turn back into courtiers, or even into evangelists! Though we may find no profound significance in the changes of identity assumed by Encina and his fellow-actors in the action of an introductory *égloga* and its successor, or even within a single *égloga*, we can easily detect, in all these plays, the intimate family pleasures of the game of charades.[4]

Only three of Encina's plays follow the familiar ritualistic pattern of the medieval European Christian drama: the second of the two Christmas eclogues which may have been performed as early as 1492 or as late as 1495 (*Égloga* II) and the solemn and moving pair on the passion, death, and resurrection of Christ, played in one of the years between 1493 and 1496 (*Églogas* III and IV). The rest of Encina's drama shows a marked deviation from the strictest lines of the medieval religious drama, and the subject-matter of most of his plays is mainly secular and even, on occasion, unashamedly and gaily pagan. Even in *Égloga* II the peasant-evangelists Juan and Mateo turn excitedly, with Marco and

Lucas, to the worship of the new-born Divine Master only after they have demonstrated at length, in the introductory *Égloga* I, their willingness and eagerness to serve the ideal worldly master and mistress, the duque and duquesa de Alba. And in the *Égloga de las grandes lluvias* (*Égloga* IX; 1498?) the angel's song, announcing the birth of the Saviour, comes only after a long, though not irrelevant, account of the misfortunes of four storm-tossed shepherds and in the middle of their game of 'odds and evens'. Apart from his Easter plays, in the early eclogues Encina wisely gives more obvious emphasis to innocent entertainment than he does to edification. The two delightfully spirited Shrovetide plays, performed as a pair in one of the years between 1494 and 1496 (*Églogas* V and VI), with their shepherds vigorously gormandising before the arrival of Lent and as a celebration of their joy at discovering that the duke will not have to go to war, are fine examples of this attitude.[5] So is the famous *Auto del repelón*, 'the hair-pulling play', in which two frightened shepherds relate their experiences in a students' raid on the market and finally wreak vengeance on a student who has found them in their hiding-place. So too are the jolly transformation-plays in which a courtier turns shepherd because of his love for a shepherdess and later turns back to the courtly life with the girl changed into a well-dressed lady; they are followed by his old shepherd-rival and the latter's wife, also in their Sunday clothes and eager to sample the pleasures of the Court (*Églogas* VII and VIII). And so is the tale of Cristino, who tries to live the religious life of a hermit but is soon, by the machinations of an outraged Cupid, made to abandon it for love of the temptress Febea (*Égloga* XI in Morales). It is, in fact, a mistake to regard Encina's drama simply as a development out of and a secularisation of religious drama. He owes less to the church plays than to the agile and frolicsome art of the fifteenth-century court mummers, the *momos*, who bounded into banqueting halls on festive occasions to perform playlets and execute a final dance, often bearing, as they entered, gifts for their patrons and for honoured guests, as Encina himself bears them to the duchess in the guise of Juan in *Égloga* I and in the role of Mingo in *Égloga* VIII.[6] In the texts of Encina's plays the final dance is represented by the *villancico*, an exit song.

The plot-structure of Encina's early plays is simple. So also is their strophic structure; they are all, from the beginning to the point at which the *villancico* starts, monostrophic. Nevertheless, simplicity in plot and strophic pattern does not indicate either dramatic or poetic primitiveness. These plays are the work of a highly skilled versifier and a good poet, a fine musician who could utilise a wide range of rhythms in his verse as well as in his melodies, and an arch-mummer who knew how to capture and hold the interest of an educated audience. Encina could not have worked out plays with neatly contrived *protasis*, *epitasis*, and *catastrophe* on a neo-Aristotelian model half a century before the *Poetics* became widely known in Europe, but he was sufficiently skilled to produce effective contrasts and tensions, which are the essence of good drama. Many modern scholars have seemed reluctant to perceive the wide variety of the ways in which he created and built up suspense, expectation, and excitement in his plays: by changes of moods, emotions, and attitudes, by clashes of temperament and contrasts of character, by quarrels and arguments, by the use of the unexpected, by delays, by repeated words, questions, and urgent commands, often in terse, cunning language:

> Digo, digo que Él es vid,
> vida, verdad y camino.
> Todos, todos le servid,
> todos comigo decid
> qu'Él es el verbo divino.   (*Égloga* II)

Encina's characters themselves are simply drawn, but they do all they need to do: they clash and contrast as much as is necessary to provide tension in such brief plays; they show control and economy, not lack of imagination, in their creator. And, when we make the effort to re-create the eclogues in our mind, they do hold our interest because of their vitality. The two Holy Week plays have been described as cold and lifeless, but, in fact, the frequent, rapid changes of emotion in *Égloga* III are carefully contrived and orchestrated as they gradually mount to their exultant climax, and even the least varied and least obviously alive of Encina's dramas, *Égloga* IV, can genuinely move us, with its solemn, melodious poetry and the struggles within each of the characters between anguish and the surging joy which finally triumphs.

The vogue of Encina's *églogas* and those of his imitators up to the middle of the sixteenth century firmly established the type of the comic shepherd as an important stock character of the theatre of the Golden Age. In Encina's plays many of the basic traits of the stage rustic become fixed: he is sometimes bashful in the presence of aristocrats, but he is proud of his lineage and of country life as opposed to life at Court; he is also proud of, and at times boastful about, his own skill at flute-playing, dancing, singing, and sports, occupations which he naturally tends to prefer to the boring business of tending his flocks; he may be somewhat lazy, in fact; he may, like Piernicurto in the *Auto del repelón*, brag about his bravery when in reality he has been chicken-hearted, but he may equally well be rash, like Pelayo, who challenges Cupid in *Égloga* x. He may be prepared to guzzle and drink prodigiously at Shrovetide, but López Morales has pointed out the injustice of over-generalising and of describing all the shepherds in Encina as habitual gluttons, cowards, sluggards, and fools.[7] The peasant *bobo* is really a creation of mid-sixteenth-century drama. Most of Encina's rustics are given a certain marked human dignity which seems to forecast Lope de Vega's Peribáñez and Calderón's Pedro Crespo. As far as their comicality is concerned, Encina's shepherds' language is supremely important. They utter a type of the quaint and stylised rustic speech which had earlier been used in the *Coplas de Mingo Revulgo* and the *Vita Christi*. It varies from author to author in some of its characteristics and is generally known as *sayagués*, because of a mistaken association with the district of Sayago (Zamora), whose inhabitants were reputed to speak a particularly execrable form of Spanish.[8] Because of the popularity of his *Cancionero*, Encina became a model for other dramatists writing pastoral dialogue, and considerably watered-down versions of his and his contemporaries' gusty rustic language were still the norm for comical stage peasants' speech in the seventeenth century.

For some purists, the 'truly Renaissance' playwriting of Encina did not begin until he started to imitate Italian models and techniques in the second part of his career. The pagan adventures of the *Égloga de Cristino y Febea* have been taken by various critics to be Italianate in inspiration. Nevertheless, no reliable indication of any Italian source for this play has been given; technically it shows no change from the dramatist's early playlets, although it is longer than any of them;[9] and the presumption that because it contains a little very mild anti-clerical satire it must have been written outside Spain is amusingly ill-founded. Encina may well have written this play in Rome, but there is nothing specifically Italian in it. He appears, in reality, to have composed only two plays that clearly show Italian influence. One of these, the *Égloga de Fileno, Zambardo y Cardonio*, is in part a close adaptation of the second eclogue of his contemporary, the Italian poet Antonio Tebaldeo.[10] The play, which in turn may have been a source of Garcilaso's *Égloga segunda*, concerns the desperation of Fileno over his unrequited love for Cefira, his two friends' inability to help him in his plight, and his consequent suicide. Written in eighty-eight resonant *coplas de arte mayor*, it is the first tragedy in the drama of the Golden Age. Encina's other Italianate play, the most ambitious of all his *églogas*, was that of *Plácida y Vitoriano*, a complex, polymetric work almost as long as the three-act *comedias* of the seventeenth century. This may have been the play by Encina which, according to a letter of the time, was the entertainment given in Rome on 6 January 1513, at the house of the archbishop of Arborea before the Spanish ambassador, Federico Gonzaga, and a large gathering of the Spanish colony:

> la comedia fu recitata in lingua castigliana, composta da Joanne de Lenzina qual intervenne lui adir le forze et accidenti di amore; et per quanto dicono spagnoli non fu molto bella, et poco delettò al S. Federico.[11]

Encina's personal appearance to speak of the power and the accidents of love might mean his acting a part in any one of several of his plays which contain such expositions. But the idea that the play was *Plácida y Vitoriano* is particularly seductive; Moratín mentioned an edition of it printed in Rome in 1514, now untraceable; the prologue declaimed by Gil Cestero, with its detailed outline of the plot and the fatal power of love in it (an explanatory technique learned from the *introito y argumento* sequence used by Torres Naharro to introduce his plays to his Roman audiences from around 1508), is in its first lines remarkably like the initial parts of the roles of Juan and Mingo which Encina wrote for himself in *Églogas* I and VIII, and Gil's action in the play itself is exactly the kind of part that Encina's early plays suggest he most enjoyed performing. Whatever the Spanish colony at Rome may have thought of it, *Plácida y Vitoriano* is varied, interesting, and usually satisfactorily tense, with the rustics Gil and Pascual providing comic relief, and with a scene derived from *La Celestina* as a sordid contrast to the main action. The noble Plácida, thinking that she has been abandoned by Vitoriano, commits suicide, and her lover, having found her dead, is about to kill himself when, in the tradition of certain Euripidean tragedies and of the Italian pastoral drama, the goddess Venus intervenes and has her brother Mercury revive the girl's corpse to provide a happy ending.

Lucas Fernández (1474?-1542), who robbed Encina of the post of *cantor* at Salamanca in 1498, was apparently less restless than his rival. Although he may have been at the Portuguese Court for some time around 1502,[12] he appears to have spent almost all his life in Salamanca, where he was Professor of Music at the university from 1522 until his death. His *Farsas y églogas* (Salamanca, 1514) are seven in number, one being a simple dialogue to be sung by two shepherds on love and its effects. Fernández may have started to write his plays around 1496. He knew the *églogas* of Encina and alluded to several of them in complimentary terms in his own *Farsa o cuasi comedia del soldado*. Encina is, in fact, clearly the principal model he used when he wrote his plays. His two Christmas eclogues are very similar to the *Égloga de las grandes lluvias* and follow Encina's device of suddenly introducing the news of Christ's birth late in the action of a hitherto secular playlet. Fernández's three amorous comedies, however, show some promising innovations. The *Comedia de Bras-Gil y Berenguella* is an amusing betrothal play which presents the first comical *viejo* of the Golden Age drama, Juan-Benito, Berenguella's crusty but goodhearted grandfather. The *Farsa o cuasi comedia de una doncella, un pastor y un caballero*, which ends with two *villancicos*, shows not a nobleman falling in love with a shepherdess but a shepherd falling into unrequited love for a courtly young lady, perhaps the first in the Spanish pastoral drama, as the play may well have been written before *Plácida y Vitoriano*. And the *Farsa o cuasi comedia del soldado* introduces amongst its peasants a boastful soldier, apparently derived from Centurio of *La Celestina*, in the long tradition of the Plautine *miles gloriosus*. There is a good deal of knockabout in Fernández's secular plays. His shepherds tend to be earthier, coarser, less dignified, more violently quarrelsome, and more spiritedly vituperative than Encina's. They speak a rather thicker, more colourful, and often less decorous form of *sayagués*, very like Encina's rustic language but probably closer to the *charro* spoken in reality by the peasants around Salamanca. And Fernández's rustics are more insistent on the details of their lineage.[13]

The most original of Fernández's plays, and perhaps his last, is his *Auto de la Pasión* for Holy Week, which is much longer than Encina's two Easter plays placed end to end and surpasses them both in dramatic quality. This *auto*, which may have been performed in a church, perhaps the Cathedral at Salamanca,[14] is the first conversion-play of the Golden Age drama and a notable predecessor of the seventeenth-century *comedias de santo*. It concerns the reactions of Dionysius the Areopagite[15] to what he gradually learns about Christ and about the meaning, causes, and circumstances of His passion and death. At the beginning, Dionysius is a troubled and questioning pagan intellectual; by the time the first quarter of the play has passed, he is a convinced but not fully informed Christian, still seeking information; at the end he is shown the sepulchre of Christ and, with the other characters, Peter, Matthew, the three Maries, and Jeremiah, he kneels to sing songs to the Saviour.[16]

The second dramatist who was to benefit from Encina's creation of the modern Spanish drama was that extraordinarily talented playwright, one of the bilingual Portuguese writers of the sixteenth century, Gil Vicente (c. 1465-1537?). If Encina was a skilful poet with a keen sense of how to create dramatic tension, Gil Vicente was, as Dámaso Alonso has observed, the most sensitive and delicate of all the dramatic poets of the Golden Age, and he has been described as the greatest dramatist in Europe before Shakespeare.[17] The exact date and the place of Vicente's birth are unknown. He almost certainly was a goldsmith and became, in 1513, mestre da balança of the Royal Mint in Lisbon; he was dramatist at the Portuguese Court from 1502 to 1536, the first literary playwright in the history of the Portuguese theatre, under Manuel I and John III. Writing for the bilingual Court of Portuguese kings who had Spanish wives, Vicente composed eleven plays in Spanish, at least seventeen in Portuguese,[18] and sixteen in a mixture of both. Some of his plays were printed separately during his lifetime and after his death; all the forty-four which are generally recognised to be his were printed together in the *Copilaçam de todalas obras de Gil Vicente* (Lisbon, 1562), of which a second edition was issued in 1586. Fortunately for the literary historian, the *Copilaçam* gives a careful though not always accurate account of the place, date, and occasion of the first performance of almost all the plays.

The first important sources of inspiration for Gil Vicente's development as a dramatist appear to have been the mummeries of the Portuguese Court, Encina's *Cancionero*, and at least one or two of Lucas Fernández's plays in manuscript.[19] Vicente did not take long to surpass the dramatic art of his Salamantine models. Waldron has divided Vicente's dramatic works into five main groups: the first group is his early rustic plays in the style of Encina and Fernández; 'after Vicente had evolved beyond his early dramatic models and produced his own type of morality, farce, allegorical fantasy and romantic comedy, he wrote plays conforming to each of these types, or combining several of them, until the end of his career'.[20] His plays in Spanish represent most of these types; in this study we deal mainly with these Spanish works.

Vicente's first three plays, all in Spanish, show him developing and making variations on the early type of play written by Encina and Fernández. The *Auto da Visitação*, often called the *Monólogo do Vaqueiro*, was the brief monologue in sayagués with which Vicente started his career as a dramatist. Performed by the playwright himself before Queen Maria on 7 June 1502, the day after the birth of her son Prince John, this gay playlet is very like Encina's *Églogas* I and VIII; it presents a flustered and amazed cowherd who has bustled his way through the palace guard into the Queen's chamber to see whether she has yet borne her child; after dancing for joy, he summons other herdsmen to present eggs, milk, cheese, and honey to the baby. The *Auto pastoril castelhano*, which was produced for Christmas 1502, shows a reserved shepherd, Gil, who, on hearing the Angel's song which his companions do not hear, leads them to the manger to adore the Child and the Virgin. His experience has transformed Gil; all of a sudden he displays a fund of biblical knowledge on Christ and Mary which neither his friends nor he himself knew he possessed. The *Auto dos Reis Magos* was performed on Epiphany 1503. A shepherd, Gregorio, who has got lost on his way to see the Child, asks a lazy friar where he must go; the friar does not know, and the problem is solved only after a gentleman from the company of the Three Kings has appeared to ask if he is on the right road to Bethlehem and told them of the star and of his masters, when the Magi enter to sing a *villancico* and give presents to the King and Queen. Vicente also wrote a very short play in Spanish for Corpus Christi 1504, the *Auto de S. Martinho*, on St Martin's cutting his cloak and sharing it with a poor man.

Just how far Gil Vicente developed beyond the art of Encina and Fernández in the next decade is clear when we consider the celebrated *Auto da Sibila Casandra*, which was probably performed in December 1513. This play is one of Vicente's masterpieces. Not only is it the best Christmas play ever written in Spanish; it is also the funniest Spanish play of the whole of the sixteenth century. The *Auto da Sibila Casandra*, with its careful, but in one important way misleading, stage directions, is an excellent example of a play whose total dramatic subtlety is not apparent when we first read it on the printed page. It demands, more than most plays, lively re-creation in the mind as spectacle. The reader can enjoy a moment of exquisite hilarity which the sixteenth-century spectators would not, at that moment, have fully appreciated, when he suddenly reads of Solomon's entrance with Isaiah, Moses, and Abraham, all four singing a *folía*:

> ¡Sañosa está la niña!
> ¡Ay Dios! ¿quién le hablaría?

Here Gil Vicente's first audience would have seen only four shepherds or farmers. The play uses Encina's technique of metamorphosis of characters much more cunningly and humorously than Encina ever did. To enjoy it to the full we must try to forget about the directions in the text which, at the beginning of each speech, tell us who each character actually is, or who he or she will become, if we are to appreciate the unexpected and extremely amusing revelations of identity which Vicente prepared for his first audience. The obstinate shepherdess of the beginning of the play, the girl who refuses to marry, is called Casandra in line 23, but only halfway through the performance would the audience have realised that she is the silly sibyl who believes she will be the virgin mother of Christ. Her aunts are named as Erutea, Peresica, and Cimeria before they appear, but it is only much later that most of the spectators could have understood that they also are sibyls. Moses reveals his identity soon after his entrance, but it must have taken the audience some time to realise that his companions were Isaiah and Abraham. The most amusing revelation is that of the identity of Casandra's suitor. Shocked by the girl's presumption that she will be the virgin mother, he tells her

> Casandra, según que muestra
> esa respuesta
> tan fuera de conclusión,
> tú loca, yo Salomón,
> dame razón:
>   ¿qué vida fora la nuestra?

Solomon's words contrast his proverbial wisdom with Casandra's foolishness. As Spitzer observed, the play's central theme is that of prophecy: 'all the dramatis personae assume the role of "prophets" and all, except Casandra, are prophets of Christ's birth from Mary'.[21] The senior sibyls and the biblical prophets all know *that* the Redeemer will be born of a virgin, but none knows *when* he will be born. Isaiah knows very well when the Last Judgment will be made, but, like all the other seers, he is surprised by the 'discovery' of the Nativity scene and the angels' sudden burst of song which puts an end to his description of the signs of Judgment (which insinuate Vicente's own social preoccupations) and the sonorous predictions of the wrath to come. This play begins lightheartedly; gradually its country people take on symbolic attributes so that the ending is serious and devotional. Strands from several sources, liturgical, literary, and artistic, have been woven together by the playwright, as Révah has shown,[22] to provide one of the most satisfying Spanish dramas of the Golden Age.

Vicente's *Auto dos Quatro Tempos*, which may have been performed in 1511 or 1516, is another play which shows an imaginative advance beyond the limits of Encina's formulae. Here we have allegorical figures. As Asensio has pointed out, this *auto* is a dramatic and lyrical commentary on the *Laudate dominum de caelis*, the *Benedicite*, and the *Te Deum*, which provided the playwright with an excellent opportunity to

contrive that an even wider range of characters than the pagan and
biblical prophets of the *Sibila Casandra* should worship the new-born
Child on the stage; in this play, the manger is visited in turn by four
angels, the four seasons (skilfully contrasted), the god Jupiter, and King
David in shepherd's dress.[23] In its structure the *auto* is simple; its
poetry is magnificent.

Gil Vicente's most internationally famous plays are the trilogy of the
Barcas, the first two *autos* of which are in Portuguese and the third, the
Auto da Barca da Glória, in Spanish.[24] For a full appreciation of their
artistry, these should be read in sequence. Conceived in the traditions of
Charon the ferryman of the Styx, of Christ and St Ursula's ship, and
of Sebastian Brant's celebrated *Narrenschiff* or *Ship of Fools* (1494),
which was repeatedly imitated all over Europe during the Renaissance
and long after it,[25] the three *Barcas* vigorously present a remarkably
wide gallery of witty and sharp social and anti-clerical satire. The
barcas themselves, in each of the three plays, are two boats moored to
the shore of an arm of the sea. The characters who must board one boat
or the other are the souls of men and women who have just died. One
boat, which is bound for Hell, is captained by a devil, a remarkably
lively barker who does his best to make sure that his craft's complement
of oarsmen is made up. The other boat is commanded by an angel, who
is to steer it to Heaven; this boat is not so easy to board, for the angel
will accept but few souls, carefully judged and found fitting. The shore
is Purgatory, and some who would sail to Heaven are left behind to
purge themselves of sin. In the *Auto de Barca do Inferno* (1517), an
hidalgo who despised the poor, a usurer, a friar who arrives with his
mistress, a sinful shoemaker, a Celestinesque bawd, a Jew, a lawyer,
a corrupt *corregidor,* and a hanged criminal are all forced to sail to
Hell; only a simpleton, whose language is atrocious but whose heart is
innocent, and four knights who have been killed in Africa in the service
of God are allowed to go aboard the ship to Heaven. In the *Auto da
Barca do Purgatorio* (1518), the souls are those of humble but not spot-
lessly virtuous peasants who meet a variety of fates. In the Spanish
Auto da Barca da Glória (1519) the souls have come from the highest
levels of human society: they have been a Count, a Duke, a King, an
Emperor, a Bishop, an Archbishop, a Cardinal, and a Pope. All have
sinned, power has corrupted them, the torments of Hell which they
deserve are chanted to them sternly, and, as they pray to Christ for
mercy, the angelic boat is about to sail away and leave them behind,
when suddenly the risen Christ appears to save them.

Vicente's *Comédia do Viuvo* (1514 according to the *Copilaçam,* but

probably written after 1521)[26] is a simple example of romantic comedy
like that of some plays by his contemporary, Torres Naharro. The
romantic comedies of Vicente are 'plays in which the theme of romantic
love is developed in a dramatic action which ends happily with the
union of the lovers'.[27] The playwright composed three such plays in
Spanish, the *Comédia do Viuvo*, *Don Duardos*, and *Amadís de Gaula*.
The widower of the title of the first of these plays is not its protagonist.
The plot concerns the dilemma of Don Rosvel, Prince of Huxonia, who
falls in love with both the widower's daughters at the same time and
cannot make up his mind which of them to marry; in the end, a *frater ex
machina* solves the problem. In order to be able to woo the daughters,
Don Rosvel had disguised himself as a peasant and entered the service
of their father. This feature of the intrigue of the *Comédia do Viuvo* is
also seen in the most delightful of Vicente's romantic comedies, *Don
Duardos* (1522?), which may have been developed out of, or refined
from, the other play.[28] *Don Duardos*, based on a novel of chivalry, the
Primaleón (1512), shows the dramatist at the summit of his achievement as a lyrical and dramatic poet and as a creator of finely shaded
characters for the stage. The English Prince, Don Duardos, assumes the
role of a gardener in order to win and test the love of Flérida; she does
not know that the peasant with whom she gradually falls in love is
really a Prince. The play is leisurely but dramatically tense. It is a
moving fantasy of high chivalric ideals and purity of spirit, which
Vicente wove with great delicacy and with a tenderness which is perhaps
uncommon in the Spanish drama. A modern editor has asserted that
only the Prince's sufferings and his taking the risk of losing the woman
he loves above all other creatures save him from being a prodigy of
selfishness.[29] This is a moralist's view, and the play was surely written
not for moralists but for sentimentalists prepared to be drawn into a
dream-world in which the idea of Don Duardos's being selfish simply
does not arise. Dámaso Alonso's acute study of this play and its poetry
provides a magnificent interpretation of Vicente's artistry in *Don
Duardos*.[30] For the last of Vicente's romantic comedies in Spanish,
Amadís de Gaula (1533?), drawn from the famous chivalresque novel
of the same name, and for a short but shrewd conspectus of this dramatist's life and art, the reader should consult the introduction to Waldron's edition.[31] Yet one ought not to take leave of Gil Vicente without
enjoying also a much simpler play, and a good reminder of the origins
of the dramatist's techniques in the court playlets in the style of Encina,
the *Farsa das ciganas* (1521 or 1525?, and not a farce as we understand

the term nowadays), with its lisping Spanish gipsy women telling fortunes for the ladies of the Portuguese royal Court.

Juan del Encina wrote his plays in Spain and later in Rome; Gil Vicente wrote his in Portugal; the third member of the great first-generation trio of Iberian playwrights, Bartolomé de Torres Naharro (c. 1485?-c. 1520), wrote most of his plays in Italy. The birth and rapid international development of the modern Spanish drama from the last decade of the fifteenth century to the third of the sixteenth perhaps reflect Spain's swiftly growing strength as a European power during that period, and also the increasing cultural contacts between the three southern European nations. Encina influenced both Gil Vicente and Torres Naharro, and Torres appears to have influenced the development of both Encina's and Vicente's dramatic art. For the evolution of dramatic writing in Spain itself during the first half of the sixteenth century, Encina was by far the most influential of the three playwrights, but for the later development of the Spanish drama Torres Naharro was perhaps more important than Encina. Lope de Vega may not have known Encina's plays at all, but almost certainly, when a youth, he must have read Torres Naharro's plays in the expurgated edition of Madrid, 1573. Between 1692 and 1694, the last notable dramatist of the Golden Age, Bances Candamo, wrote that 'Los Poetas Españoles dieron principio bien pocos años ha a sus comedias, . . . imitando en algo a las Latinas y en más a las Italianas',[32] but the Italianisation of the Spanish drama began, in reality, long before Bances thought it did, and quite a long time before Boscán and Garcilaso established Italian rhymes and rhythms in Spanish poetry. The Italianisation of the drama may be considered to have begun with Encina's *Fileno, Zambardo y Cardonio*; it started as a serious movement when Torres Naharro wrote the first of his five-act plays, which was probably the *Comedia Seraphina* (1508-09, according to Gillet's chronology).[33]

Of Torres Naharro's life little is known and much has been conjectured.[34] He was born in the village of La Torre de Miguel Sesmero (Badajoz) and may have studied philosophy and classics at Salamanca, living as servant to a richer student. He became a priest but possibly turned soldier and served in Seville and in Valencia, whence he may have sailed for Italy. He was captured by Moorish pirates and later ransomed, perhaps after a period as a galley-slave. He reached Rome, possibly around 1508, and there he may have written his first full-length play, which Gillet believed to be the *Comedia Seraphina*. He became one of the members of the large Spanish colony in Rome and perhaps between 1509 and 1510 went on to write, for his fellow-countrymen's entertainment, the *Comedia Soldadesca*. Perhaps as early as 1513 he belonged to the household of a great patron (Cardinal Giulio de' Medici?), but he may never have risen to high status as a courtier, even when in the service of the Spanish Cardinal Bernardino de Carvajal. In Rome he seems to have gone on writing plays and poetry. Gillet claimed that Torres wrote at least three more *comedias* there, the *Trophea* (1514?), the *Jacinta* (1514-15?), the *Tinellaria* (1516?), and perhaps also his most celebrated play, the *Ymenea* (1516?). By 1517 he appears to have moved to Naples, where, in March, he published a collection of his drama and verse, the *Propalladia*, dedicated to a new patron, the marquis of Pescara. He may have returned to Spain, for the second edition of the *Propalladia* was printed in Seville in 1520 and included another *comedia*, the *Calamita*, which contains frequent allusions to that city. It is possible that he wrote another play in Seville, the *Aquilana* (*c.* 1520-23?), and that he died in Spain. Several more editions of the *Propalladia* were issued, in Seville and abroad, before the book was banned by the index of 1559. An expurgated version was published in Madrid in 1573.

The *Prohemio* of the *Propalladia* contains the first important statement of dramatic theory in the Golden Age and, indeed, in Renaissance Europe. After a brief account of classical definitions of comedy and tragedy, Torres declares that

Según Acrón, poeta, hay seis géneros de comedias, scilicet: stataria, pretexta, tabernaria, palliata, togata, motoria; y cuatro partes, scilicet: *prothesis, catastrophe, prologus, epithasis;* y como Horacio quiere, cinco actos; y sobre todo que sea muy guardo el decoro, etc. Todo lo cual me parece más largo de contar que necesario de oír. Quiero ora decir yo mi parecer, pues el de los otros he dicho. Y digo ansí: que comedia no es otra cosa sino un artificio ingenioso de notables y finalmente alegres acontecimientos, por personas disputado. La división de ella en cinco actos, no solamente me parece buena, pero mucho necesaria; aunque yo les llamo jornadas, porque más me parecen descansaderos que otra cosa, de donde la comedia queda mejor entendida y recitada. El número de las personas que se han de introducir, es mi voto que no deben ser tan pocas que parezca la fiesta sorda, ni tantas que engendren confusión. Aunque en nuestra *Comedia Tinellaria* se introdujeron pasadas veinte personas, porque el sujeto de ella no quiso menos, el honesto número me parece que sea de seis hasta a doce personas. El decoro en las comedias es como el gobernalle

* *

en la nao, el cual el buen cómico siempre debe traer ante los ojos. Es decoro una justa y decente continuación de la materia, conviene a saber: dando a cada uno lo suyo, evitar las cosas impropias, usar de todas las legítimas, de manera que el siervo no diga ni haga actos del señor, *et e converso*; y el lugar triste entristecello, y el alegre alegrallo, con toda la advertencia, diligencia y modo posibles, etc. De dónde sea dicha comedia, y por qué, son tantas opiniones, que es una confusión. Quanto a los géneros de comedias, a mí parece que bastarían dos para en nuestra lengua castellana: comedia a noticia y comedia a fantasía. A noticia se entiende de cosa nota y vista en realidad de verdad, como son *Soldadesca* y *Tinellaria*; a fantasía, de cosa fantástiga o fingida, que tenga color de verdad aunque lo lo sea, como son *Seraphina*, *Ymenea,* etc. Partes de comedia, ansí mesmo bastarían dos, scilicet: introito y argumento. Y si más os pareciere que deban ser, ansí de lo uno como de lo otro, licencia se tienen para quitar y poner los discretos.[35]

This passage, which continues with a defence, on the grounds of verisimilitude, of the use of Italian words in certain of Torres's plays, shows a broad culture, a knowledge of classical theory, and a common-sensical independence of mind which are remarkably similar to those demonstrated, almost a century later, by Lope de Vega in the *Arte nuevo.* Though here he might possibly be said to be speaking only of comedy and not of *comedia* in its normal Golden Age sense (= a play of any genre, several acts long, usually three from the end of the sixteenth century onwards), Torres effectively combines within his wide definition of the term characteristics of both ancient comedy (*finalmente alegres*) and ancient tragedy (*notables*). For him, the *comedia* encompasses historical incidents (held by many Renaissance and seventeenth-century theorists to be subjects for tragedy) and invented intrigues. The basic distinction between *comedia a noticia* and *comedia a fantasía* is precisely that which Bances Candamo makes in 1689 or 1690.[36] Torres initiates the use of the word *jornada* to describe an act of a play, and by the seventeenth century the word becomes universally accepted in Spain. He does not indicate that there ought to be any restriction, as in the classical drama, of the social rank of characters in different types of play, that gods, kings, and heroes should figure in tragedy and no one above the middle range of the nobility in comedy. He emphasises the importance of one of the basic classical literary principles which is to become extraordinarily influential in seventeenth-century Spanish drama, that of decorum (what ought to be), though, like many Renaissance theorists, he does not clearly indicate the difference between decorum and verisimilitude (what seems probable or feasible).[37]

Torres wrote nine plays, craftily and with a range and depth of human experience which is far greater than that shown in Encina's or Fernández's art. Apart from the simple *Diálogo del Nacimiento,* Salamantine in inspiration and form, all Torres's *comedias* are divided into five acts, in the classical manner, and preceded by the *introito y argumento* to win over the audience and explain the plot. All of them, except the *Diálogo,* are monostrophic, like Encina's early eclogues, though the strophe used in *Ymenea* is Italianate. Torres's dramatic techniques reveal a sound knowledge of classical dramatic practice;[38] his language is rich and heady, distilled by a keen ear from the polyglot southern Europe of the Renaissance.

Amongst the *comedias a fantasía, Seraphina,* derived from the tradition of the *Romance del Conde Alarcos,* is a grim and tense bourgeois play in which the problem posed by what is, in reality, bigamy is solved by the arrival of the bigamist's brother. *Ymenea,* the best of the *comedias a fantasía,* is derived mainly from three acts of *La Celestina.* The drama is carefully contrived, and tension rapidly mounts to the climax when, just as the outraged Marquis is about to kill his sister Phebea, her lover Ymeneo appears, prevents the execution, and declares that he and she are man and wife. This *comedia* introduces into the Spanish drama one of its most fruitful themes, that of honour and vengeance. With its problems of courtship and honour, its mysterious night-scenes, and its frightened servants, *Ymenea* has been described as a notable predecessor of the seventeenth-century *comedia de capa y espada* (see below, p. 51). This is true, but we must not forget that, in many ways, so also are *Seraphina* and the neatly constructed *Calamita.* The *comedia de capa y espada* is the Spanish, decorous version of the middle-class comedy modelled on Plautus and Terence, and to this long tradition of European comedy all three of these plays belong.

The best of the *comedias a noticia,* amongst which we might place the festival-play *Trophea,* are the *Soldadesca* and the *Tinellaria.* Both are apparently realistic social *tableaux vivants.* Both have clear satirical and moralising purpose, pointing at abuses in Rome. *Soldadesca,* which concerns the mustering of a company of soldiers for the wars, exposes the brutality, corruption, and criminality of the soldiery at various levels. *Tinellaria,* a fine macaronic poem in various Spanish dialects, Portuguese, Latin, Italian, and French, describes the preparation and consumption of a meal in the *tinelo* or common refectory under a Cardinal's palace and reveals sloth, parasitism, and vice where there ought to be gratitude, honesty, and piety. Torres raises the stone, and we see the slugs writhe and crawl. The climax of the play is magnificent.

The modern reader can best taste the flavour of the Spanish drama of the rest of the first part of the sixteenth century by reading the fine collection of *Autos, comedias y farsas* of the Biblioteca Nacional, published in facsimile.[39] Religious drama, festival plays, and romantic comedy flourished, quietly. Only two really notable dramatists emerged. The first, Fernán López de Yanguas, wrote a *Nunc dimittis* which was attached, in a *suelta,* to Encina's *Plácida y Vitoriano.* He also wrote four plays, two in the tradition of Encina's *églogas* and two allegorical *farsas.*[40] The other playwright, Diego Sánchez de Badajoz, has justly been called, by Crawford, 'the outstanding figure in the Spanish religious drama of the first half of the sixteenth century'.[41] Sánchez, who was curate at Talavera (Badajoz) between 1533 and 1549, wrote twenty-eight plays which were published after his death, by his nephew, in the *Recopilación en metro* (Seville, 1554). Ten of these works were written for celebrations of Corpus Christi in Badajoz, and Wardropper has shown them to be important precursors of the fully-fledged *auto sacramental* (see below, p. 114). As he observed, Diego Sánchez modified significantly the traditional pastoral eclogue, putting universalised characters in place of the conventional shepherds, developing the use of allegory even in the plays which he wrote for occasions other than Corpus Christi, and greatly increasing anti-clerical satire in the drama.[42]

One might, tentatively, add a third important dramatist to this pair. In Chapter 58 of the Second Part of *Don Quixote,* the knight and Sancho meet a group of youths and maidens who are trying to revive the pastoral life and are rehearsing 'dos églogas, una del famoso poeta Garcilaso, y otra del excelentísimo Camoens . . . , las cuales hasta ahora no hemos representado'. All three of Garcilaso's eclogues are actable. The first and the third would not lend themselves to very lively movements, but the *Égloga segunda,* with the fountain as its focal point and its varied and sometimes amusing action, seems a natural, and a worthy, successor to Encina's *Fileno, Zambardo y Cardonio.* It would be difficult to reject Lapesa's opinion that the *Égloga segunda* is conceived as a dramatic work and not to believe that Garcilaso, when he wrote it, was consciously thinking of at least one of the eclogues of his predecessor as poet to the Alba family.[43]

Several other particularly striking plays were composed in this period. Among them are Micael de Carvajal's *Tragedia Josefina* (published in 1535), on the tribulations of the youthful Joseph, and a long play which Carvajal began and Luis Hurtado de Toledo finished in 1557, *Cortes de la Muerte*. In this drama, as in Gil Vicente's *Barcas,* the dead come to judgment; but here, at the Court of Death, the World, the Flesh, and the Devil are the prosecuting counsel and the defence counsel is formed by saints. The macabre and fascinating theme of the Dance of Death also passed from the Middle Ages into the Renaissance drama, in such works as the anonymous *Coplas de la Muerte* (printed *c.* 1530), Diego Sánchez's *Farsa de la Muerte* (probably written in 1536), and Juan de Pedraza's *Farsa llamada Danza de la Muerte* (1551). Another noteworthy play is Luis de Miranda's roguishly moralising *Comedia pródiga* (printed 1554; possibly written soon after 1532), on the chastening of a youth who keeps bad company. Finally, it should be noted that the influence of *La Celestina* at this time is not confined to the few plays which we have cited as derivative from it. Some of the works which imitated *La Celestina* were too long to be acted, but a number of playable plays of this period, Pedro Manuel Ximénez de Urrea's *Égloga de la tragicomedia de Calisto y Melibea,*[44] the *Comedia Ypólita* (printed 1520-21), Jaime de Güete's *Comedia Tesorina* and *Comedia Vidriana* (both probably printed by 1535), and others, are its direct descendants, and it was important in the foundation of the tradition of main plot plus sub-plot in the Spanish drama.

The period closes on a sombre note. The Toledan Index of 1559 banned many printed plays in Spain. The exact reasons why most of them were prohibited remain uncertain, but the index must have forced playwrights after 1559 to write with much more close attention to doctrine and decorum than they had needed before its publication.

NOTES

1. In 'Cronología de las primeras obras de Juan del Encina', *Archivum* (Oviedo) IV (1954), 362-72, José Caso González has argued that the poet entered the service of the duque de Alba as late as the summer or autumn of 1495, and that the dates which most modern scholars have tentatively accepted for his early plays should be changed to the following: *Égloga VII*, summer of 1495; *Églogas I* and *II*, Christmas 1495; *Églogas V* and *VI*, February 1496; *Églogas III* and *IV*, Holy Week 1496; *Égloga VIII*, summer 1496. The 'patriarca del teatro español' begat the first generation of the host of chronological problems which make it impossible to write a truly systematic history of the drama of the Golden Age.

2. In the only other edition of Encina's complete dramatic works, that of Cañete and Barbieri (Madrid, 1893), *Fileno, Zambardo y Cardonio* is printed as the eleventh *égloga,* before the *Auto del repelón, Plácida y Vitoriano,* and *Cristino y Febea.* Oliver T. Myers has denied the authenticity of the *Auto del repelón* (*HR,* XXXII [1964], 189-210). López Morales has denied the validity

of Myers's arguments and conclusion and has promised a further study of the problem. See John Lihani on the possible influence of Lucas Fernández on Encina (*HR*, XXV [1957], 255).

3. The anonymous *Égloga interlocutoria* published by Urban Cronan (*RH*, XXXVI [1916], 475-88), has been attributed to Encina but it is now considered to be no more than an imitation of Encina's style and techniques.

4. See Bruce W. Wardropper, 'Metamorphosis in the Theatre of Juan del Encina', *SPh*, LIX (1962), 41-51.

5. See Charlotte Stern, 'Juan del Encina's Carnival Eclogues and the Spanish Drama of the Renaissance', *Renaissance Drama*, VIII (1965), 181-95.

6. For the art of the *momeries* or mummings of the fifteenth and sixteenth centuries, see N. D. Shergold, *A History of the Spanish Stage* (Oxford, 1967), pp. 126-36. Mingo's gift to the duchess may be the first edition of the *Cancionero*. For the staging of Encina's plays, see Shergold, op. cit., pp. 26-8, 40, 144-5.

7. On the figure of the shepherd, see Humberto López Morales, *Tradición y creación en los orígenes del teatro castellano* (Madrid, 1968), pp. 147-72.

8. For *sayagués*, see H. López Morales, op. cit., pp. 172-90, and 'Elementos leoneses en la lengua del teatro pastoril de los siglos XV y XVI', *Actas II*, 411-19; John Lihani, 'Some Notes on *sayagués*', *HBalt*, XLI (1958), 165-9; Paul Teyssier, *La langue de Gil Vicente* (Paris, 1959), pp. 23-73; Charlotte Stern, 'Sayago and *sayagués* in Spanish History and Literature', *HR*, XXIX (1961), 217-37.

9. The play has 600 lines of verse, plus a *villancico* of 31. The shortest of the plays printed in the 1496 *Cancionero* is *Égloga I*, which has 180 lines and no *villancico* (*Églogas* II and IV both have 180 lines plus *villancicos*), and the longest is the Easter *Égloga III*, with 350 lines plus a *villancico* of 18.

10. See J. P. Wickersham Crawford, 'The Source of Juan del Encina's *Égloga de Fileno y Zambardo*', *RH*, XXXVI (1916), 475-88, and 'Encina's *Égloga de Fileno, Zambardo y Cardonio* and Antonio Tebaldeo's Second Eclogue', *HR*, II (1934), 327-33.

11. See Othón Arróniz, *La influencia italiana en el nacimiento de la comedia española* (Madrid, 1969), pp. 40-1.

12. See John Lihani, 'Personal Elements in Gil Vicente's *Auto pastoril castelhano*', *HR*, XXXVII (1969), 297-303.

13. See J. Lihani, 'Lucas Fernández and the Evolution of the Shepherd's Family Pride in Early Spanish Drama', *HR*, XXV (1957), 252-63.

14. See Shergold, op. cit., p. 29.

15. See Acts, 17, 34.

16. See Alfredo Hermenegildo, 'Nueva interpretación de un primitivo; Lucas Fernández', *Seg*, II, núm. 3 (1966), 10-43, and Shergold, op cit., pp. 28-9.

17. See Gil Vicente, *Tragicomedia de Don Duardos*, ed. Dámaso Alonso, I [no more published] (Madrid, 1942), 33; A. R. Milburn in *The Penguin Companion to Literature*, II, *European*, ed. A. K. Thorlby (Harmondsworth, 1969), 800b.

18. I. S. Révah, in *Deux 'autos' de Gil Vicente restitués à leur auteur* (Lisbon, 1949), published two anonymous Portuguese plays which he attributed to Vicente, but not all critics agree with these attributions.

19. It has been suggested that Lucas Fernández spent some time in Portugal and knew Gil Vicente personally.

20. Gil Vicente, *Tragicomedia de Amadís de Gaula*, ed. T. P. Waldron (Manchester, 1959), pp. 7-10.

21. Leo Spitzer, 'The Artistic Unity of Gil Vicente's *Auto da Sibila Casandra*', *HR*, XXVII (1959), 57.

22. See I. S. Révah, 'L'*Auto* de la Sibylle Cassandre de Gil Vicente', *HR*, XXVII (1959), 167-93. On this play, see also Mia I. Gerhardt, *La pastorale* (Assen, 1950), pp. 141-5.

23. See Eugenio Asensio, 'El *Auto dos quatro tempos* de Gil Vicente', *RFE*, XXXIII (1949), 350-75.

24. Révah, in his *Recherches sur les oeuvres de Gil Vicente*, I (Lisbon, 1951), 76-80, has argued that the *Auto da Barca da Glória* is the work not of Gil Vicente but of his son Luis.

25. See Edwin H. Zeydel's introduction to his verse translation of the *Ship of Fools*, 2nd ed. (New York, 1962), pp. 1-54. Zeydel does not mention Gil Vicente.

26. See I. S. Révah, 'La *comedia* dans l'oeuvre de Gil Vicente', *Bulletin d' Histoire du Théâtre portugais*, II (1951), 1-39.

27. Gil Vicente, *Tragicomedia de Amadís de Gaula*, ed. cit., p. 10.

28. ibid., p. 14.

29. Gil Vicente, *Obras dramáticas castellanas*, ed. T. R. Hart, CC 156 (Madrid, 1962), p. XLIV.

30. See above, p. 19, note 17. See also Elias L. Rivers, 'The Unity of *Don Duardos*', *MLN*, LXXVI (1961), 759-66.

31. See above, note 20.

32. Francisco Bances Candamo, *Theatro de los theatros de los passados y presentes siglos*, ed. Duncan W. Moir (London, 1970), p. 49.

33. See vol. IV, 473, of Joseph E. Gillet's excellent edition of *Propalladia and Other Works of Bartolomé de Torres Naharro* (Bryn Mawr-Philadelphia, 1943-61). The fourth volume, *Torres Naharro and the Drama of the Renaissance*, was transcribed from Gillet's manuscript and brought to a conclusion by Otis H. Green.

34. ibid., 401-17, and the notable study by M. Menéndez y Pelayo in vol. II of the Madrid 1880-1900 edition of the *Propalladia*.

35. ed. Gillet, I, 142-3. Gillet's commentary is in vol. IV, 427-44. The text is also in F. Sánchez Escribano and A. Porqueras Mayo, *Preceptiva dramática española del renacimiento y el barroco* (Madrid, 1965), pp. 61-2, henceforth referred to as *Preceptiva*.

36. See below, p. 139.

37. On decorum and verisimilitude up to the end of the seventeenth century, see Bances Candamo, op. cit., pp. lxxiv-lxxxviii.

38. For a good analysis of these, see *Propalladia*, ed. cit., IV, 480-562. In Torres's time Aristotle's *Poetics* were still generally unknown in Europe.

39. 2 vols., Madrid, 1962-64. See also *Teatro español del siglo XVI*, I, ed. Urban Cronan (Madrid, 1913). For a detailed account of the development of the drama in this period, see J. P. Wickersham Crawford, *Spanish Drama before Lope de Vega*, 3rd ed. (Philadelphia, 1968), pp. 38-106.

40. See F. López de Yanguas, *Obras dramáticas*, ed. F. González Ollé, CC 162 (Madrid, 1967); the review by A. I. Watson in *BHS*, XLVI (1969), 60-1; B. W. Wardropper, *Introducción al teatro religioso del Siglo de Oro*, 2nd ed. (Madrid, 1967), pp. 176-82. González Ollé (*Seg*, III, 1 and 2 [Nos. 5-6, 1967], 179-84) considers Yanguas's *Farsa sacramental* to be the first Spanish *auto sacramental*.

41. op. cit., p. 40. At last Sánchez's *Recopilación en metro* can be read not in black letter but in modern print, in the fine edition by Frida Weber

de Kurlat (Buenos Aires, 1968). On his work, see José López Prudencio, *Diego Sánchez de Badajoz: estudio crítico, biográfico bibliográfico* (Madrid, 1915), and Wardropper, op. cit., pp. 185-209.

42. ibid., pp. 185-8. For a very brief but very shrewd survey and bibliography of the religious drama of this period, see Jean-Louis Flecniakoska, *La formation de l' 'auto' religieux en Espagne avant Calderón* (1550-1635) (Paris, 1961), pp. 6-14.

43. On the actability of the *Égloga segunda*, see Rafael Lapesa, *La trayectoria poética de Garcilaso*, 2nd ed. (Madrid, 1968), pp. 110-13.

44. Logroño, 1513; see his works, *Cancionero* (Saragossa, 1878), pp. 452-80.

Chapter 2

FROM RUEDA TO CERVANTES

EXCEPT FOR THE YOUNG AND MATURING LOPE DE VEGA, the later part of the sixteenth century could boast of no dramatic genius of the stature of Gil Vicente. Nevertheless, this was a period of very great importance in the development of the two major art-forms of the Spanish drama, the *comedia* and the *auto sacramental*. Social change influenced this development. The trade guilds, which had been weak in Castile in the Middle Ages but had been reorganised under Ferdinand and Isabella, gained great strength and security as the sixteenth century advanced; and the increasing prosperity and prestige of the guilds did much to determine the form and expensive pageantry of the Corpus *autos*. The growth and nature of the *comedia* were in large measure decided by the systematic commercialisation of much of the secular drama, by the establishment, in the booming towns and cities, of fixed theatres for the populace, and by consequent demand for more and more plays which led, by the 1580s and 1590s, to the flood which perhaps exceeded, in the sixteenth and seventeenth centuries, the dramatic output of all other European nations combined.[1]

The first notable figure in this period was Lope de Rueda (1509?-65), who was not only an important dramatist but also one of the first, if not the first, professional actor-manager in Spain. Rueda and his company of actors moved up and down the country from around 1540 till his death, performing plays not only in the dining-halls of the nobility but also, on improvised stages in inn-yards and patios, for the people.[2] The best-known account of his activities was given by Cervantes, who, talking of a conversation about *comedias* in the prologue to his own volume of *Ocho comedias y ocho entremeses nuevos*, said

> Tratóse también de quién fue el primero que en España las sacó de mantillas y las puso en toldo y vistió de gala y apariencia; yo, como el más viejo que allí estaba, dije que me acordaba de haber visto

representar al gran Lope de Rueda, varón insigne en la representación y en el entendimiento. Fue natural de Sevilla y de oficio batihoja, que quiere decir de los que hacen panes de oro; fue admirable en la poesía pastoril, y, en este modo, ni entonces ni después acá ninguno le ha llevado ventaja; y aunque, por ser muchacho yo entonces, no podía hacer juicio firme de la bondad de sus versos, por algunos que me quedaron en la memoria, vistos agora en la edad madura que tengo, hallo ser verdad lo que he dicho; y, si no fuera por no salir del propósito de prólogo, pusiera aquí algunos que acreditaran esta verdad. En el tiempo de este célebre español, todos los aparatos de un autor de comedias se encerraban en un costal, y se cifraban en cuatro pellicos blancos guarnecidos de guadamecí dorado, y en cuatro barbas y cabelleras y cuatro cayados, poco más o menos. Las comedias eran unos coloquios como églogas entre dos o tres pastores y alguna pastora; aderezábanlas y dilatábanlas con dos o tres entremeses, ya de negra, ya de rufián, ya de bobo y ya de vizcaíno, que todas estas cuatro figuras y otras muchas hacía el tal Lope con la mayor excelencia y propiedad que pudiera imaginarse. No había en aquel tiempo tramoyas, ni desafíos de moros y cristianos a pie ni a caballo; no había figura que saliese o pareciese salir del centro de la tierra por lo hueco del teatro, al cual componían cuatro bancos en cuadro y cuatro o seis tablas encima, con que se levantaba del suelo cuatro palmos; ni menos bajaban del cielo nubes con ángeles o con almas. El adorno del teatro era una manta vieja tirada con dos cordeles de una parte a otra, que hacía lo que llaman vestuario, detrás de la cual estaban los músicos, cantando sin guitarra algún romance antiguo. Murió Lope de Rueda, y por hombre excelente y famoso le enterraron en la iglesia mayor de Córdoba (donde murió), entre los dos coros, donde también está enterrado aquel famoso loco Luis López.[3]

Cervantes wrote these words in 1615, when *tramoyas* or stage machinery, trap-doors, and cloud-machines were common to most civic theatres, and Shergold has shown clearly that, except for performances hurriedly improvised by the troupe in the most adverse of conditions, Cervantes appears to exaggerate the primitiveness of Rueda's staging techniques and resources. Four of Rueda's *comedias*, *Eufemia*, *Armelina*, *Los engañados*, and *Medora*, together with two of his *coloquios pastoriles*, *Camila* and *Tymbria*, were published in 1567, in amended and expurgated form, by his friend and fellow-dramatist, Juan de Timoneda, who in the same year edited a selection of seven prose *pasos* or brief

comic pieces by Rueda under the title of *El deleitoso* and in 1570 issued
at least three more in the *Registro de representantes*. Certain of the long
plays, which also are all in prose except for occasional songs in the
coloquios, contain features which suggest that Rueda and his players
performed them on stages set against houses, using their doors and
windows for special effects, that the dramas' casts required at least eight
or nine actors, doubling up in some parts, and that the actors' costumes
were more varied than Cervantes says they were. Moreover, Rueda
appears to have employed skilled musicians. Nevertheless, Cervantes's
description is very useful; it tells us a certain amount of essential
information about Rueda the actor, and this information may lead to
interesting speculation about his work as a dramatist and his policy as
actor-manager.

Of the Corpus *autos* which Rueda is known to have performed we
know no more than that he performed them. The six full-length plays
which have been preserved in Timoneda's versions do not show that
Rueda was acquainted with Aristotle's *Poetics* or Horace's *Ars poetica*.
On the other hand, at least four of them do show him to have read
Italian plays and *novellas* and all demonstrate that he was, in his
dramatic techniques, an *italianizante*, a typically well-read writer of the
Spanish Renaissance and a clear illustration of Shergold's statement
that 'the early history of the *comedia* as a dramatic entertainment must
be sought in Italy and not in Spain'.[4] *Los engañados* has been shown to
be a fairly careful *refundición* or recasting of the anonymous Italian
play *Gl'Ingannati*, which was first performed in 1531, in the famous
academy of the Intronati at Siena;[5] in Rueda's play appears, perhaps
for the first time in the Golden Age drama, the woman in man's dress
who was, by virtue of her leg-show (even though, in Rueda's time she
may have been played by a boy), to become one of the favourite figures
of the Spanish drama. *Medora* was devised from another Italian play,
La Cingana, by Giancarli. And both of Rueda's most famous plays, the
Comedia llamada Eufemia and the *Comedia llamada Armelina*, have
Italian sources. Neither of these plays shows the artful construction nor
the instinctive realisation and grasping of sources of tension which we
find in the work of the dramatic masters of the first part of the century.
Eufemia and *Armelina* do not race; they amble. In both plays a modern
audience, if not prepared for a dramatic problem by the explanatory
introito, would probably be bored or puzzled until a great part of the
action has passed. *Eufemia*'s source is the same as that of Shakespeare's
Cymbeline, the brilliantly amusing ninth story of the second day of
Boccaccio's *Decameron*, one of the most influential books for the in-

trigues of plays in Italy, Spain, and England. But it would be futile to seek, in *Eufemia*, the verbal and emotional glories of *Cymbeline*. Rueda's treatment of his subject is both simple and leisurely. The *introito* warns us that there will be a dramatic problem in the play, but we do not discover until the sixth of its eight *escenas* exactly what this problem will be. Yet the solution of the problem is cleverer in Rueda than in Boccaccio. In *Armelina*, for which Rueda borrowed some details of Cecchi's *Il servigiale* and many more from Raineri's *L'Altilia*, the dramatist does little, until the fourth of the six *escenas*, to inform us that his heroine is really desperately unhappy about the prospect of marrying her shoemaker suitor. Though Rueda's plays amused the nobility from time to time, he wrote for ordinary, simple people, fascinated by the stage and prepared to accept even the rhetoric of Neptune's speech to Armelina, though to us it resembles that of Bottom and his mates in *A Midsummer-Night's Dream*.

Yet Rueda's *comedias* are not to be despised. Careless though he was about dramatic construction, he shone as a writer of colourful dialogue and as a creator of lively comic characters. Several of the best parts of *Eufemia* and *Armelina* are the comic scenes or *pasos* which are interspersed, perhaps indiscriminatingly, between serious events. The *paso* is a short amusing dramatic fragment, involving a small number of comical and usually humble characters. As Timoneda described it in an *octava* at the beginning of the *Registro de representantes*, the *paso* was a ready-made comic unit which actors could use to enliven their longer plays. *Pasos* could serve as light relief, or as interludes, as 'curtain-raisers' (though there was no proscenium curtain), or to end a performance merrily. In the evolution of the Golden Age *comedia*, the *pasos* of Rueda and his contemporaries and disciples were the predecessors not only of the comic sub-plots of serious plays but also of the interludes or *entremeses*.

As Cervantes's account of his acting suggests, Rueda appears to have excelled in *paso* roles. Some of his *pasos* are very funny. One of the best is the *Paso tercero* of the *Deleitoso*, in which an unscrupulous doctor encourages, for his own profit, the illusions of a stupid man, Martín de Villalba, who is being cuckolded by a student, his wife's cousin. The student has convinced Martín that, because in the eyes of God he and his wife are one flesh, the husband ought to take the medicine for the woman's ailments, which are feigned. Martín, who has swallowed and suffered from the purge which the doctor prescribed for his wife, finally agrees to her going off on what he believes to be a novena but will really be an escapade with her lover. The *Paso quinto* of the same collection is also very amusing. Its plot, which coincides with that of an Italian *commedia dell'arte*,[6] concerns the way in which two thieves contrive to eat the food which a simpleton is carrying to gaol to give to his wife, imprisoned for being a procuress. Speaking in turn, each of the thieves distracts the poor man's attention with extraordinary tales of the imaginary luxuries of life in the 'land of Jauja' (the city which, as a health resort for the miners of the riches of Peru, came to symbolise paradise on earth for the Golden Age); as one thief talks, the other gobbles up the food. The most celebrated of all Rueda's *pasos* is the *Paso séptimo* of the *Deleitoso*, often called *Las aceitunas*. It is about the family quarrel which arises, in the home of the simple-minded peasant Toruvio, over the price at which his daughter will sell the produce of some olives which he has newly planted or perhaps has even forgotten to plant. This play, with its final pricking of the swelling balloon of illusion, is a good example of a long tradition in Spanish literature, a tradition which reached its highest point in *Don Quixote*.

Rueda's posthumous editor, Juan de Timoneda, was a bookseller and publisher in Valencia who also issued volumes of plays by other dramatists: the *Turiana*, a collection of anonymous *comedias*, *farsas*, and *entremeses*, in 1565; three plays by Alonso de la Vega in 1566; and what he called the *Segundo ternario sacramental* in 1575, containing three *autos* of uncertain authorship. But Timoneda was a creative writer in his own right. He is perhaps best known nowadays for his *Patrañuelo*, a collection of *patrañas* or tales retold from many sources, principally Italian. But he was also a noteworthy dramatist. In 1558 he published his *Ternario spiritual*, which comprised two plays entirely of his own devising, the *Auto del nacimiento* and the *Auto de la quinta angustia*; the third play in the book, the *Auto de la oveja perdida*, has been polished and lengthened by him from an earlier play. In 1559 he published his *Tres comedias*, *Amphitrión*, *Los Menemnos*, and *Cornelia* (or *Carmelia*). These plays, in prose like Rueda's, are his greatest achievement. The first two, which are lively free versions of the *Amphitruo* and the *Menaechmi* based on earlier Spanish translations, have been described as 'the first appearance of Plautus on the Spanish stage', even though plays in the Plautine tradition were already common in Spain.[7] The *Cornelia* is a reworking of Ariosto's play *Il Negromante*.[8] In 1575 Timoneda issued another volume of his own plays, the *Ternario sacramental*, containing the previously published *Auto de la oveja perdida* plus the *Auto del castillo de Emaús* and the *Auto de la Iglesia*.

The most important collection of sixteenth-century religious plays is contained in one of the codices of the Biblioteca Nacional which comprises ninety-five dramas written approximately between 1550 and 1575; they were all published in 1901 by Léo Rouanet.[9] Each begins with a *loa* or *argumento* to prepare the audience for the spectacle, almost all of them have comic relief provided by a *bobo* or *simple*, most of them end with a *villancico* and some are divided into two parts by the inclusion of an *entremés*. Only three are in prose, and seventy-six are, like many other plays of the period 1530-75, written entirely in *quintillas*; one (XXXI) is entirely in *redondillas*, a form which is found in parts of various others.[10] The range of their subject-matter is great. Some (e.g. XLVIII, XLVI, LXIV, LVI) deal with events in the life of Christ and others with His passion, death, and resurrection (e.g. LIV, XCIII, LX). Several, for example the *Coloquio de Fenisa* and the *Coloquio de Fide Ypsa* (LXV and LXVI),[11] are devoted to the cult of the Virgin Mary. Twelve deal with the lives of saints, many with Old Testament material, and many are allegorical and deal with the mystery of the Sacrament.[12] In fact, the Rouanet collection shows clearly that the Spanish religious drama of the middle of the sixteenth century already treated the whole variety of subjects which were to be more skilfully developed in the *comedias a lo divino*, the *comedias de santo*, and the *autos sacramentales* of the seventeenth.[13] Doctrinally sound and emotionally moving religious plays were amongst the best literary products of Counter-Reformation Spain. And, at this time, a religious theme can play second fiddle to a moral social theme, such as that presented in Fray Ignacio de Buendía's *Triunfo de Llaneza*,[14] which protests against the migration of the peasants from the countryside to the towns and cities in search of lucre, in an age of financial inflation and corruption.

In the sixteenth century the School drama appears to have flourished. The universities recognised the usefulness of performances of plays as part of the academic programme, for training students to fluency in colloquial Latin, for instruction in rhetoric and in Christian and moral doctrine, for the celebration of Christmas, Shrovetide, Easter, and Corpus Christi, and also for what St Thomas Aquinas and later theologians recognised to be the permissible and desirable result of morally sound drama: *eutrapelia*, or moderate and innocent entertainment. In the earlier part of the century, the plays performed at the universities of Alcalá, Salamanca, and Valencia were usually in Latin: Plautus, Terence, and modern Latin plays sometimes based on Italian dramas or written from scratch by university teachers. As one might expect, at least one of these plays, *Ate relegata et Minerva restituta*, concerned a problem of university politics; it was probably written by one of the most celebrated School dramatists, Juan Pérez, who was Professor of Rhetoric at Alcalá from 1537 till 1545. As the century wore on, some academic plays were composed with Spanish speeches and scenes amongst the Latin, and some were entirely in Spanish. The most prominent of the School dramatists, Juan Lorenzo Palmyreno (1514?-79), professor at Valencia, made no secret of his indebtedness to Spanish plays, and Francisco Sánchez de las Brozas wrote a Spanish play for Corpus Christi at the request of the University of Salamanca.

Also very important in the academic drama were the plays performed in the many colleges or schools founded in Spain in the sixteenth century by the Jesuits, who wished in their plays to replace boring sermons by living dialogue accompanied by actions: clearly a much more effective method of instilling doctrine into their pupils, who were the actors and the spectators. The Jesuit dramatists wrote a wide range of edifying plays both sacred and profane, often with a good measure of skill. The most celebrated of the Jesuit playwrights of the sixteenth century were Padre Pedro Pablo de Acevedo and Padre Juan Bonifacio. The most famous Jesuit play of the time is the anonymous *Tragedia de San Hermenegildo*, performed in the college at Seville. This is a five-act drama written in a variety of Spanish strophes; it follows a notable new tradition in the drama of the second half of the century, that of treating material drawn from Spanish history.[15]

The School drama contributed much to the formation of the *comedia nueva* and the *auto sacramental*. It did so not only through the nature of the plays the academics wrote, but also through the nature of the men who were educated in the universities and the Jesuit colleges. The number of Spaniards of the sixteenth and seventeenth centuries who could boast (perhaps better than Polonius to Hamlet) of at least a rudimentary academic dramatic education must have been considerable. The School drama thus formed a substantial educated element of the audiences in the public theatres; it also formed aspirant dramatists, including Calderón. It must seem strange and unfortunate that the Society of Jesus, so enthusiastic about the use of drama in its own colleges, was in the vanguard of the many attacks directed against public plays in the course of the Golden Age and beyond it. The Jesuits recognised, with St Thomas Aquinas, that performing and watching plays were in themselves 'neutral acts', capable of being used for good or for ill; but they could not, as an order, accept the idea that the popular drama could be anything but a stimulant to depravity, acted as it was by professionals who had for centuries been considered to be *infames*. The attacks on the public theatre by the Jesuits and by other severe moralists did, however, have a useful effect: they were the main cause of the theatrical legislation and the stage censorship system which gradually became tighter and better organised as the Golden Age advanced and which perhaps made most Spanish plays of that age, in Rennert's phrase, 'cleaner and on a higher moral plane' than those of other European countries.[16]

As we have seen, classical comedy had a long as well as profound influence on the sixteenth-century Spanish drama. On the other hand, the deep and extensive influence of classical tragedy came remarkably late. It is true that the academic Hernán Pérez de Oliva's free prose versions of Sophocles' *Electra* (*La venganza de Agamenón*) and of Euripides' *Hecuba* (*Hécuba triste*) were composed, and the former one printed, in the first half of the century,[17] and that, from Encina onwards, Renaissance dramatists did write plays of a tragic nature. Nevertheless, it was not till the 1570s that a school of deliberately classicising Spanish tragedians grew up. When this school did appear, its main stylistic source was not Greek tragedy but Seneca, the great model of all the Renaissance and seventeenth-century European schools of tragedy.[18]

The impetus was given to the Spanish school by a Portuguese dramatist, Antonio Ferreira (1528-69), who in his play *A Castro*, started a new tradition amongst Peninsular classicising tragedians, that of writing dramas not only on classical and mythological subjects but on Peninsular history.[19] *A Castro* is a five-act, polymetric tragedy on a subject which itself was to be repeatedly treated in European drama, the love of Prince Peter of Portugal for the noble Inês de Castro and her murder in 1355, for reasons of state, at the behest of the prince's father, King Alfonso IV. *A Castro*, a beautiful and moving tragedy, was not printed until 1587, but before then it was read in manuscript and closely imitated, in Spanish, by the Dominican friar Jerónimo Bermúdez, in his *Nise lastimosa*, published in Madrid in 1577. Bermúdez restricted the role of the chorus, which had been of great importance in the Portuguese original; he changed the pattern of scenes slightly within the five acts, and his tragedy is less truly poetic and more cluttered with Senecan rhetoric than *A Castro*. But Bermúdez went on to write a continuation to *Nise lastimosa*, *Nise laureada*, also in five acts. In this play, Peter, after his father's death, comes to Coimbra to be crowned king, but he has the assassins of Inês brought back from Castile to Portugal, has Inês's corpse disinterred and crowned queen, and orders her killers to be brutally put to death. Poetically and structurally this play is not as good as *Nise lastimosa*; it is even more weighed down with heavy rhetoric. But both plays of Bermúdez show quite a rich

polymetric system, with a wide variety of Italian verse-forms.[20] Their
subject was treated in the seventeenth century, in Luis Vélez de
Guevara's excellent play *Reinar después de morir* and, in the twentieth,
not only in Henry de Montherlant's celebrated *La Reine morte* but also
Alberto Caraco's French drama *Inès de Castro* (Rio de Janeiro, 1941).

Other tragedians followed Bermúdez. A Valencian, Cristóbal de
Virués, wrote five tragedies, strongly Senecan for the most part. *La
gran Semíramis* energetically dramatises, in three acts, the bloody story
of the ambitious Queen of Assyria. *La cruel Casandra,* the most complex
of Virués's plays, set in Spain, is a story of vindictiveness ending in
calamity. *Atila furioso* is equally full of neo-Senecan horror. *La infelice
Marcela,* whose source is part of Ariosto's *Orlando furioso,* likewise
accumulates horrors and ends with the poisoning of Princess Marcela.
The most strictly classical of Virués's plays is *Elisa Dido,* on Dido's
suicide. This play is in five acts of blank verse (*versos sueltos*), mainly
in hendecasyllables but occasionally in heptasyllables, with various forms
of *estancias* in the choruses. His other plays are in three acts or *jornadas*
and are polymetric, with a skilful use of different Italian and Spanish
strophes to suit different situations.[21]

Lupercio Leonardo de Argensola (1559-1613) was another poet who
wrote tragedies in the Senecan manner. He is known to have written
three, *Filis, Alejandra,* and *Isabela,* but the text of *Filis* has not been
preserved. The other two are in three acts. *Alejandra* is a grim drama
of intrigue at the Court of ancient Egypt. Its most horrifying moment
comes when the Queen, Alejandra, who has been poisoned at her
husband's order, bites her own tongue off in her agony and throws it at
the King. The plot of *Isabela* takes place at the Court of Alboacén, a
Moorish King of Saragossa. Isabela, a Christian maiden, must decide
whether to sacrifice her body to the King's lust in order to prevent him
from persecuting the Christians in the city. When Alboacén, seeking to
impress her, shows her the bloody corpses of her father, mother, and
sister, she decides to die the death of a martyr.

Other notable tragedians of this time were Micer Andrés Rey de
Artieda and Diego López de Castro, who wrote their plays in four acts.
But it is a mistake to think, as some scholars have done, that the influence of Seneca on the Golden Age drama ends around 1590; in reality
it was a rich source of inspiration for many dramatists of the seventeenth
century. The Spaniards were too proud of their fellow-countryman not
to be influenced, when they wrote their plays, both by his philosophy
and by his rhetorical and dramatic techniques.[22]

Travelling companies of players, like Rueda's troupe, continued to take plays far and wide in Spain in the late sixteenth and throughout the seventeenth centuries. These companies were known as *compañías de la legua* and were prodigiously important in bringing drama, and with it the measure of instruction which the responsible Spanish dramatists always intended to convey in their plays, to all parts of the country. In a novel which he published in Madrid in 1603, the *Viaje entretenido*, the actor Agustín de Rojas Villandrando gives a fascinating account of the lives of strolling players and their *autores de comedias* or managers at the turn of the century. For example, his character Solano says, of the different kinds of company, that

Habéis de saber que hay bululú, ñaque, gangarilla, cambaleo, garnacha, boxiganga, farándula y compañía. El bululú es un representante solo, que camina a pie y pasa su camino, y entra en el pueblo, habla al cura y dícele que sabe una comedia y alguna loa; que junte al barbero y sacristán y se la dirá, porque le den alguna cosa para pasar adelante. Júntanse éstos, y el súbese sobre una arca y va diciendo: 'Agora sale la dama y dice esto y esto', y va representando, y el cura pidiendo limosna en un sombrero, y junta cuatro o cinco cuartos, algún pedazo de pan y escudilla de caldo que le da el cura, y con esto sigue su estrella y prosigue su camino hasta que halla remedio. Ñaque es dos hombres . . .: éstos hacen un entremés, algún poco de un auto, dicen unas octavas, dos o tres loas, llevan una barba de zamarro, tocan el tamborino y cobran a ochavo, y en esotros reinos a dinerillo (que es lo que hacíamos yo y Ríos), viven contentos, duermen vestidos, caminan desnudos, comen hambrientos y espúlganse el verano entre los trigos, y en el invierno no sienten con el frío los piojos. Gangarilla es compañía más gruesa; ya van aqui tres o cuatro hombres, uno que sabe tocar una locura; llevan un muchacho que hace la dama, hacen el auto *de la oveja perdida*, tienen barba y cabellera, buscan saya y toca prestada (y algunas veces se olvidan de volverla), hacen dos entremeses de bobo, cobran a cuarto, pedazo de pan, huevo y sardina y todo género de zarandaja (que se echa en una talega); éstos comen asado, duermen en el suelo, beben un trago de vino, caminan a menudo, representan en cualquier cortijo, y traen siempre los brazos cruzados . . . ; porque jamás cae capa sobre sus hombros. Cambaleo es una mujer que canta y cinco hombres que lloran; éstos traen una comedia, dos autos, tres o cuatro entremeses, un lío de ropa que le puede llevar una araña; llevan a ratos a la mujer a cuestas y otras en silla de manos; representan en los cortijos por hogaza de pan, racimo de uvas y olla de berzas; cobran en los pueblos a seis maravedís, pedazo de longaniza, cerro de lino y todo lo demás que viene aventurero (sin que se deseche ripio); están en los lugares cuatro o cinco días ... Compañía de garnacha son cinco o seis hombres, una mujer que hace la dama primera y un muchacho la segunda; llevan un arco con dos sayos, una ropa, tres pellicos, barbas y cabelleras y algún vestido de la mujer de tiritaña. Estos llevan cuatro comedias, tres autos y otros tantos entremeses; el arca en un pollino, la mujer a las ancas gruñendo, y todos los compañeros detrás arreando. Estan ocho días en un pueblo ... En la bojiganga van dos mujeres y un muchacho, seis o siete compañeros, y aun suelen ganar muy buenos dineros ... Estos traen seis comedias, tres o cuatro autos, cinco entremeses, dos arcas, una con hato de la comedia y otra de las mujeres; alquilan cuatro jumentos, uno para las arcas y dos para las hembras, y otro para remudar los compañeros a cuarto de legua, conforme hiciere cada uno la figura y fuere de provecho en la chacota ... Este género de bojiganga es peligrosa, porque ay entre ellos más mudanzas que en la luna y más peligros que en frontera (y esto es si no tienen cabeza que los rija). Farándula es víspera de compañía; traen tres mujeres, ocho y diez comedias, dos arcas de hato; caminan en mulos de arrieros, y otras veces en carros, entran en buenos pueblos, comen apartados, tienen buenos vestidos, hacen fiestas de Corpus a doscientos ducados, viven contentos (digo los que no son enamorados) ... En las compañías hay todo género de gusarapas y baratijas, entreban cualquiera costura, saben de mucha cortesía, hay gente muy discreta, hombres muy estimados, personas bien nacidas y aun mujeres muy honradas (que donde hay mucho, es fuerza que haya de todo); traen cincuenta comedias, trescientas arrobas de hato, diez y seis personas que representan, treinta que comen, uno que cobra y Dios sabe el que hurta ... Sobre esto suele haber muchos disgustos. Son sus trabajos excesivos, por ser los estudios tantos, los ensayos tan continuos y los gustos tan diversos.[23]

It is hard to tell whether Rojas's terms for various sizes of company are more than inventions of his own or slang of his group, but his description of the actors and of their life is witty and vivid. It has a sharp flavour which is not altogether satisfactorily recaptured in the novel's French adaptation, Scarron's *Roman comique*.

But it was in this period that the fixed public theatres grew up, not only in the great theatrical centres of the Golden Age, Madrid, Valencia, and Seville, but also in other towns and cities. Travelling players had to continue to act on improvised stages in villages and in small towns, throughout the seventeenth century. But the actors in the cities wanted permanent theatres with good facilities and better and better stage equipment and machinery. These the cities were very willing to give them, as from the revenue of carefully organised and administered theatres the municipal authorities could maintain hospitals and other charitable institutions. The main reasons why, apart from temporary closures because of plagues or following the death of a king or queen, most of the municipal theatres were kept open through the end of the sixteenth and the seventeenth centuries despite often feverish attacks by moralists, appear to have been the economic usefulness of the theatres and the fact that the hospitals were dependent on their revenue.

Between 1565 and 1635, the year of Lope de Vega's death, the municipal theatres or *corrales* were established and gradually improved their amenities and equipment. In 1565 a charitable organisation, the Cofradía de la Pasión y Sangre de Jesucristo, was formed in Madrid in order to care for the poor. This Cofradía maintained a hospital, and the city granted it the right to sponsor the performance of plays, in its own yards or *corrales*, to raise funds for the hospital's upkeep. The Cofradía eventually hired yards for this purpose, including the famous Corral de la Pacheca, in various parts of Madrid. In 1574 a second organisation, the Cofradía de la Soledad de Nuestra Señora, which also had plays performed for its charitable purposes, came to an agreement with the Pasión y Sangre, with official sanction, to share the profits from performances in the city. In that year the Italian *Commedia dell'arte* player Alberto Ganassa, who was with his troupe in Madrid,[24] helped the Cofrades to have a stage and covered platform built in the Corral de la Pacheca, for the performance of his plays. In 1579 the Corral de la Cruz was founded, in 1582 the Corral del Príncipe, and these two, ousting the Pacheca, were to remain the two Madrid public theatres throughout the seventeenth century and well beyond it.

The main characteristics of a typical Spanish *corral* of the Golden Age were that it was a yard (normally rectangular) with a stage at one end, its apron projecting into the pit. The Madrid *corrales* and most others in Spain were exposed to the sky and the weather, except for parts of the stage area and certain rows of seats along the sides and at the back. In most *corrales* the commoners in the pit, or *patio*, had to stand. Along the sides of the theatre towards the back ran covered rows of *gradas* or benches in tiers, and above these the windows of the houses at the sides of the yard formed boxes, *aposentos*, which could be hired by the year by the wealthy. The lower level of the back building of the yard was occupied by the entrances, one for men and one for women, and the theatre bar (*fruteria* or *alojeria*). Above this level were the areas for women of the lower classes, who (unlike the ladies in the boxes) were strictly segregated from the men. The floors reserved for women were known as the *cazuela* or *cazuelas*. One fee was charged for entrance to the theatre itself and other fees were paid inside, for admission to the spectators' areas.

The stage was suited for a great variety of spectacle. It consisted not only of the projecting apron, the mid-stage, and the backstage or *foro* but also of the various balconies and windows of the wall behind it. At either side of the backstage were the *vestuarios* or green-rooms, from which the actors went on-stage through curtains or doors. There was no proscenium arch or proscenium curtain, but part of the back-stage was generally curtained off, and its curtains could be used for sudden 'discoveries', the main stage-device of this period. The action of a play could take place at various levels. Battles and jousts, some-times with real horses, could be held in a roped-off area of the pit itself, with ramps whereby the riders could reach the stage. Ramps and ladders could also connect the stage with the various balconies above it. The top balcony might represent Heaven, with cloud-machines descending from it to bring down angels, and trapdoors in the stage, belching smoke and flames, might represent the pit of Hell. There may have been a fairly wide range of props and machinery. Transform-ation-devices could suddenly hide an actor or reveal another. Imitation rocks could open. Curtains could be whipped back to reveal a startling spectacle. Drop-scene effects were sometimes used. The players' costumes were often rich, colourful, and varied. In the richer companies there seems to have been an abundance of luxurious contemporary clothing; indeed leading actors and actresses may have spent a great deal of their salaries on their costumes. The realism of the costumes was, however, limited. Characters of whatever period were presented in seventeenth-century Spanish dress: doublet, breeches, cloak, and sword. There may sometimes have been deliberate policy in such anachronisms in treating historical subjects. Golden Age dramatists were sometimes creating social and political parables for their own times, and the use of contemporary costume may have served to under-line the contemporary point of the plots. Whatever their moral or didactic purpose, however, it is clear that performances offered vivid, interesting, and remarkably varied spectacle.[25]

The afternoon's entertainment in a *corral* (heavy fines were imposed if the performance went on till dusk) followed a set pattern. First the musicians might play and sing; then the introductory *loa* would be recited, mainly as a compliment to the audience but sometimes outlining the *comedia* to come; the *loa* might end with a dance. Then would come the various *jornadas* of the play, and between the acts brief farces called *entremeses*, *sainetes*, or, with the characters in animal masks, *mojigangas*. After the last *jornada* would come a lively *fin de fiesta* ending with a dance. The continuous but varied entertainment left no gaps in which an audience could become restive or bored: wisely, for the *mosqueteros* or groundlings of the *patio* were quick to show their disapproval, and violent in expressing it. A week was a long run; a run of more than two or three days was more usual. The public's demand for more and more plays was insatiable.

The actors, whose life appears often to have been picturesquely and squalidly immoral, were organised in *compañías* in the cities. Madrid's two companies, for the two *corrales*, were made up during Lent and began the theatrical year at Easter. After Easter, the *corrales* were opened for the season, which did not end until Lent came round again. At the head of each company was the manager, called *autor de comedias*, who obtained his plays either directly from the dramatists (called *poetas* or *ingenios*) or from existing texts. Each company would have about four young actors, led by the *primer galán*, with two men to play elderly parts (*barbas*) and two comedians (*graciosos*); the actresses included the *primera dama* and five others. There was no royal troupe of actors in Spain. For court performances, in the simple palace theatres and the elaborate Italianate Coliseo del Buen Retiro which opened in the 1630s, the palace authorities simply ordered one or other, or both, of the town companies to do the work. Sometimes, and particularly in the late seventeenth century, these demands of the court theatre seriously frustrated the *arrendadores* who ran the Príncipe and the Cruz and also annoyed the theatregoing public, who might be deprived of *comedias* in the *corrales* for weeks on end. Nevertheless, itinerant companies must often have filled the gap.[26]

One of Lope de Vega's most notable predecessors, Juan de la Cueva (1550?-1610), appears to have written his fourteen tragedies and comedies for the early public theatres of Seville where they were performed between 1579 and 1581. Cueva is a disappointing dramatist. He could create an effective individual scene, but he could not contrive dramatic wholes. Like many other late sixteenth-century *ingenios* he suffered from dramatic myopia, unable to see the dramatic wood for the trees. His metrical variety is interesting.[27] In addition he appears to have been one of the first playwrights to introduce Spanish history and legend to the Spanish drama, treating his historical themes with great freedom. He begins, in fact, one of the great traditions of the Golden Age, that of dramatising popular national history, drawn from chronicles and from the ballad-cycles, and of treating it in such ways as to produce effects that are not only emotional but also didactic. His *Comedia de la muerte del rey don Sancho y reto de Zamora* dramatises King Sancho II of Castile's siege of Zamora, a well-known balladsubject. The *Comedia de la libertad de España por Bernardo del Carpio* treats a very popular ballad-subject, Bernardo's turning back the French invaders at Roncesvalles and saving Spain from Charlemagne. The most famous of Cueva's plays on Spanish history and legend is the *Tragedia de los siete infantes de Lara*, which retells an old story of treachery and bloody vengeance. Cueva's audiences, who knew the whole legend from ballads, doubtless revelled in the *dramatismo* of individual scenes, without worrying about the structure of the play as a whole. Nowadays, we find it episodic and clumsily constructed, though not without fine moments, scenes, and effects. The magnificent legend was better treated in the anonymous *Gran comedia de los famosos hechos de Mudarra*, written between 1583 and 1585, and better still in Lope de Vega's moving and lyrical tragedy, *El bastardo Mudarra*.

Cueva also wrote three plays on subjects from Greek and Roman history. The best of these, the *Tragedia de la muerte de Virginia y Appio Claudio*, is much more tightly and effectively constructed than most of his dramas. He composed light comedies, for example the *Comedia del tutor*, a celestinesque comedy of student life and love, and dark *comedias* such as the *Comedia del degollado*, drawn from the Italian original of Giraldi Cinthio. This Italian short-story writer, dramatist, and literary theorist, whose influence on the Spanish drama was probably greater than has been supposed, would have called *El degollado* a *tragedia di lieto fine*, a tragedy with a happy ending, such as we find in certain of Euripides' plays and Cinthio's own.[28] Such plays were to be frequently cultivated in seventeenth-century Spain. It is to this category of play, and not to the *comedia de capa y espada* (plays of amorous intrigue), that Cueva's very well-known play *El infamador* belongs. In this drama the dissolute Leucino defames the chaste Eliodora when she resists his advances. Eliodora's life and honour are saved by the intervention of the goddess Diana, who has Leucino buried alive. The play, which contains many details and characters drawn from the tradition of *La Celestina*, has some dramatic tension, but it is clumsily contrived.

Despite the carelessness with which he devised his plots, Cueva was the most important representative of the sixteenth-century dramatists writing plays in four *jornadas*. His importance, however, may be even greater than this. Some of the inconsistencies of the intrigues may have been deliberately intended by the playwright, as part of the techniques of political drama. Cueva may have been presenting to his Sevillian audiences a series of veiled political commentaries directed against Philip II's campaign to take over the throne of Portugal, after the death of Sebastian of Portugal at Alcazarquivir. It has been suggested that Cueva's history-plays and novelesque plays alike were political allegories treating this problem and that he adapted his sources to suit the needs of this treatment. If this is correct, Cueva was the first of many dramatists who appear to have used the Spanish *corrales* of the Golden Age for political satire and propaganda.[29] That he knew about the classical theory of satire is shown by his important poem on literary and dramatic theory and practice, *Ejemplar poético*, which he wrote in 1609, long after the last of his plays.[30]

Cervantes[31] was also a prolific dramatist in the 1580s. He left off writing plays for some years, but his *Ocho comedias y ocho entremeses nuevos* (printed in Madrid, 1615) are in the new style of Lope de Vega. In the prologue to this collection of his late dramatic works, Cervantes says that in the early part of his career

> se vieron en los teatros de Madrid representar *Los tratos de Argel*, que yo compuse, *La destruición de Numancia* y *La batalla naval*, donde me atreví a reducir les comedias a tres jornadas, de cinco que tenían; mostré, o, por mejor decir, fui el primero que representase las imaginaciones y los pensamientos escondidos del alma, sacando figuras morales al teatro, con general y gustoso aplauso de los oyentes; compuse en este tiempo hasta veinte comedias o treinta, que todas ellas se recitaron sin que se les ofreciese ofrenda de pepinos ni de otra cosa arrojadiza: corrieron su carrera sin silbos, gritas ni baraúndas. Tuve otras cosas en que ocuparme, dejé la pluma y las comedias, y entró luego el monstruo de naturaleza, el gran Lope de Vega, y alzóse con la monarquía cómica.[32]

Only two of his early plays have been preserved, *Los tratos* (or *El trato*) *de Argel* and *El cerco de Numancia*, both in four acts, although one manuscript of *El trato* has five. *El trato de Argel* is a weakly constructed play whose principal interest nowadays is in its documentary value concerning Cervantes's five years of slavery in Algiers. But *El cerco de Numancia* is his best play by far. True, it is not a perfect dramatic poem by any means. Cervantes was not a good poet. As he himself wryly confessed in the prologue to the *Ocho comedias*, a bookseller once told him he would have bought his new plays for printing, had the manager of a company of actors not told him 'que de mi prosa se podía esperar mucho, pero que del verso, nada'. In the *Numancia* there are many bad lines and rhymes. Yet the plot, though not remarkably skilful or at all involved, holds our interest throughout. The play concerns the siege of the Spanish city of Numantia by Scipio Africanus. There are few signs of individualised characterisation, and few are needed, for Numantia the community is the protagonist. Antonio Buero Vallejo has rightly stressed the importance of the element of hope in tragedy.[33] And the secret of the success of Cervantes's *Numancia* is precisely that it treats of human hope, that is frustratable but is also indomitable. The play presents, in fact, a series of hopes, each of which is dashed until the last, which results in a terrible triumph.

Cervantes seems at first to have resented Lope de Vega's rise to fame and expressed his resentment in the famous tirade by the priest in Chapter 48 of the First Part of *Don Quixote*:

En materia ha tocado vuestra merced, señor canónigo, ... que ha despertado en mí un antiguo rencor que tengo con las comedias que agora se usan, tal, que iguala al que tengo con los libros de caballerías; porque habiendo de ser la comedia, según le parece a Tulio, espejo de la vida humana, ejemplo de las costumbres e imagen de la verdad, las que ahora se representan son espejos de disparates, ejemplos de necedades e imágenes de lascivia. Porque, ¿qué mayor disparate puede ser en el sujeto que tratamos que salir un niño en mantillas en la primera escena del primer acto, y en la segunda salir ya hecho hombre barbado? Y ¿qué mayor que pintarnos un viejo valiente y un mozo cobarde, un lacayo retórico, un paje consejero, un rey ganapán y una princesa fregona? ¿Qué diré, pues, de la observancia que guardan en los tiempos en que pueden o podían suceder las acciones que representan, sino que he visto comedia que la primera jornada comenzó en Europa, la segunda en Asia, la tercera se acabó en Africa, y aun si fuera de cuatro jornadas, la cuarta acabara en América, y así se hubiera hecho en todas las cuatro partes del mundo?

And so on. Nevertheless, the priest and his crony the canon do not necessarily represent their creator's views but may rather express his dilemma with respect to the aesthetics of the new dramatic system.[34] At all events, Cervantes eventually overcame any resentment he may have felt for Lope, and in 1615 he praised him both generously and highly. Cervantes indeed wrote his own *Ocho comedias* in three acts and in what appears to have been a simple and rather clumsy attempt at Lopesque style. As he admitted in one of them, *El rufián dichoso*, times change, the techniques of art change with them, and the fact that men's minds are agile ('el pensamiento es ligero') fully justifies the breaking of the neo-classical unities of time and place.[35] The *Ocho comedias* are not great drama. The most interesting of them are the three which use material drawn from Cervantes's memories of his captivity in Africa (*Los baños de Argel, El gallardo español, La gran sultana*) and the picaresque *Pedro de Urdemalas*. None of them has the tension of the *Numancia*. The best of Cervantes's late plays are really his humorous and ironical *entremeses*, all but two of which are in prose; and, amongst these, four stand out as excellent: two playlets on matrimonial problems, *El juez de los divorcios* and *El viejo celoso*, and the remarkably funny *La cueva de Salamanca* and *El retablo de las maravillas*.[36]

The last important date in the history of the sixteenth-century drama is 1596. How well acquainted the majority of the late sixteenth-century Spanish dramatists were with the classical dramatic theory of Aristotle and Horace cannot be determined. Argensola's *loa* for his *Alejandra* mentions Aristotle, whose *Poetics* were not published in Spanish translation until the seventeenth century, although they were available in a Latin version from 1536 and could be read, from 1570, in the Italian translation by Castelvetro. In 1591 and 1592 two Spanish translations of Horace's *Ars poetica* were published, the first in Madrid and the second in Lisbon.[37] It is possible that most of the tragedians knew little of the classical theorists and simply imitated Seneca, but it is more probable that, because of the very close cultural contacts between Spain and Italy in their time, they knew not only the texts of the two great theorists but also many of the Italian commentaries on them. Whatever be the truth of this, in 1596 there was published in Madrid the first of the great Spanish commentaries on and explanations of Aristotle and Horace, Alonso López Pinciano's *Philosophía antigua poética*, a long, eloquent, and sensible work written in typical Renaissance fashion, as a dialogue. It must have stimulated fruitful debate among the rising dramatists.[38]

NOTES

1. Hugo Albert Rennert, *The Spanish Stage in the Time of Lope de Vega*, 2nd ed. (New York, 1963), p. xi. This book, though superseded by Shergold, op. cit., is still valuable and readable.

2. The best studies of Rueda's art are contained in Shergold, op. cit., pp. 151-67; R. L. Grismer, *The Influence of Plautus in Spain before Lope de Vega* (New York, 1944), pp. 166-87; Arróniz, op. cit., pp. 73-134; E. Cotarelo y Mori, 'L. de R. y el teatro español de su tiempo', *Estudios de historia literaria de España* (1901), pp. 183-290; and the introduction by A. Cardona and G. Pallardó to L. de R., *Teatro completo* (Barcelona, 1967).

3. Cervantes, *Comedias y entremeses*, ed. Schevill and Bonilla, I (Madrid, 1915), 5-6; *Preceptiva*, pp. 142-3. As Shergold has shown, Cervantes's partially eyewitness account is probably based in part on Juan Rufo (*Preceptiva*, p. 83) and Agustín de Rojas (*Preceptiva*, pp. 98-9).

4. Shergold, op. cit., p. 144.

5. See Arróniz, op. cit., pp. 73-89, and ff. for the other three plays for which precise Italian sources have been identified.

6. See Allardyce Nicoll, *The World of Harlequin. A Critical Study of the Commedia dell'arte* (Cambridge, 1963), pp. 146, 232 n. On the evolution of *paso* character-types, see María Rosa Lida de Malkiel, 'El fanfarrón en el teatro del Renacimiento', *RPhil*, XI (1957-58), 268-91; Frida Weber de Kurlat, 'Sobre el negro como tipo cómico en el teatro español del siglo XVI', *RPhil*, XVII (1963-64), 380-91, with its bibliographical notes.

7. On the two plays, see Grismer, op. cit., pp. 187-93.

8. See Arróniz, op. cit., pp. 134-42.

9. *Colección de autos, farsas y coloquios del siglo XVI*, 4 vols. (Macon, 1901). See Crawford, *Spanish Drama*, pp. 142-50.

10. See S. Griswold Morley, 'Strophes in the Spanish Drama before Lope de Vega', *Homenaje ofrecido a Menéndez Pidal*, I (Madrid, 1925), 517-18.

11. See J. L. Flecniakoska, 'De cómo un coloquio pastoril se transmuta en dos coloquios a lo divino', *Actas* I, 271-80.

12. See Wardropper, op. cit., pp. 226-8.

13. For the development of the *auto* in this period see J. L Flecniakoska, *La formation de l' 'auto'*, and Wardropper, op. cit., pp. 211-74.

14. ed. E. M. Wilson (Madrid, 1970).

15. For the School drama, see Crawford, *Spanish Drama*, pp. 155-8; A. Bonilla y San Martín, 'El teatro escolar en el renacimiento español...', *Homenaje ofrecido a Menéndez Pidal*, III (Madrid, 1925), 143-55; Flecniakoska, *La formation de l' 'auto'*, pp. 225-68; Grismer, op. cit., pp. 88-100; Justo García Soriano, 'El teatro de colegio en España', *BRAE*, XIV (1927), 234-77, 374-411, 535-65, 620-50; XV (1928), 62-93, 145-87, 396-446, 651-69; XVI (1929), 80-106, 223-43; XIX (1932), 485-98, 608-24, and *El teatro universitario y humanístico en España* (Toledo, 1945); Félix González Olmedo, *Las fuentes de 'La vida es sueño'* (Madrid, 1928).

16. See Rennert, op. cit., pp. 120-1, 266 and note 2. The controversies over the permissibility of public play-acting in Spain need much further research. E. Cotarelo y Mori's *Bibliografía de las controversias sobre la licitud del teatro en España* (Madrid, 1904) is valuable but incomplete. See J. C. J. Metford, 'The Enemies of the Theatre in the Golden Age', *BHS*, XXVIII (1951), 76-92; E. M. Wilson, 'Las "Dudas curiosas" a la Aprobación del Maestro Fray Manuel de Guerra y Ribera', *Estudios escénicos*, No. 6 (1960), 47-63, and

'Nuevos documentos sobre las controversias teatrales: 1650-1681', *Actas II*, 155-70; Bances Candamo, op. cit. For the workings of the censorship system in the seventeenth century, see E. M. Wilson, 'Calderón and the Stage-censor in the Seventeenth Century. A Provisional Study', *Sym*, XV (1961), 165-84.

17. See Hernán Pérez de Oliva, *Teatro*, ed. William Atkinson, *RH*, LXIX (1927), 521-659; W. Atkinson, 'H.P. de O. A Biographical and Critical Study', *RH*, LXXI (1927), 309-484; Alfredo Hermenegildo, *Los trágicos españoles del siglo XVI* (Madrid, 1961), pp. 95-118.

18. For Seneca and his wide influence, see F. L. Lucas, *Seneca and Elizabethan Tragedy* (Cambridge, 1922); *Les tragédies de Sénèque et le théâtre de la Renaissance*, ed. Jean Jacquot (Paris, 1964); Karl Alfred Blüher, *Seneca in Spanien* (Munich, 1969), pp. 244-52.

19. See A. I. Watson, 'George Buchanan and A. F.'s *Castro*', *BHS*, XXI (1954), 65-77; H. G. Whitehead, 'A. F.: *Ines de Castro*, 1587', *Atlante*, III (1955), 205-6.

20. On Bermúdez, see Mitchell D. Triwedi, 'Notas para una biografía de J. B.', *Hisp*, núm. 29 (1967), 1-9; Hermenegildo, op. cit., pp. 149-80, 553-5; J. P. W. Crawford, 'Influence of Seneca's Tragedies on Ferreira's *Castro* and B.'s *Nise lastimosa* and *Nise laureada*', *MP*, XII (1914-15), 171-86.

21. On Virués, whose plays can be read in *Poetas dramáticos valencianos*, ed. Eduardo Juliá Martínez, I (Madrid, 1929), 25-178, see Hermenegildo, op. cit., pp. 213-80, 590-5; W. C. Atkinson, 'Séneca, Virués, Lope de Vega', *Homenatge a Antoni Rubió i Lluch*, I (Barcelona, 1936), 111-31; Cecilia Vennard Sargent, *A Study of the Dramatic Works of Cristóbal de Virués* (New York, 1930).

22. See, for example, R. R. MacCurdy, 'La tragédie néo-sénéquienne en Espagne au XVIIe siècle, et particulièrement le thème du tyran', in Jacquot, op. cit., pp. 73-85.

23. *NBAE*, XXI, 497b-9a. See Shergold, op. cit., pp. 508-12.

24. See N. D. Shergold, 'Ganassa and the "Commedia dell' Arte" in Sixteenth-Century Spain', *MLR*, LI (1956), 359-68.

25. See Shergold, *History*, pp. 177-235, 360-414.

26. For the life of the actors and the organisation of their work, see Shergold, *History*, pp. 503-43, and Rennert, op. cit., passim.

27. See E. S. Morby, 'Notes on Juan de la Cueva: Versification and Dramatic Theory', *HR*, VIII (1940), 213-18.

28. For the *tragedia di lieto fine*, see Marvin T. Herrick, *Tragicomedy*, ed. of Urbana, 1955, pp. 63-124; Bernard Weinberg, *A History of Literary Criticism in the Italian Renaissance*, I (Chicago, 1961), 210-12; P. R. Horne, *The Tragedies of Giambattista Cinthio Giraldi* (Oxford, 1962), passim and in particular, pp. 28, 36-9, 114. There are useful translations from Giraldi's theoretical writings in *Literary Criticism. Plato to Dryden*, ed. and trans. A. H. Gilbert, 2nd ed. (Detroit, 1962), pp. 242-73. His influence on Virués has been noted by Crawford, *Spanish Drama*, pp. 183-4, and on others by Arróniz, op. cit., pp. 70, 72, 136, 297-300.

29. See A. I. Watson, *Juan de la Cueva and the Portuguese Succession* (London, 1971).

30. See Hermenegildo, op. cit., pp. 281-325, 564-70; Marcel Bataillon, 'Simples réflexions sur J. de la C.', *BH*, XXXVII (1935), 329-36 (and in translation in his *Varia lección de clásicos españoles* [Madrid, 1964], pp. 206-14); E. S. Morby, 'The Influence of Senecan Tragedy in the Plays of Juan de la Cueva', *SPh*, XXXIV (1937), 383-91; Shergold, *History*, pp. 191-2, and 'J. de la C. and the early theatres of Seville', *BHS*, XXXII (1955), 1-7; Crawford, *Spanish Drama*, pp. 164-70.

31. See R. O. Jones, *A Literary History of Spain: The Golden Age: Prose and Poetry*, pp. 168-85.

32. Cervantes, *Comedias y entremeses*, ed. cit., I, 7-8. The entire prologue is printed, with a few errors, in *Preceptiva*, pp. 142-6.

33. See A.B.V., 'La tragedia', in *El teatro*, ed. G. Díaz-Plaja (Barcelona, 1958), pp. 74-8, and also his *comentario* to the first Alfil edition of his own tragedy *Hoy es fiesta* (Madrid, 1957), pp. 99-109.

34. See Wardropper, 'Cervantes's Theory of the Drama', *MP*, LII (1955), 217-21.

35. See *Preceptiva*, pp. 139-42.

36. On Cervantes's drama, see Bibliography, p. 149, and also Wardropper's studies of the *comedias* in *Suma cervantina*, ed. J. B. Avalle-Arce and E. C. Riley (London, 1971).

37. See Duncan Moir, 'The Classical Tradition in Spanish Dramatic Theory and Practice in the Seventeenth Century', in *Classical Drama and its Influence. Essays presented to H. D. F. Kitto*, ed. M. J. Anderson (London, 1965), pp. 191-228.

38. El Pinciano's treatise is best read in the edition by Alfredo Carballo Picazo, 3 vols. (Madrid, 1953). See Sanford Shepard, *El Pinciano y las teorías literarias del Siglo de Oro* (Madrid, 1962); Margarete Newels, *Die dramatischen Gattungen in den Poetiken des Siglo de Oro* (Wiesbaden, 1959), passim.

Chapter 3

THE DRAMA OF LOPE DE VEGA

THE SPANISH *comedia* OF THE SEVENTEENTH CENTURY, a neat and satisfying art-form which could be the vehicle for many different kinds of play, was the ultimate result of technical and poetic experimentation carried out by many dramatists in the late sixteenth. But the basic characteristics of the form (three acts and a well-developed polymetric system) and the custom of the play's having, whether it be comedy, tragedy, or tragicomedy, at least one fully-fledged *gracioso* character in it, and very often a comic or serious sub-plot relevant to the *comedia's* main theme, were fixed and established as norms because they became the practice of one prodigiously successful dramatist, Lope de Vega Carpio. The sixteenth-century poets moved towards the form; Lope, drawing on their experience, perfected it and gave it authority. After his death, his polymetric system might be gradually simplified and modified, but the *comedia*-form itself, the Spanish dramatic mould *par excellence*, remained unchanged until the eighteenth century was well advanced.

Lope's was an extraordinarily powerful and many-sided talent.[1] His amazing passion and vitality as a man and his markedly extrovert nature are reflected not only in his poems and prose-works but also, very clearly, in his plays, which always have dash and fire (even the many potboilers). They often contain a character, called Belardo or some other stock name, who obviously represents Lope himself and may tell us details of his doings in life and love at the times when the dramas were being written.[2] Spontaneity and naturalness are the hallmarks of Lope's genius. Cervantes called him a prodigy of nature (*monstruo de naturaleza*), and long after Lope's death Fray Manuel de Guerra y Ribera called Calderón a prodigy of intellect (*monstruo del ingenio*). Modern comparisons of the two great dramatists have often tended, unjustly, to make Lope seem naïve, and intellectually second-class. Although it is quite true that he could, and often did, both think and write naïvely, and wrote many mediocre plays which he

43

appears to have dashed off carelessly in a couple of days, Lope had one of the first brains in an age which prided itself on its intellectual sharpness, and his best plays often reveal upon careful reading both subtlety and depth. For his contemporaries, he was the intellectual Phoenix, 'el Fénix de España', 'el Fénix de los ingenios'.

In his long career as a dramatist, which started in earnest in the 1580s and continued until just before his death in 1635, Lope wrote an astonishingly large number of plays. In the prologue of the first edition of his novel *El peregrino en su patria* (1604) he himself gave the titles of 219 *comedias* which he had composed by that date. In later lists the number mounts until at last, in the posthumously printed *Égloga a Claudio*, he laid claim to 'mil y quinientas fábulas'. Finally, in his *Fama póstuma*, his protégé Juan Pérez de Montalbán said that 1,800 *comedias* and over 400 *autos sacramentales* by his master had been acted. Modern scholars are sceptical. Many plays with titles mentioned by Lope in his lists have been lost. Also, there are many plays attributed to him in seventeenth- and eighteenth-century printed and manuscript texts which are not in fact by Lope. Carelessness, ignorance, doubt, presumption, and also the mercenary motives of hack playwrights, *autores de comedias*, and speculating printers who realised, in an age when '¡Es de Lope!' was a very common colloquial expression for 'It's excellent!', that any play attributed to Lope might sell, whoever its real author might be—all these have contributed to our present confusion about the exact number of Lope's plays whose texts have been preserved. Specialists nowadays generally agree with Morley and Bruerton that we have texts (pure and corrupt, in manuscript and in print) of around 314 *comedias* which are definitely by Lope; and that of 187 which have been attributed to him 27 are probably his, 73 may be his, and 87 are probably not his.[3] *El sufrimiento premiado*, a fine romantic comedy, has also been convincingly claimed for him by Dixon.[4] Certain striking and well-known plays which have been said to be by Lope, for example *La estrella de Sevilla*, do not in fact appear to be his.[5]

Seventeenth-century plays are often difficult to date, and chronology is perhaps the greatest problem of all those which face students of the history of the Golden Age drama. Dramatists did not always sign or date their manuscripts. Printed plays often bear no date or place of publication; and such dates, when they are given (the dates of *Partes* are good examples), can usually only be regarded as *termini ad quos* of composition. In the case of Lope de Vega's *comedias*, invaluable work has been done by Morley and Bruerton, who analysed the development of the playwright's use of different types of strophe in his undoubtedly authentic and datable plays, along with other relevant evidence, in order to give approximate and tentative dates to his otherwise undatable *comedias* (and also to eliminate from the *corpus* of his work plays which, on stylistic grounds, they do not consider to be his).[6] Their method is not infallible; but it gives us a most useful guide to the development of Lope's dramatic art as well as credible approximate dates for each play whose date of composition is not certain.

Lope wrote copiously about his dramatic principles.[7] Any serious study of his plays ought to be preceded by the study of his *Arte nuevo de hacer comedias en este tiempo*, which he wrote for the Academia de Madrid and published in 1609. This poem in 389 lines is not a young man's manifesto; Lope had been writing plays for many years before he composed it. Nor is it a completely authoritative and infallible guide to all details of his dramatic art; what he says in it about his polymetric system, for example, is very sketchy and incomplete, especially as this system changed considerably between the 1580s and 1635. Nevertheless, the *Arte nuevo*, ironic, elliptical in its style, tells us what Lope thought and felt in 1609 about the art of writing for the wide social range of spectators who flocked to the *corrales*. The poem, which has something in common with Boileau's *Art poétique*, shows Lope to be well within the great classical tradition of the European drama. Lope, Tirso de Molina, Calderón, and other good Spanish dramatists of the seventeenth century certainly did not always observe the neo-classical unities of time and place in the *comedia* (although Lope wrote at least six regular plays and Calderón and other *ingenios* also wrote within the unities more often than has been supposed), but they were, in their own fashion, classicists.[8] Also, the *Arte nuevo* shows that Lope, who in his dramatic practice followed and elaborated on the tendency of sixteenth-century playwrights to introduce comic scenes and incidents into serious plays, defended this practice in theory which appears to be derived from Giambattista Guarini and perhaps from other Italian defenders of the genre of tragicomedy. The *Arte nuevo* is partly a defence of Lope's *comedia nueva* against its neo-classicist attackers, for in Spain the new dramaturgy was the subject of sometimes bitter aesthetic controversy which began at least as early as 1605 and seems to have gone on for most of the rest of the first quarter of the century, until the neo-classicists gave up their written attacks.[9] But the poem is also a practical guide, written by an expert, for dramatists aspiring to please the theatrically experienced Madrid public in 1609.

Having saluted the members of the Academy in the first lines of the *Arte nuevo*, Lope says, ironically, that it would be easy for any of them to write a popular dramatic *Art* but that it is more difficult for him, as he has written plays without observing the precepts of the neo-classicists. He studied the relevant books as a young man and has written a few regular plays:

> mas luego que salir por otra parte
> veo los monstruos, de apariencias llenos,
> adonde acude el vulgo y las mujeres
> que este triste ejercicio canonizan,
> a aquel hábito bárbaro me vuelvo,
> y, cuando he de escribir una comedia,
> encierro los preceptos con seis llaves;
> saco a Terencio y Plauto de mi estudio,
> para que no me den voces, que suele
> dar gritos la verdad en libros mudos,
> y escribo por el arte que inventaron
> los que el vulgar aplauso pretendieron,
> porque, como las paga el vulgo, es justo
> hablarle en necio para darle gusto.[10]

He gives a brief definition of comedy and tragedy and their basic constituents (without insisting that tragedy should have an unhappy ending). He speaks of Lope de Rueda's influence in the formation of the new dramaturgy and goes on to talk of the origins of the different genres of play in classical antiquity. For classical playwriting, he recommends the study of the Italian Francesco Robortello's famous commentary on the *Poetics* of Aristotle (Florence, 1548) and his treatise on comedy which was bound along with it.

Then Lope turns to the most useful purpose of his poem: to give advice on the writing of new plays for the *corrales*. The playwright should first select his subject and not worry about whether or not he is writing a *comedia* with kings in it; he reminds his readers that, despite all that theorists may say about the separation of social classes between tragedy and comedy, Plautus put the god Jupiter into his comedy *Amphitryon*. Then comes one of the crucial passages of the *Arte nuevo*:

> Lo trágico y lo cómico mezclado,
> y Terencio con Séneca, aunque sea

como otro Minotauro de Pasife,
harán grave una parte, otra ridícula,
que aquesta variedad deleita mucho;
buen ejemplo nos da naturaleza,
que por tal variedad tiene belleza.

In these lines Lope is not recommending his pupils to make all their plays tragicomedies; some of his own best plays are in fact tragedies, with a few or even no comic elements. What he appears to be doing here is using one of Guarini's arguments in defence of *Il pastor fido* and the genre of tragicomedy in order to justify the use of comic relief, characters, scenes, and sub-plots in serious Spanish plays, as well as the writing of tragicomedies if playwrights want to write them. Lope could scarcely have been unaware of the long controversy that was waged in Italy over the validity and permissibility of Guarini's pastoral tragicomedy *Il pastor fido*, which was by far the most famous, influential, and most frequently translated and adapted play of the Renaissance in Europe. *Il pastor fido* was composed between 1580 and 1585. Some critics believed it to be a monstrous violation of the principle of the separation of genres and that tragicomedy as a genre did not (and should not) really exist. Guarini and other writers passionately but sensibly defended both the play and the genre, and in his revised and definitive pamphlet on the subject, the *Compendio della poesia tragicomica* (published 1601; reprinted with the play in 1602), Guarini argued that the mixture of tragic and comic elements in plays was justified because there were in nature many admirable mixtures of diverse and contrary things.[11] What Lope seems to be doing in the *Arte nuevo* is using Guarini's theory to justify his own dramatic practice, which itself may have been influenced by the popularity of *Il pastor fido* in Italy and Spain.

Lope's true didactic intention in the *Arte nuevo* appears to be to tell young dramatists: 'write whatever sorts of plays you want to—comedies, tragedies, tragicomedies, or what you will; but, when you write them, do observe certain principles which commonsense dictates.' He insists on the observance of the unity of action but does not try to enforce the neo-classical unities of time and place. Of place he says nothing. Of time he says that the action of the *comedia* should occupy as little time as possible, except in historical plays, which may require a long time-span. He jokingly defends this freedom on the grounds of his fellow-countrymen's temperament,

3 * *

> porque, considerando que la cólera
> de un español sentado no se templa
> si no le representan en dos horas
> hasta el Final Juïcio desde el Génesis,
> yo hallo que, si allí se ha de dar gusto,
> con lo que se consigue es lo más justo.

He does, however, recommend a new unity of time of his own invention: that the events of each act should not, if possible, exceed the limits of one day.

Lope goes on to advise dramatists to write out their plots first in prose and divide them into three acts, corresponding to the classical concepts of protasis (exposition), epitasis (complication), and catastrophe (unravelling);

> pero la solución no la permita
> hasta que llegue a la postrera escena,
> porque, en sabiendo el vulgo el fin que tiene,
> vuelve el rostro a la puerta y las espaldas
> al que esperó tres horas cara a cara,
> que no hay más que saber que en lo que para.

He says the stage should very rarely be left empty, for the audience gets impatient if it does not hear and see something going on and gaps retard the pace of the performance. He emphasises the importance of verisimilitude in the speeches given to different types of character. He briefly treats of decorum:

> Las damas no desdigan de su nombre,
> y, si mudaren traje, sea de modo
> que pueda perdonarse, porque suele
> el disfraz varonil agradar mucho.

He warns writers to avoid improbabilities, impossibilities, and illogicalities in their plots and suggests that the intrigue should lead the spectators to expect events to turn out otherwise than in fact they will do. Then he gives a short account of the use of different strophes to suit different types of situation:

> Acomode los versos con prudencia
> a los sujetos de que va tratando;
> las relaciones piden los romances,
> el soneto está bien en los que aguardan,
> las décimas son buenas para quejas,
> aunque en octavas lucen por extremo;

> son los tercetos para cosas graves,
> y para las de amor las redondillas.[12]

He points out the usefulness of the traditional rhetorical devices in
dramatic dialogue. In particular he advises the employment of tactics
to keep the audience guessing what will happen without realising
what in fact will happen. On the choice of plots, he makes two sug-
gestions, both of them shrewd:

> Las casos de la honra son mejores,
> porque mueven con fuerza a toda gente;
> con ellos las acciones virtüosas,
> que la virtud es dondequiera amada.

He warns poets not to make their plays too long and, recognising the
political function of the drama of his time, he advises them to be careful when they put in satirical material:

> en la parte satírica no sea
> claro ni descubierto, pues que sabe
> que por ley se vedaron las comedias
> por esta causa en Grecia y en Italia;
> pique sin odio, que si acaso infama,
> ni espere aplauso ni pretenda fama.

He gives a few observations on staging and on costume, pretends to
mock at himself for being anti-classical, and then clearly reveals his
justified pride in his own plays:

> Sustento, en fin, lo que escribí y conozco
> que, aunque fueran mejor de otra manera,
> no tuvieran el gusto que han tenido,
> porque a veces lo que es contra lo justo
> por la misma razón deleita el gusto.

But pleasure is not all that can be derived from the *comedia nueva*.
And Lope, who wrote his plays not just to amuse commoners and
noblemen but also to teach them useful truths, ends the *Arte nuevo*
with a declaration of the Spanish drama's didactic function. Ten lines
of this statement are in Latin and concern the *comedia* as a mirror of
life and its expressing serious ideas in the midst of its jokes. The last
three lines are in Castilian and are telling:

> Oye atento, y del arte no disputes,
> que en la comedia se hallará de modo
> que, oyéndola, se pueda saber todo.[13]

Deleitar aprovechando, the phrase which forms the title of one of Tirso de Molina's books, expresses concisely the dual function which the drama had in the opinion of responsible seventeenth-century Spanish playwrights and theorists. It was generally accepted, in accordance with classical thought, that the pleasurable aspect of literature and the drama was essential and its didactic element incidental, but the latter element is present in the great majority of Golden Age plays, to a greater or lesser extent in individual cases. The theme, or the ideas expressed in a play, is therefore usually important, and in many plays it may be supremely important. In an instructive (and controversial) study, Parker has argued that the structure of the Spanish drama of this period is governed by five principles:

> (1) the primacy of action over character drawing; (2) the primacy of theme over action, with the consequent irrelevance of realistic verisimilitude; (3) dramatic unity in the theme and not in the action; (4) the subordination of the theme to a moral purpose through the principle of poetic justice, which is not exemplified only by the death of the wrongdoer; and (5) the elucidation of the moral purpose by means of dramatic causality.[14]

It may be doubted whether, in many of Lope's plays (and especially in his early ones), there is really primacy of theme over action. Lope, a voracious reader, simply appears to have come across, and also thought up, stories which would make lively plays and proceeded to write these plays, weaving in what doctrine he thought appropriate. Yet in many of his mature *comedias* we see him moving towards what we find in most Calderonian plays, a drama of ideas in which both action and characterisation are determined by the demands of the theme.

There is continuous, and apparently conscious, improvement in Lope's style and techniques between *Los hechos de Garcilaso de la Vega y el moro Tarfe* (Morley and Bruerton: 1577-83?), his only four-act play, and the late masterpieces such as *El castigo sin venganza* (1631). Lope's early plays often show the dramatic myopia which we have noted in other examples of sixteenth-century drama. Some of them are very far from observing his own dicta of 1609 about perfect construction and lack of episodic, unconnected fragments. In such plays there are some brilliant scenes and flashes of exhilarating poetry, but there are also arid wastes of mediocrity. Some of the early plays are also morally irresponsible. Bances Candamo noted this of *Los donaires de Matico* (M and B: before 1596), which contains some pretty scurrilous material and some remarkably plebeian behaviour by a Princess of León.[15] In his maturity, however, Lope produced much better and subtler plays. His dramatic craftsmanship became surer. He developed the figure of the *gracioso*, the comic servant who is a humorous parody of his master in some ways and a complete contrast to him in others, whose down-to-earth philosophy can form a fine continuous counterpoint to the elevated ideas of the man he serves.[16] Lope also developed the sub-plot into a meaningful complement to a main plot.[17] He greatly improved the dramatic structure of his *comedias*, their effectiveness as varied but coherent dramatic poems, and their didactic content.

The subject-matter of Lope's plays is of a very wide range. The largest group which he wrote were amorous cloak-and-sword comedies, *comedias de capa y espada*, defined by Bances Candamo as follows:

> Las [comedias] de capa y espada son aquéllas cuyos personajes son sólo Caballeros particulares, como Don Juan, o Don Diego, etcétera, y los lances se reducen a duelos, a celos, a esconderse el galán, a taparse la Dama, y, en fin, a aquellos sucesos más caseros de un galanteo.[18]

The *comedia de capa y espada* is, then, a form of the tradition of comedy which runs from Plautus and Terence on to the middle-class domestic comedy of our own times. No stranger to love, even in his years as a priest, Lope excelled at these frothy comedies of intrigue, which could, we must remember, sometimes reveal serious practical moral doctrine under the froth. One of his most delightful plays of this type is *La dama boba* (1613), an expression of the old idea that love can make the simpleminded clever. Much of the pleasure is in the characterisation of the two sisters, Nise the erudite and Finea the ignorant and silly girl who learns wisdom and shrewdness.[19] Another very fine *comedia de capa y espada* is *Los melindres de Belisa* (M and B: 1606-08), which pokes fun at the astonishingly finical young girl, Belisa, who finds fault with every suitor who seeks to win her hand. It also pokes fun at her mother, a still-young widow who does not realise that she is still a prey to amorous passion. Both mother and daughter fall in love, in spite of their middle-class-consciousness, with a man who, they think, is a slave: the play is, in fact, a witty, lightly-handled satire on snobbishness. In *La discreta enamorada* (M and B: 1606-08 [probably 1606]) the young minx Fenisa pretends to agree to marry an old man in order to make his son fall in love with her. In the end, not only does she capture her young beloved but even contrives to make his father marry her mother. Rather more idealistic than these plays, but nevertheless a good comedy of intrigue, is *Amar sin saber a quién* (M and B: 1616-23), which starts with a duel, a killing, and the arrest of an innocent man. *El acero de Madrid* (M and B: 1606-12 [probably 1608-12]), in which the heroine pretends to be ill so that her lover, pretending to be a doctor, can have access to her at all times, exploits the improper situation very funnily. Other notably amusing *comedias de capa y espada* by Lope are *El sembrar en buena tierra, Quien todo lo quiere, La noche toledana,* and *Las bizarrías de Belisa,* perhaps the last play he wrote. In this type of play we see Lope at his most amusing, treating deftly, lightly but often satirically the customs, taboos, and prejudices of his own social class. Not only the 'caballeros de capa y espada' but also the commoners must have relished these comedies.

Lope also wrote many interesting amorous comedies outside the strict class-limitations of the *comedia de capa y espada,* as their main characters are of higher social position than the lower reaches of the nobility. Bances Candamo would have included such plays as these in the category which he called *comedias de fábrica.*[20] The most celebrated of this group of plays by Lope is the brilliant *El perro del hortelano* (M and B: 1613-15). It concerns the problems which face Doña Diana, Countess of Belflor, as she becomes infatuated with her secretary, the commoner Teodoro, who does not even know who his parents were. The code of honour tells her to stifle her growing passion, as social convention would not allow her to marry such a man. But she cannot suppress it. In her tense state, she is, in the words of the proverb which provides the play's title, 'el perro del hortelano, que no come ni deja comer'. Unlike the imaginary honour-problem which faces the mother and daughter in *Los melindres de Belisa,* Diana's dilemma is real, and it is heartrending. Suitable noble suitors for her hand plot to kill Teodoro. This is dark comedy, and Lope treats his subject and his characters with care and with true insight, but also with irony. In the end, after Teodoro's servant Tristán (one of the most brilliantly drawn of all Lope's *graciosos*) has, by an outright lie, convinced all except Diana that his master is a Count, and after Teodoro has told the lady that he will go away because he cannot face the prospect of a life of deceit, Diana tells him that, for her, this statement is sufficient proof of his nobility for her to marry him. By marrying a Countess, the fake Count will become a real Count. The ending of the play is wonderfully ambiguous and ironic. It is clearly hinted that Diana realises fully that her recognition of Teodoro's *nobleza* is a convenient pretence. As Pring-Mill has observed, the use of a faked solution is part of Lope's comment on the conventions of honour; 'the point is that honour, in the sense of public reputation, *is* satisfied by the fake, and that since such a conception of honour can be satisfied by a sham that conception of honour is itself hollow'.[21] Characterisation and intrigue are both magnificent in this work. Another fine play in this category is *La hermosa fea* (M and B: 1625-32 [probably 1630-32]), in which a prince wins the love of a haughty lady by pretending that he disdains her and thinks her ugly.[22] Another good *comedia*, especially notable for the intricacy of its plot, is *El sufrimiento premiado*.[23] Others are *La moza de cántaro* (M and B: originally written before 1618 and partially revised in 1625) and, smutty as it is, *Los donaires de Matico*.

Especially in the early part of his career, Lope also wrote amorous plays in the pastoral mode, as was to be expected in an age when both the pastoral novel and pastoral poetry were extremely popular. None of his plays of this type for the *corrales* is particularly good. *El verdadero amante* is the best-known of these *comedias*, for Lope claimed that he wrote it at the age of twelve or thirteen; Morley and Bruerton, however, have argued that he probably composed it much later, between 1588 and 1595. It is pretty thin stuff and clumsily constructed. The elder Moratín was right when he stated, in the eighteenth century, that this play shows 'excelente y pestilente versificación'. Much more interesting is *Belardo el furioso* (M and B: 1586-95). As its title suggests, this *comedia* is a pastoral burlesque of Ariosto's *Orlando furioso*, but what makes the play amusing is that the character Belardo very clearly is a pseudonym for Lope himself. That *Belardo el furioso* is really an autobiographical skit is what saves it from being totally obscured by the many better plays its author wrote. The best of Lope's pastoral plays for the *corrales* is in fact *La Arcadia*, written well after the others (M and B: 1610-15; probably 1615) and a dramatic recasting of Lope's own pastoral novel of the same title.

He also drew plots from chivalresque novels and poems. A vigorous play of this type is *La mocedad de Roldán* (M and B: 1599-1603), which tells of the parentage, birth, early military exploits, and love of the future hero Roland. *Los celos de Rodamonte* (M and B: before 1596) is also on Roland but is a much inferior play, based on fragments of Boiardo's *Orlando innamorato* and Ariosto's *Orlando furioso*. Very much more skilfully written than either of the two *comedias* we have mentioned, however, is *El marqués de Mantua* (M and B: 1598-1603, probably 1600-02), drawn from the *romances* on the treacherous murder of Valdovinos, who dies in the arms of the Marquis after revealing that he is his relative. The play is gloriously written. The lyricism of the love-scenes between Valdovinos and his bride, the Infanta Sevilla, and of Lope's treatment of her premonitions of the calamity that will befall Valdovinos, contrasts strongly but effectively with the heroic poetic tones of the later part of the play, of the Marquis's solemn oath to take vengeance for the murder, and of the trial and death-sentence of the traitor Carloto. Tension is carefully prepared and accumulates steadily and ominously as the play pursues its course. This is a fine and noble tragedy based on legend, and, within the context of this study, it serves to lead us away from Lope's comedy and light drama of adventure to consider another aspect of his art, his serious plays.

A great deal of nonsense has been talked about Lope de Vega's alleged incapacity in the genre of tragedy. Indeed, it has been a commonplace of literary history that seventeenth-century Spanish dramatists could not or would not write real tragedy. This very shortsighted view is now undergoing revision.[24] Seventeenth-century dramatists appear, in accordance with common Renaissance theory, to have treated all historical subjects with a seriousness that they did not grant, on the whole, to invented stories. Lope himself said in the *Arte nuevo*:

> Por argumento la tragedia tiene
> la historia, y la comedia el fingimiento.

And Torres Naharro's division of plays into *comedias a noticia* and *comedias a fantasía* may have been simply the first statement in Spanish dramatic theory of a fundamental division in Golden Age playwrights' minds between different types of intrigue—on the one hand, historical plots, which must be treated with a certain seriousness and are really types of tragedy, whether they may have unhappy endings or not; on the other hand, invented plots, which can be treated lightly and frivolously and are therefore usually comedy. At the end of the seventeenth century, Bances Candamo divides the bulk of Golden Age *comedias* into two primary categories, *comedias historiales* and *comedias amatorias*, the latter being 'pura invención o idea sin fundamento en la verdad'; from these two categories he keeps apart only what he calls *fábulas*, mythological plays, although for most seventeenth-century dramatists it would seem that the mythological play was really treated seriously, as in the Greek drama, as tragedy.[25] As a useful provisional working rule Golden Age plays from Lope onwards may be broadly classified as historical/tragedy or invented/comedy. But the division is not hard and fast, and there are exceptions. The terminology used by dramatists or their editors is not always helpful. Usually they used the nowadays often misleading term *comedia*, although they might use *tragicomedia* as a word to describe what is perhaps best described as tragedy with a happy ending (*tragedia di lieto fine*) and *tragedia* to describe tragedy with an unhappy ending.

This is not a quibble: these terms are important in that they guide our expectations and hence our response. We should be particularly careful in our use of what Styan has justly called 'the spurious term "tragicomedy", which invites us to measure a play by two widely different yardsticks simultaneously, regardless of their possible irrelevance'.[26] Whatever Guarini and the seventeenth-century dramatists and theorists may have thought about it, 'tragicomedy' is a concept which is difficult to define satisfactorily. Like Shakespeare, the seventeenth-century Spanish playwrights usually but not always employed comic relief in their tragedies. This, in the best plays, was usually relief in two senses simultaneously—emotional (temporary relaxation from accumulating tension) and intellectual or artistic (the adding of a comic perspective to material treated from a tragic point of view). It should also be noted that, though these playwrights treated historical material seriously, they did treat it freely, changing details to suit their didactic purposes. This freedom to change and adapt should not be lightly dismissed as 'poetic licence' in a trivial sense. The seventeenth-century *ingenios* usually altered historical detail because they believed, with Aristotle (*Poetics,* IX and XXV), that historical or particular truth is inferior to universal or poetic truth.[27] Their modifications of the details of their sources deserve attention for they were often made carefully to suggest specific moral, philosophical, or political points. Lope seems to have known this Aristotelian doctrine well and used it craftily in various good tragedies. Lope was skilful in comedy; he came to excel at tragedy.

For the Golden Age, the Bible was undoubtedly history, and Lope wrote many good plays on biblical subjects and lives of saints. Such plays were very popular. *Comedias a lo divino* and *comedias de santo* often lent themselves to startling scenic effects and religious plays were amongst the most remarkably spectacular of the *comedias* performed in the *corrales*. The moralists thought such plays to be particularly scandalous, acted as they were by often dissolute professional actors. Nevertheless, Lope and other good playwrights of the seventeenth century had a manifestly pious intent in writing such plays, which they regarded as a means of instruction in practical Christian doctrine and frequently subtle theology. The *corrales* may have taught the basic principles of Christianity to some who did not go regularly to church. In a country in which the great mass of the populace was illiterate, the popular drama was certainly one of the three greatest educational forces, the others being the public storytellers and the Church.

The range of Lope's biblical *comedias* was very wide. Custom and decorum placed one important limitation on the subject-matter of these plays. It was considered that the character of the adult Christ would not decently be acted in the *corrales*, and therefore biblical *comedias*, though they could run through the subject-matter of the entire Old Testament, could dramatise from the New only the birth and infancy of Christ. His later life was, however, thought fitting material for plots of Corpus Christi *autos*, the performances of which were more strictly supervised than the plays in the *corrales* could be. Lope wrote a large cycle of plays on subjects drawn from Genesis onwards. It was probably Lope who made an interesting play out of the first four chapters of the Book of Genesis, *La creación del mundo y primera culpa del hombre*, demonstrating the concept of original sin, its consequences, and its moral implications for Christian life. As Glaser has shown, the playwright has systematically altered his biblical material to suit the demands of his artistic and doctrinal intentions, and he presents the disasters which befall Abel and Cain as direct consequences of Adam and Eve's depravity.[28] Another impressive play from Genesis, this one definitely by Lope, is *El robo de Dina* (M and B: 1615-22), on the rape of Dinah by Shechem and the terrible vengeance by Jacob's sons. This is strong and tense drama, with particularly well-conceived contrasts in the characterisation. In Glaser's words,

> Lope . . . envisages the tale from Genesis as a clash between a courtly attitude toward life and a rural one, a contrariety around which he builds some of his finest plays during the period coinciding roughly with that of the composition of *El robo de Dina*. The two systems of values operating in the Biblical drama are very similar to those in *Fuenteovejuna, Peribáñez y el Comendador de Ocaña*, and *El mejor alcalde el rey*, though, admittedly the opposition is here less sharply drawn and the frequent recourse to the supernatural, well-nigh indispensable in a religious work, tends to blur the basic struggle.[29]

But perhaps the most beautiful of all Lope's biblical plays is his dramatisation of the Book of Esther, *La hermosa Ester* (1610), the autograph manuscript of which is in the British Museum. This play shows the dramatist at his most sensitive, and amongst all his *comedias* there can be very few which leave us so contented, aesthetically and spiritually. It is glorious stuff, both poetically and dramatically.[30] Other good biblical plays by Lope include *Los trabajos de Jacob* (M and B: 1620-30) and *La historia de Tobías* (M and B: 1606-15; probably *c*. 1609).

Of the *comedias de santo*, three stand out. The most startlingly fascinating of these is *La buena guarda* (1610: dated autograph), which is not about a canonised saint at all. It is a simple but moving (and very amusing) dramatisation of a legendary tale of a nun who runs away with a lover. As a reward for her devotion to the Virgin, her absence goes unnoticed, for an angel representing the Virgin assumes the appearance of the delinquent and stands in for her until she returns. This play is one of the most delightful of all the many Spanish literary works dedicated to the cult of the Virgin Mary. And it is certainly the funniest of them. *La buena guarda*, though fundamentally serious, illustrates the cultured Spaniard's capacity for taking religion both humorously and seriously at the same time.

The second *comedia de santo* of Lope which is particularly striking is *El divino africano* (M and B: *c*. 1610). It is a dramatisation of the conversion of St Augustine, based on the account given in his *Confessions*, and of his subsequent miracles. At the close he is revealed in Heaven trampling on Heresy. Menéndez Pelayo considered the first two acts of this play excellent but objected to the third because he believed that Lope should have contented himself with, and amplified into three acts, the story of the conversion.[31] Such a procedure might not have satisfied either Lope or his audiences. Their view was probably that a great conversion ought to be seen to produce great miracles, and when the play is looked on from this point of view it clearly hangs together very well both as drama and as doctrine.

The third outstanding play amongst Lope's *comedias de santo* has an interest far beyond the usual limits of religious drama. This is *Lo fingido verdadero* (M and B: *c*. 1608), which Lope dedicated to his great disciple Tirso de Molina. The play concerns the conversion and martyrdom, under the Roman emperor Diocletian, of the actor saint Genesius, to whom the *representantes* and the *ingenios* of the Golden Age drama were devoted. But the play also presents the rise of Diocletian from soldier to emperor and the fall of various emperors who reigned before he did. Some critics (and especially those who have sought to suggest that the French dramatist Rotrou's *Saint Genest* is superior to Lope's play, which is its main source) have thought Lope's play to be haphazardly constructed. In particular the First Act, concerning the deaths of emperors and the rise of Diocletian, has been thought irrelevant to the main theme of the drama.[32] But such opinions are based on a misconception. The main theme of *Lo fingido verdadero* is the philosophical and religious idea of the great theatre of the world: 'all the world's a stage' on which all men are actors playing their brief parts in life until they are summoned before God for judgment on their performance.[33] In the light of this, the First Act, with its emperors falling one after the other in rapid succession like Aunt Sally figures in a fairground, has an obvious relevance to the rest of the play and serves to make its main moral teachings clear. The drama is, indeed, deftly constructed. Its two plays-within-a-play, disturbed as they are by Genesius's sensibility and his tendency to be taken over by his part, are magnificently conceived. It is lively, it grows tense, and it moves at a cracking pace. It is superior both to Rotrou's play (which has a feeble sub-plot of no significant relevance to its main theme) and to Calderón's famous *auto, El gran teatro del mundo*. But there is more than 'all the world's a stage' in *Lo fingido verdadero*. In its two main characters, Diocletian and Genesius, it shows two entirely different kinds of actor, and in the contrast between them the playwright suggests ideas about the actor's art which are subtle and penetrating.

Lope wrote several other excellent plays drawn from ancient history. The best of these is *Contra valor no hay desdicha* (M and B: 1620-35, probably 1625-30), on the rise of the great and arrogant Cyrus of Persia, drawn from Herodotus. This *comedia* is constructed with great skill and shows Lope at the height of his maturity as a dramatic poet. Another interesting and vigorous tragedy, though it lacks the masterful construction of the later plays, is *Roma abrasada* (M and B: 1594-1603; probably 1598-1600), which treats of Nero. Seneca, whose dramatic tradition has had a deep influence on the nature of *Roma abrasada*, appears in it as a character. Some of its poetry is brilliant.

Lope also wrote plays about other subjects from foreign history of later periods. In *La imperial de Otón* (M and B: 1595-1601; probably October 1598) he treated, majestically and with excellent characterisation, the rebellion of Otto of Bohemia against the newly elected Emperor Rudolph. And there is another good play by Lope on events in eastern Europe in his own times, *El Gran Duque de Moscovia y Emperador perseguido* (M and B: 1606?). In such plays, with the entertainment is mingled instruction on social rights and obligations from which high and low might learn.

Lope was especially eager to find lessons for the present from the past history of Spain and Portugal. He wrote numerous plays on Spanish historical subjects. In general, their lessons were on moral integrity, loyalty, patriotic spirit, respect for properly established authority, and the nature and responsibilities of lordship and kingship.[34]

It is impossible, in a brief space, to give a comprehensive account of Lope's plays on Peninsular history and to relate them to Spanish society and its problems from the 1580s to 1635. Their subjects range from the Visigothic period (e.g. *La vida y muerte del rey Bamba*, M and B: 1597-98; *El postrer godo de España*, M and B: 1599-1603, perhaps 1599-1600) up to Lope's own times, although he and his contemporaries could not represent the reigning monarch on the stage and had to be careful in their treatment of his immediate predecessors. The sources of these history-plays, at least of those which have pre-Renaissance subjects, are chronicles, legends, and traditional ballads.

One of the finest of these dramas is *El bastardo Mudarra* (1612: autograph), on the grim legend of the Siete Infantes de Lara.[35] This play has the richness of a trilogy of Greek tragedies compressed into three acts. It tells the whole story of the legend, in a carefully unified intrigue unfolded in superb heroic and lyrical poetry. In the bitter, ironical First Act Lope shows the sources of the squalid family feud which will lead to the slaughter of the Infantes. In particular, the rancorous Doña Lambra is magnificently characterised, as she incites her husband, Ruy Velázquez, to avenge the slight which she resents so bitterly:

> Ponerte fuera mejor,
> en vez del acero limpio,
> aquestas sangrientas tocas
> y aquesta cofia de piños;
> crenchas en vez de penachos
> rojos, blancos y amarillos;
> chapines en vez de espuelas,
> y por pendones moriscos
> arcas de afeite y color,
> y una rueca en vez de filo;
> por rótulo tus infamias,
> y entre ellas, que Gonzalillo,
> el menor de los de Lara,
> te ha muerto dos deudos míos,
> y con un halcón terzuelo,
> que le arrebató atrevido
> de la mano a un escudero
> que de las montañas vino,

delante del conde, en Burgos,
te cruzó ese rostro lindo,
vertiendo sangre, a su golpe,
boca, narices y oídos.
Vete, y no me veas más,
ni vuelvas a Barbadillo,
pues que sufres en tus barbas
las afrentas que te han dicho.

The second *jornada* comes to a powerfully moving climax as Gonzalo Bustos mourns over the heads of his seven sons, in a fine gloss on Garcilaso's line 'Ay, dulces prendas, por mi mal halladas'. In the Third Act, some eighteen years later, the bastard Mudarra hears who his father is and of the treachery which led to the killing of his half-brothers. He, the living image of the youngest of the seven Infantes (probably played by the same actor), leaves Córdoba for Castile, to execute terrible vengeance on Ruy Velázquez and Doña Lambra and bring comfort to the aged Gonzalo Bustos, whose lost eyesight is (not insignificantly, for the honour-symbolism of the play) restored by the appearance of his son and the restoration of his honour by bloody revenge. This play is a great family tragedy.

Another striking historical tragedy by Lope is *Las paces de los reyes y judía de Toledo* (M and B: 1604-12, probably 1610-12). This play concerns the disastrously imprudent love-affair of Alfonso VIII of Castile with a Jewess, Raquel, with whom he becomes so besotted that he neglects the proper government of the state; the Queen, Doña Leonor, incensed by Alfonso's infidelity and misgovernment, incites loyal nobles to assassinate Raquel, and after the Jewess's death the King and Queen are finally reconciled—a symbolic representation of the restoration of harmony in the state. Some critics have found the construction of *Las paces de los reyes* to be imperfect, and the First Act, on the *mocedades* of Alfonso, to be superfluous and ill-connected to the rest of the play, for the King meets Raquel only in the second *jornada*. Nevertheless, as in the case of *Lo fingido verdadero*, there is a good thematic reason for the inclusion of the at-first-sight-irrelevant First Act. It shows Alfonso's positive qualities as a ruler and that he had great political virtues, which could create harmony in the state— harmony which would be disrupted by his disastrous misconduct after his meeting with the Jewess. The clear sequence of harmony/disharmony/restoration of harmony in this play is ultimately much more important than (and is the artistic justification of) the looseness of construction in the plot. The impressive and exciting subject which it treats, and the relevance of this subject to the central problems of government in a monarchy, led to the plot of *Las paces de los reyes* being repeatedly rewritten by other dramatists. In the seventeenth century important dramatic versions of the story were made by Mira de Amescua and Diamante. In the eighteenth century it produced the best political play of that age, García de la Huerta's *Raquel*. It also had influence abroad, and Lope's play was recast by Grillparzer to form his famous drama *Die Jüdin von Toledo*.[36]

One of Lope's most masterful and dark tragedies comes from Portuguese history. This is *El Duque de Viseo* (M and B: 1604-10, probably 1608-09). In it also we find warnings for rulers and kings. Its theme is the difficulty of administering justice when so often appearances may deceive. The Duke, innocent of any treason, and in fact the epitome of loyalty and patriotism, is undone by a conjunction of suspicion in the King of Portugal, envy, and a series of unfortunate chances. This is high tragedy and a moving play.[37]

The political chaos of Spain in the fifteenth century, before the establishment of order in the reign of Ferdinand and Isabella, provided Lope and his contemporaries with material for many plays on the need for loyalty, justice, and harmony within the state. Such a play is Lope's *Fuenteovejuna* (M and B: 1611-18, probably 1612-14), the best known of all his plays and one of his masterpieces. The source of its plot is a fragment of a chronicle of the three Military Orders of Santiago, Calatrava, and Alcántara, although the process of the play's creation may have started with Lope's reflecting on a common proverb 'Fuenteovejuna lo hizo' or on an emblem in Sebastián de Covarrubias Horozco's *Emblemas morales* (Madrid, 1610).[38] The play tells of the disorder caused both in the state and in the village of Fuenteovejuna by Fernán Gómez de Guzmán, a villainous Comendador Mayor of the Order of Calatrava, the revolt of the villagers, their pact not to reveal the identity of the persons who actually killed him, the failure of the Catholic Monarchs' justices to extort, by torture, evidence of the killers' identity, and the final pardon of the villagers by King Ferdinand because the culprits cannot be identified by the law.

In this play Lope seeks to express various important ideas. Not the least important by any means concerns honour. Problems of honour were amongst the most fruitful sources of dramatic situations in the Golden Age theatre. Exactly to what extent the drama reflected real preoccupations and real problems in seventeenth-century Spanish society is not clear. The many honour-plays which were written may not be reliable in the impression they give of a society obsessed by a fantasy; yet it is clear that in that society there must have been real problems of class, of reputation, and of self-respect. Lope's statement in the *Arte nuevo* that plots on honour-problems 'mueven con fuerza a toda gente' doubtless reflects real preoccupations in the public for which he wrote. The 'code of honour' which the plays express may not have existed, as such and in all its details, in the everyday life of seventeenth-century Spaniards, but it was compounded of real fears, real prejudices, real social values, and real legal statutes.

Honour, in the strictest sense of the word, is respect, esteem, or reverence accorded to virtue, worthiness, or high rank. By extension, an honour is a mark or sign of recognition given to a man because of such qualities. And one's sense of honour is one's consciousness of the extent to which other people, and also oneself, give one due respect. Spanish legislation, from Visigothic times onwards, gave abundant reasons for worry about one's honour. The dishonoured man, as the medieval law expressed it, 'aunque no haya culpa, muerto es cuanto al bien y a la honra de este mundo'. In other words, a dishonoured person, whether the dishonour was his own fault or not, was, though physically alive, socially dead. He could, however, recover lost honour, either by legal means or by drawing blood, killing the dishonourer being a legally acceptable method of reinstating oneself socially. There were many ways in which a man might be dishonoured—for example, by being called a liar (the *mentís* being taken very seriously, as a negation of one's integrity), by being slapped in the face, by having his beard pulled, or by the infidelity or violation of his wife or daughter. It was legally accepted that family ties implied the obligation to avenge dishonour done to another member of one's family. Public dishonour had to be publicly avenged, but various honour-plays make the basically sensible point that dishonour not publicly known should be avenged secretly. The law condoned the killing of both one's unfaithful wife and her lover. It also tended to condone such killings in cases where adultery was not proven but genuinely suspected. Such legislation was not without its sensible causes, for the legislators realised the usefulness of a system of giving honour and of taking it away as a binding and consolidating force in society, and as a curb on vice.

But such a system was open to grave abuse, and it was more often, perhaps, by the possible and probable abuses of the honour-system that Lope and other responsible seventeenth-century dramatists were preoccupied than by the system itself. In plays like the vigorous drama *Los comendadores de Córdoba* (M and B: 1596) and *La locura por la honra* (M and B: 1610-12), Lope may seem cheerfully to approve of the killing of an adulterous wife and her accomplice or accomplices, but the playwright may really have considered it better for the husband to seek milder remedies, like the thrashing which the gentleman in *El castigo del discreto* (M and B: 1598-1601) gives in the dark to his wife, who thinks she is being beaten by the gallant she adored up to that moment.[39] There was an obvious conflict between Christian doctrine and the principle by which a husband could kill his erring wife. It may well be, in fact, that Lope's true advice about the solution of the problem of a wife's unfaithfulness is contained in his *auto sacramental*, *La adúltera perdonada*, a work which certainly has social as well as religious significance. And, carefully and subtly, seventeenth-century dramatists attack other abuses of the honour-system, such as impulsiveness, over-suspiciousness, etc.

What is attacked in *Fuenteovejuna* is the aristocratic conviction that commoners are not entitled to a sense of honour. Fernán Gómez jeers at the villagers:

> ¿Vosotros honor tenéis?
> ¡Qué freiles de Calatrava!

There were certain medieval legal and theoretical precedents for, and causes of, this scornful attitude towards commoners and the belief that honour was an exclusive prerogative of the nobility. The *Siete partidas* of Alfonso el Sabio, for example, instruct kings to love and honour (*amar e honrar*) their nobles both great and small, learned men, citizens of the towns (the bourgeois, we might say), and merchants; but, when it comes down to day-labourers and farm-labourers, the law changes its wording from 'amar e honrar' to 'amar e amparar':

> E amar e amparar deben otrosí a los menestrales, y a los labradores, porque de sus menesteres, e de sus labranzas se ayudan e se gobiernan los Reyes, e todos los otros de sus señoríos, e ninguno non puede sin ellos vivir.

Their work was essential, but without honour! The anti-commoner prejudice survives into doctrinal works of the sixteenth century. For example, Fray Antonio de Guevara stated that

> La culpa de un rústico en él se acaba, mas la del hidalgo redunda en su generación toda, porque amancilla la fama de los pasados, desentierra las vidas de los muertos, pone escrúpulo en los que agora viven y corrumpe la sangre de los que están por venir.

However, between the late sixteenth century and the middle of the seventeenth a change appears to have taken place in the minds of sensitive intellectuals in Spain with regard to the commoner's right to a sense of honour and dignity. The change is admitted openly about 1640 by the erudite Diego Saavedra y Fajardo who, when he composed a commentary on Alfonso's law in his emblem-book, *Idea de un príncipe político-cristiano*, stated that the king must honour not only nobles and great Ministers, 'sino también a los demás vasallos'; in other words, he must honour all his virtuous subjects. In the great theatre of the world all men are fundamentally equal; their ranks or social roles are quite extraneous to their essential being. Nobility, for the seventeenth-century thinkers, was a matter of virtue rather than of social position. García Valdecasas has expressed their point of view concisely and aptly:

(1) Nobility consists only in virtue. Wherever there is or can be virtue there will be or may be nobility. All other conditions are secondary to this one.

(2) Noble lineage does not imply nobility; it only implies the obligation to be noble and, at most, a credit-balance of trust: one expects noble behaviour of a person who is of noble descent.

(3) Virtue is proved by works, as the tree is known by its fruits. Consequently, every man is the son of his own deeds.

(4) Works consist in resolute action, not in its result or success.[40]

This is Lope de Vega's point of view in *Fuenteovejuna*, one of the main functions of which is to convince us that every virtuous man or woman, however humble his or her station in life, is entitled to a sense of honour and dignity, to self-respect, and to the respect of others. Who are the noble of spirit in this play? The Catholic Monarchs, the regenerate Master of Calatrava, and the peasants of Fuenteovejuna. Who is the base villain? The Comendador, Fernán Gómez. There is, in the delicately but colourfully woven poetic imagery of this work, a great deal of subtle play on these ideas. The Comendador calls Frondoso a dog ('¡Perro! ¡Villano!') and so Frondoso is, in the sense that the dog is a symbol of fidelity. But who is a low dog and dies like a dog? Fernán Gómez de Guzmán. The animal-imagery which runs through *Fuenteovejuna*, as through a bestiary, should be carefully studied; it can tell us a great deal. And the honour-theme of *Fuenteovejuna* is not irrelevant to our own times. Honour problems are not confined to the seventeenth century or to the Mediterranean countries.[41]

But *Fuenteovejuna* treats of more than honour. It treats also of even more vital and unifying forces in society and the universe—trust and true love. The debate between Barrildo and Mengo in Act I about the nature of love is central to this aspect of the play's theme. Barrildo's words

> Sin amor, no se pudiera
> ni aun el mundo conservar

are, in reality, the core of the arguments which Lope puts forward in the drama. The Comendador represents the antithesis of that true love which holds the whole universe and its contents, both macrocosm and microcosm, together in perfect harmony. And what the peasants of Fuenteovejuna learn, as the play proceeds, is to trust one another and to submerge their individual self-interest and self-love in harmonious love of their neighbours and of the community. The play is beautifully conceived and constructed, as poetry and as drama. It is full of ironies and of power, and it mounts majestically to two fine climaxes, the emotional climax, which is the killing of the Comendador, and the intellectual climax, the pardon granted to the villagers. Fundamentally, it is a Christian play. The Comendador is surrounded by Devil-imagery. When he dies, we feel an exultant religious triumph. When the villagers are pardoned, we are reassured by the mercy of God, whose prime representatives in the state are the King and Queen. This is great theatre, the work of a true genius.

Fuenteovejuna may tend to overshadow other admirable plays on peasant-honour themes which Lope wrote. A comparative study of these plays and their ideas can be fruitful, as Salomon's important work has shown.[42] Nevertheless, in order fully to appreciate these plays as drama, which ought to be our prime concern, it is advisable to read or see on the stage each one on its own, in isolation from the others. Only then can we savour their artistry and participate in their emotion. A warning is perhaps needed: in reading these plays the reader must not confuse fiction with reality. The hunger and the squalor of real life are not in the plays. The view of peasant life which they present is Arcadian. They derive from the tradition of classical pastoral poetry and in particular from Horace's *Beatus ille*, versions of which are frequently amongst the best fragments of their verse. In their characterisation and their social themes they are not realistic or naturalistic, but markedly idealised. As Salomon has neatly put it, these plays show simultaneously 'un reflet du réel, une négation du réel et une idéalisation du réel'.[43] It may be that, as a group, with their exaltation of the virtues of country life as opposed to the misery and vice of city life, they were written by Lope for the *corrales* of the capital as propaganda-plays, as part of a campaign to lure the immigrants to Madrid back to the underpopulated countryside of Castile.[44] But, whatever their immediate political purposes may have been, they cannot fail to stir us as plays.

One of the best of these dramas is *El mejor alcalde, el Rey* (M and B: 1620-23), yet another chronicle-play. It concerns the predicament of a Galician peasant (of noble stock, come down in the world) when his master, a great noble, who believes himself to be omnipotent in his domains, snatches off his bride in the course of their wedding and, in the baronial castle, unsuccessfully tries to seduce her. Sancho, the peasant, appeals for help to the King of León, in person. The King sends the potentate a letter commanding him to release the girl, but Don Tello arrogantly tears it up. After a second appeal from Sancho, the King, in the guise of an officer of justice, goes himself to confront the insubordinate offender. Don Tello has raped Elvira. But the ultimate source of justice and honour in León is at hand. The ending of the play is at once a striking *coup de théâtre*, and an ironic comment on the honour-system. Having revealed his true identity, the King commands Don Tello to take Elvira's hand and marry her on the spot. Then, at once, the King orders his attendants to execute Don Tello. In a few seconds a desperate, poor, dishonoured, and therefore un-marriageable peasant girl is transformed into the rich and honourable widow of a great noble, and she will bring honour to Sancho by marrying him. Simply but carefully constructed, its poetry enriched by the same sorts of animal-imagery that we find in *Fuenteovejuna* and with an excellent *gracioso*, Pelayo, the swineherd who sees all the world in terms of pigs, *El mejor alcalde, el Rey* is one of Lope's most satisfying plays. It vividly expresses three sets of important ideas: (1) the ideal of the monarchy as the ultimate source of honour and justice in the state, and of the personal responsibility of the monarch for dispensing justice to all his subjects (perhaps an ironic comment on the inaccessible and irresponsible Philip III); (2) the necessity, in society, of the giving of honour, by king to subjects, by overlord to subjects; (3) the right of every good-loving person to dignity, self-respect, and the respect of others.

And there is *Peribáñez y el Comendador de Ocaña* (M and B: 1605-12, probably 1605-08), one of Lope's most lyrical and moving plays. *Peribáñez* is not a tragicomedy (as some term it), but what neo-classical theoreticians of Lope's time would have called a double tragedy: the tragedy of the nobly spirited peasant, Peribáñez, *primus inter pares*, who is tortured by the discovery that his young wife is, despite her virtue, being courted by the Comendador, and the tragedy of the basically honourable young Comendador (no Fernán Gómez) who, falling in love with the beautiful Casilda, brings about his own death by the sword of Peribáñez, the commoner whom he has justly ennobled for his own ends. The poetry of this play is very fine; so also is the characterisation of Peribáñez, who subtly but strikingly changes in his attitude and in his language when he ceases to be just the noble peasant and becomes the ennobled peasant.[45]

Another fine play on the country life and its virtues is *El villano en su rincón* (M and B: 1611), which gives a skilful characterisation of Juan Labrador, the dignified and sententious peasant who is content with his lot and so impressively virtuous that the King, who tests his loyalty in various ways and envies him his stoicism, his tranquillity and integrity, finally summons him to a high place of honour at Court. This play, as Bataillon has shown, begins as a dramatic illustration of the traditional *Menosprecio de corte y alabanza de aldea* theme, but later changes course and ends as a sort of *auto sacramental* 'a lo profano' illustrating not the power of God but the omnipotence of His vicegerent, the King.[46]

We have still to deal with the two greatest of Lope's tragedies. One of these is *El caballero de Olmedo* (M and B: 1615-26, probably 1620-25), a disturbing play built up out of an earlier drama of the same name (perhaps by Cristóbal de Morales), out of *La Celestina*, whose most distinguished dramatic descendant it is, and from a popular refrain which is employed to great dramatic effect in the third *jornada*:

> Que de noche le mataron
> al caballero,
> la gala de Medina,
> la flor de Olmedo.

This drama is undeniably beautiful and powerful, though some have considered that it is uneven in tone and that it 'starts as a comedy and ends as a tragedy'. It has even been maintained that Lope does not prepare his audience sufficiently early or well for the murder of Don Alonso, and that this ending comes as too much of a surprise. But careful attention to the play's poetic imagery inevitably leads us to other conclusions. Lope's audiences, already knowing the song, would be led by the title to expect a tragedy. In addition, at least the literate spectators would realise, when near the beginning of Act II the *gracioso* calls Don Alonso Calisto and Inés Melibea, that the play is a version of *La Celestina* and could be expected to have as disastrous an ending. But even a sensitive reader of our own times who had never heard of the song or *La Celestina* would, at an early stage of the play, be made uneasy by hints and omens in the text. Don Alonso very clearly prepares his own tragedy by a series of rash and imprudent actions. From very early in the play the poetry touches more and more on death and destruction. In the imagery, violent images and contrasts of life and death, of love and war steadily accumulate. The language of the play not only repeatedly contrasts life and death but also repeatedly equates love and death. As a skilfully constructed tragedy, *El caballero de Olmedo* is excellent; as a carefully unified and disturbing dramatic poem, it is superb.[47]

Very late in life, Lope de Vega wrote an exceptionally sombre, ironical, and moving tragedy, *El castigo sin venganza* (1631: autograph). The play is based on a *novella* by Bandello which gives a version of a historical event. In Lope's drama there are three protagonists: the libidinous Duke of Ferrara; his bastard son Federico; and the young noblewoman, Casandra, whom the Duke marries for reasons of state. None of them is a pleasant character; yet we can, almost despite ourselves, understand their motives and to a certain extent sympathise with them for what they do. Lope exposes, in them, the moral squalor which underlies the fine appearances of a great Court. The Duke neglects his young wife to go whoring; then he is summoned by the Pope to go to a Holy War. He returns to Ferrara, in his own opinion reformed and purged of his fatal vice, determined now to be faithful to his wife. But an anonymous letter informs him that Casandra has taken vengeance for his neglect of her by committing what is, technically, incest, with his son. Lope has taken pains to aggrandise the Duke, to make him a worthy central figure of the tragedy. When the Duke reflects on the letter, there comes to him, in a flash, the tragic *anagnorisis*, the sudden realisation of his own guilt and responsibility for what has happened:

> El vicioso proceder
> de las mocedades mías
> trujo el castigo, y los días
> de mi tormento, aunque fue
> sin gozar a Bersabé
> ni quitar la vida a Urías.

The Duke secretly ascertains that the report was true, and then, acting, as he believes, as the supreme justiciary in Ferrara rather than as a dishonoured husband and father, he plans the punishment without vengeance. Federico is secretly tricked into killing Casandra without knowing whom he is killing; then Federico is publicly executed for killing the Duchess. The Duke is condemned to live on, knowing that he has had killed the person he loved most, his son.[48]

Apart from writing plays for the *corrales*, Lope wrote mythological and other plays for the Court, as the court theatres developed rapidly in the reigns of Philip III and Philip IV to form, by the middle of the seventeenth century, the main centre of dramatic creativity in Spain and the centre for which, as time went on, many more plays were written than were being composed for the public theatres.[49] Of Lope's court plays, we should note, in particular, *El vellocino de oro*, on Jason and the Golden Fleece, which was given a lavish production at the palace at Aranjuez in 1622; *El amor enamorado*, on the myth of Daphne, which was performed at Court in 1635; and the pastoral play, *La selva sin amor*, part recited, part sung, which was performed before the king and queen in 1629 and has been called the first Spanish opera.[50] Money was lavished, both by nobles and from the royal purse, on elaborate productions such as these, with spectacular and costly visual effects which the *corrales* could never have afforded. It is, perhaps, a pity that Lope died five years before the opening, in 1640, of the most technically advanced theatre in Spain, the Coliseo, in Philip IV's new pleasure-palace of the Buen Retiro, just outside Madrid. Unlike the *corrales*, the Coliseo had a proscenium arch and curtain and the new, Italianate picture-stage, with scenery in perspective provided by painted back-cloths and changeable flats running in slots.

Lope de Vega did not have the opportunity, which Calderón had, fully to develop his talents for court drama on the stage of the Coliseo. We must remember him as the greatest genius of the *corrales*, the entertainer and teacher of his public, and, with plays like *La adúltera perdonada*, *La venta de la Zarzuela*, *La siega*, and *El pastor lobo y cabaña celestial*, one of the greatest creators of the pre-Calderonian *auto sacramental* for Corpus Christi, that allegorical devotional *comedia* reduced to one act, as Flecniakoska has described it.[51] Lope, in his drama, well deserved Montalbán's description of him in his *Fama póstuma*:

fénix de los siglos, príncipe de los versos, Orfeo de las ciencias, Apolo de las musas, Horacio de los poetas, Virgilio de los épicos,

Homero de los heroicos, Píndaro de los líricos, Sófocles de los trágicos y Terencio de los cómicos.

For coruscating poetry, for facility and originality of invention, the theatre of the Golden Age would not see his like again.

NOTES

1. For his life, poetry, and prose, see Jones, op. cit., pp. 158-61, 63-4, 185-6.
2. See S. Griswold Morley, 'The Pseudonyms and Literary Disguises of Lope de Vega', *University of California Publications in Modern Philology*, XXXIII (1951), 421-84.
3. S. Griswold Morley and Courtney Bruerton, *Cronología de las comedias de Lope de Vega* . . . (Madrid, 1968).
4. ed. by Victor Dixon (London, 1967).
5. See J. L. Brooks, '*La estrella de Sevilla:* "admirable y famosa tragedia" ', *BHS*, XXXII (1955), 8-20; Morley and Bruerton, op. cit., 463-5. Another play Lope's authorship of which has been disputed is *La fianza satisfecha* (the source of John Osborne's *A Bond Honoured* [London, 1966]); see Daniel Rogers, ' "Not for insolence, but seriously": J. O.'s Adaptation of *La fianza satisfecha*', *Durham University Journal*, LX (1968), 146-70; Morley and Bruerton, op. cit., 466-7. In their edition of this *comedia* published by the Cambridge University Press, 1971, W. M. Whitby and R. R. Anderson make a strong plea for Lope's authorship.
6. op. cit.
7. See Luis C. Pérez and F. Sánchez Escribano, *Afirmaciones de Lope de Vega* . . . (Madrid, 1961).
8. See Duncan Moir, 'The Classical Tradition . . .'. On the unities in Calderón and others, see Duncan Moir, 'Las comedias regulares de Calderón: ¿unos amoríos con el sistema neoclásico?', to be published in the *Actas* of the Second Colloquium of British and German *calderonistas*, held at the University of Hamburg, July 1970.
9. See Duncan Moir, 'The Classical Tradition . . .'; Joaquín de Entrambasaguas, 'Una guerra literaria del Siglo de Oro. L. de V. y los preceptistas aristotélicos', in his *Estudios sobre L. d V.*, I (Madrid, 1946), 63-580, and II (Madrid, 1947), 7-411. For defences of Lope's system, see *Dramatic Theory in Spain*, ed. H. J. Chaytor (Cambridge, 1925); *Preceptiva*, pp. 125-204.
10. Chaytor, op. cit., pp. 14-29, gives the entire text of the *Arte nuevo*, with useful notes; also *Preceptiva*, pp. 125-36. By *apariencias*, Lope means 'discoveries', startling sights revealed by the use of curtains or other means.
11. For extracts from the *Compendio* see A. H. Gilbert, ed. cit., 504-33. For the controversy in Italy, see Weinberg, op. cit., II, 1074-105; Herrick, op. cit., pp. 135-42.
12. The evolution of Lope's polymetric system is studied in detail by Morley and Bruerton, op. cit., and by Diego Marín, *Uso y función de la versificación* . . . (Valencia, 1962). See also P. N. Dunn, 'Some Uses of Sonnets in the Plays of L. de V.', *BHS*, XXXIV (1957), 213-22.
13. On the *Arte nuevo*, see M. Romera-Navarro, *La preceptiva dramática de Lope de Vega* (Madrid, 1935); Ramón Menéndez Pidal, 'L. de V.—El *Arte nuevo y la Nueva biografía*', in his *De Cervantes y Lope de Vega*,

Colección Austral 120 (Madrid, 1940, etc.), pp. 69-143; Joseph-S. Pons, 'L' "Art nouveau" de Lope de Vega', *BH*, XLVII (1945) 71-8.

14. See A. A. Parker, *The Approach to the Spanish Drama of the Golden Age*, Diamante VI (London, 1957), 27; R. D. F. Pring-Mill, introduction to Lope de Vega, *Five Plays*, trans. Jill Booty (New York, 1961); Parker, in a note to his article 'Towards a Definition of Calderonian Tragedy', *BHS*, XXXIX (1962), 225-6, replies to one of Pring-Mill's objections and is answered in Pring-Mill, 'Los calderonistas de habla inglesa y *La vida es sueño:* Métodos del análisis temático-estructural', in *Litterae hispanae et lusitanae*, ed. Hans Flasche (Munich, 1968), pp. 369-413.

15. See Bances Candamo, op. cit., pp. lxxx-lxxxi, 29-30.

16. See José F. Montesinos, 'Algunas observaciones sobre la figura del donaire en el teatro de L. de V.', *Homenaje ofrecido a Menéndez Pidal*, I, 469-504; Charles David Ley, *El gracioso en el teatro de la Península (siglos XVI-XVII)* (Madrid, 1954).

17. See Diego Marín, *La intriga secundaria en el teatro de Lope de Vega* (Toronto and Mexico City, 1958).

18. *Theatro de los theatros*, ed. cit., p. 33.

19. For a good edition of this play see Rudolph Schevill, *The Dramatic Art of Lope de Vega* (Berkeley, 1918).

20. See below, p. 126.

21. Pring-Mill, in Lope de Vega, *Five Plays*, p. xxviii.

22. Morley and Bruerton, op. cit., p. 478, wonder whether this play is by Lope because it was printed in the posthumous *Parte XXIV* of his works (Saragossa, 1641). This is scarcely a reason for doubt.

23. See above, p. 44, and note 4.

24. See A. A. Parker, 'Towards a Definition of Calderonian Tragedy'; Moir, 'The Classical Tradition . . .'; C. A. Jones, 'Tragedy in the Spanish Golden Age', *The Drama of the Renaissance. Essays for Leicester Bradner*, ed. E. M. Blistein (Providence, 1970), pp. 100-7; Edwin S. Morby, 'Some observations on *tragedia* and *tragicomedia* in Lope', *HR*, XI (1943), 185-209; Antonio Buero Vallejo, 'La tragedia', in *El teatro, Enciclopedia del arte escénico*, ed. G. Díaz-Plaja (Barcelona, 1958); R. R. MacCurdy, 'La tragédie néo-sénéquienne en Espagne au XVIIᵉ siècle . . .'

25. On Bances's categories, see op. cit., pp. lxxxviii-xc, 33-6.

26. J. L. Styan, *The Dark Comedy. The Development of Modern Comic Tragedy*, 2nd ed. (Cambridge, 1968), p. vi.

27. See A. A. Parker, 'History and Poetry: the Coriolanus theme in Calderón', *Hispanic Studies in Honour of I. González Llubera* (Oxford, 1959), pp. 211-24; F. Bances Candamo, op. cit., pp. lxxxvi-lxxxviii, 35, 82; S. H. Butcher, *Aristotle's Theory of Poetry and Fine Art*, 4th ed. (New York, 1951), pp. 34-7, 96-107, 163-97.

28. See Glaser, '*La creación del mundo y primera culpa del hombre*', *AIUN*, Sez. Rom., IV (1962), 29-56. Morley and Bruerton, op. cit., pp. 440-1, cast doubts on Lope's authorship of this play, because it has no *décimas*, which are very important in Lope's versification from about 1596 onwards.

29. See Glaser, 'L. de V.'s *El robo de Dina*', *RJahr*, XV (1964), 315-34.

30. On this play, see Glaser, 'L. de V.'s *La hermosa Ester*', *Sef*, XX (1960), 110-35.

31. Marcelino Menéndez Pelayo, *Estudios sobre el teatro de Lope de Vega*, I (Santander, 1949), 333. The *Estudios* are invaluable aids though unreliable as criticism.

32. See, for example, Jean Rotrou, *Le véritable Saint Genest*, ed. R. W. Ladborough (Cambridge, 1954), p. xiv.

72 THE GOLDEN AGE: DRAMA

33. See Antonio Vilanova, 'El tema del gran teatro del mundo', *BRABLB*, XXIII (1950), 157-88, and, in particular, 172-4. See also Alan S. Trueblood, 'Rôle-playing and the Sense of Illusion in Lope de Vega', *HR*, XXXII (1964), 305-18.

34. See Menéndez Pelayo, *Estudios*, III-VI. The political purposes of Lope's *comedias* need further study.

35. See Eva Rebecca Price, 'The Romancero in *El bastardo Mudarra*', *HBalt*, XVIII (1935), 277-92, 301-10.

36. See Arturo Farinelli, *Lope de Vega en Alemania* (Barcelona, 1936), pp. 156-80.

37. See the edition by Francisco Ruiz Ramón, Alianza 26 (Madrid, 1966).

38. See Duncan Moir, 'Lope de Vega's *Fuenteovejuna* and the *Emblemas morales* of Sebastián de Covarrubias Horozco (with a few remarks on *El villano en su rincón*)', in *Estudios y ensayos sobre el teatro antiguo hispánico, y otros ensayos . . .*, ed. A. D. Kossoff (Madrid, 1971). Essential studies on the play are M. Menéndez Pelayo, *Estudios*, V, 171-82; C. E. Aníbal, 'The historical elements of L. de V.'s *Fuenteovejuna*', *PMLA*, XLIX (1934), 657-718; Wardropper, '*Fuenteovejuna: el gusto* and *lo justo*', *SPh*, LIII (1956), 159-71; Pring-Mill, introduction to Lope de Vega, *Five Plays*, pp. xxii-xxvi, and 'Sententiousness in *Fuente Ovejuna*', *TDR*, VII (1962), 5-37; and essays in *El teatro de Lope de Vega*, ed. J. F. Gatti (Buenos Aires, 1962).

39. Menéndez Pidal, 'Del honor en el teatro español', in *De Cervantes y Lope de Vega*, Austral 120 (Madrid, 1940, etc.), pp. 145-73, and, in particular, 164-7. See also William L. Fichter's essay, 'Conjugal Honor in the Theatre of Lope de Vega', in his edition of *El castigo del discreto* (New York, 1925), pp. 27-72.

40. Alfonso García Valdecasas, *El hidalgo y el honor*, 2nd ed. (Madrid, 1958), pp. 9-10.

41. On honour, see also Américo Castro, 'Algunas observaciones acerca del concepto del honor en los siglos XVI y XVII', *RFE*, III (1916), 1-50, 357-86, and *De la edad conflictiva*, 2nd ed. (Madrid, 1961); G. Correa, 'El doble aspecto de la honra en el teatro del siglo XVII', *HR*, XXVI (1958), 99-107; C. A. Jones, 'Spanish Honour as Historical Phenomenon, Convention and Artistic Motive', *HR*, XXXIII (1965), 32-9; *Honour and Shame. The Values of Mediterranean Society*, ed. J. G. Peristiany (London, 1965).

42. Noël Salomon, *Recherches sur le thème paysan dans la 'comedia' au temps de Lope de Vega* (Bordeaux, 1965).

43. ibid., p. 914.

44. Monsieur Aubrun suggested as much in an unpublished lecture, delivered, under the title of '*Fuenteovejuna* y la realidad histórica española de hacia 1612', at King's College, London, on 14 March 1963.

45. See E. M. Wilson, 'Images et structure dans *Peribáñez*', *BH*, LI (1949), 125-59; Victor Dixon, 'The Symbolism of *Peribáñez*', *BHS*, XLIII (1966), 11-24.

46. See Marcel Bataillon, '*El villano en su rincón*', *BH*, LI (1949), 5-38, and in his *Varia Lección . . .* (Madrid, 1964).

47. On this play, see I. I. Macdonald, 'Why Lope?', *BHS*, XII (1935), 337-52; Parker, *The Approach . . .*, pp. 10-12; Pring-Mill, in *Five Plays*, pp. xxviii-xxxi; Marcel Bataillon, '*La Célestine*' *selon Fernando de Rojas* (Paris, 1961), pp. 238-50; Everett W. Hesse, 'The Rôle of the Mind in Lope's *El Caballero de Olmedo*', *Sym*, XIX (1965), 58-66; Diego Marín, 'La ambigüedad dramática en *El caballero de Olmedo*', *Hisp*, núm. 24 (1965), 1-11; Frank P. Casa, 'The Dramatic Unity of *El caballero de Olmedo*', *N*, L (1966), 234-43; Lloyd King, ' "The Darkest Justice of Death" in Lope's *El*

caballero de Olmedo', *FMLS*, V (1969), 388-94; E. Nagy, *Lope de Vega y 'La Celestina'* (Mexico, 1968).

48. See E. M. Wilson, 'Cuando Lope quiere, quiere', *CHA*, 161-2 (1963), 265-98; T. E. May, 'L. de V.'s *El castigo sin venganza*: The Idolatry of the Duke of Ferrara', *BHS*, XXXVII (1960), 154-82; Victor Dixon and A. A. Parker, '*El castigo sin venganza*: Two Lines, Two Interpretations', *MLN*, LXXXV (1970), 157-66.

49. On the development of the court theatres and drama up to 1640, see Shergold, *History*, pp. 236-97.

50. ibid., 272-4, 225-6, 285; 275-6.

51. Flecniakoska, *La formation de l' 'auto'* . . ., p. 443, and 'Les rôles de Satan dans les "autos" de Lope de Vega', *BH*, LXVI (1964), 30-44. See also Wardropper, *Introducción al teatro religioso* . . ., pp. 275-92.

Chapter 4

THE SCHOOL OF LOPE DE VEGA

THE NUMBER OF DRAMATISTS who wrote their plays under the influence of the style of Lope de Vega's *comedia nueva* was very great indeed.[1] The last years of the sixteenth century and first half of the seventeenth were a period in which the *corrales* flourished, providing a source of vigorous entertainment and instruction for Spaniards, the vogue of which can be reasonably compared only to that of the cinema in our own century. The *corrales* had a very rapid turnover of plays. Their public was eager for novelty and quick to tire of more than a few days' run of any *comedia*, however good it might be. There was therefore, in this period and after it (even when, in the second half of the seventeenth century, most talented dramatists found it more advantageous and profitable to write for the court theatres), a very great demand for new *comedias* and *entremeses*.

The playwrights responded with enthusiasm. Even a potboiler might get a showing for a couple of days until the audiences stayed away or clamoured for something better, and mercenary motives were certainly not absent from many an *ingenio*'s mind. Countless poor plays have survived from this period, together with the many very good ones.

Sloman has observed that

> The history of the Spanish drama in the last decade of the sixteenth century and the first two decades of the seventeenth is largely the history of the development of a *comedia* lacking unity of action to one in which that unity is achieved. Lope's later plays have dramatic unity; so have the best plays of Tirso de Molina and his contemporaries. But most of the plays written between, say, 1590 and 1610 are carelessly and loosely constructed.[2]

The change for the better must have been produced, in part, by the demands of an increasingly exigent type of audience. Undoubtedly, however, incessant debates on the principles of dramatic art contributed to the change, as did the publication of a series of treatises on dramatic and poetic practice in which Lope's *Arte nuevo* has a prominent place, but which also includes two very important books by neo-classical thinkers, Francisco Cascales's *Tablas poéticas* (Murcia, 1617) and Jusepe Antonio González de Salas's *Nueva idea de la tragedia antigua, o ilustración última al libro singular de Poética de Aristóteles Stagirita* (Madrid, 1633).[3] Lope's dramatic theoretical writings and, in particular, his dramatic practice, as it evolved, did a very great deal in themselves to inspire the writing of good plays by other poets; it is just, for that reason, to talk of the dramatic school of Lope de Vega, even though it should be remembered that the master must have learned much from the pupils as well as they from him.

Another important factor in the prodigious development of the popular Spanish drama in this period was national pride. The *ingenios* were deeply conscious of Spain's greatness as an international and colonising power, and they appear also to have been convinced that Spain had produced a drama which excelled that of ancient Greece and Rome and also of modern Italy. Their justified pride in this achievement was a further stimulus to their writing better and better plays. It was eloquently expressed by several writers, and particularly well by Tirso de Molina in his *Cigarrales de Toledo* (1621) and by the jurist Francisco de Barreda in the fascinating 'Invectiva a las comedias que prohibió Trajano y apología por las nuestras' which he published in his book *El mejor Príncipe Trajano Augusto* (Madrid, 1622).[4] National pride shines through Barreda's eulogy of the *comedia nueva* of his times:

Salga hoy al teatro la más graciosa, la más aliñada, la más hermosa comedia de Plauto, la más elegante de Terencio, reducida a nuestra lengua, y tendrá tantos acusadores como ojos la miraren. Acusaránla todos con el ceño de desabrida y mal aliñada, de poco entretenida, porque ha llegado tiempo en que el atrevimiento dichoso de los ingenios de España, adorno de este siglo, la ha engalanado nuevamente, la ha hecho discreta y entretenida, y como abeja que labra dulcísimo panal de la quinta esencia de las flores la ha labrado con los esmaltes de todo género de agudeza, sacando de la filosofía natural lo más sublime; de la moral, lo más prudente; de las historias, la más conforme; de las fábulas descortezadas, lo más provechoso; de la elocuencia, lo más puro. Todo con apacible estilo, desnudo de la severidad y aspereza con que nos la dejaron los antiguos. Finalmente, ha aventajado a las comedias antiguas con las suyas. De manera que ya no parecen aquéllas sino diseños o sombras de éstas.

For Luis de Morales Polo, the Spanish *comedia* was 'un convite que el entendimiento hace al oído y a la vista'.[5] It is hard to dissent.

The Spanish drama of the first half of the seventeenth century was deeply involved in contemporary political problems.[6] After the death in 1598 of Philip II, who had devoted himself almost overscrupulously to his duties of state, his successors, beginning with the indolent Philip III, delegated the task of government to favourites. The favourite, called *privado* or *valido,* under the weak monarchs of the seventeenth century came to exercise great power: Olivares was for many years the effective ruler of Spain. Favouritism was never popular in seventeenth-century Spain, however. The problems of whether the king had the right to choose a favourite, whether it was advisable for him to have one, and, if so, what the proper functions of a royal favourite might be, were heatedly debated in the course of the century. They were, in fact, amongst the most crucial political problems of that age,[7] and the popular drama of the first half of the century took the debates on *la privanza* into the theatres, in a remarkably large number of plays concerned with the rise and the inevitable fall of royal favourites. Lope de Vega himself may have initiated this type of play, with *Los Guzmanes de Toral* (M and B: 1599-1603, if it is indeed by Lope) or with *Las mudanzas de fortuna* (M and B: 1597-1608). Damián del Poyo's plays *La próspera fortuna de Ruy López d'Ávalos el bueno* and its sequel *La adversa fortuna de Ruy López* ... were performed in the *corrales* as early as 1605, and Lope and his contemporaries went on to write many pointed dramatic commentaries on aspects of favouritism. Particularly notable plays of this type are Antonio Mira de Amescua's *El arpa de David, No hay dicha ni desdicha,* and *La segunda de Don Álvaro (Adversa fortuna de don Álvaro de Luna)*; Tirso de Molina's *Privar contra su gusto;* Juan Pérez de Montalbán's *Cumplir con su obligación*; Luis Vélez de Guevara's *El conde don Pero Vélez* and *El gran Jorge Castrioto*; and Juan Ruiz de Alarcón y Mendoza's *Ganar amigos, Los favores del mundo, La amistad castigada,* and *Los pechos privilegiados.* Even Quevedo contributed to this very important dramatic sub-genre, with a dramatically mediocre but politically interesting *comedia, Cómo ha de ser el privado.* The *comedias de privanza* appear to have been most frequently written in the period between 1604 and 1635, the year of Lope's death, but they did continue to be composed long after that date. One of the most interesting *comedias* of this type, though it is so in a cunningly veiled manner, is Bances Candamo's masterpiece, *El esclavo en grillos de oro* (1692).

Valencia was one of the great centres of the growing *comedia,* and in the late sixteenth century and early seventeenth the Valencian school of drama flourished, producing, amongst others, two gifted minor playwrights, Gaspar de Aguilar (1561-1623) and Dr Francisco Tárrega, who was a canon of the cathedral there. But the best of the Valencian dramatists, and one of the most talented of Lope's generation and school, was Guillén de Castro y Bellvís (1569-1631), who wrote his plays first in his native city and later in Madrid. His most famous plays are the two which he wrote under the title of *Las mocedades del Cid, Primera parte* and *Segunda parte,* drawn from the ballad-cycles on the legends of the great national hero and published in 1618.

The first of these two plays presents with dignity and fire the celebrated apocryphal tale of the feud which temporarily prevents the newly knighted Rodrigo from marrying the beautiful Doña Ximena. The lady's father, the Count Lozano, publicly slaps Rodrigo's father, Don Diego, in the face because he is jealous of him for being appointed tutor to the King's son. Don Diego is too old to take vengeance himself and he gives Rodrigo the task of doing so. Rodrigo is at first torn between the desire to restore the family's honour and his love for the daughter of the man he must kill. Nevertheless, he steels himself for the task and kills the Count. Despite her love for Rodrigo, Ximena demands that he be brought to justice; but, although he begs her to kill him, she cannot bring herself to strike the blow. In the course of a well-devised plot which develops skilfully the mental and emotional torments of its male and female protagonists, Rodrigo slays the champion of Ximena, who finally consents to marry him. This play was the source of Corneille's *Le Cid* (1636). French critics have often tended to underrate Castro's play in order to exalt the value of Corneille's. The more impartial scholar will, however, probably be more inclined to recognise the excellence of both within the different dramatic traditions which brought them forth. The first part of *Las mocedades del Cid* is a fine epic play, with many passages of very good dramatic and lyrical poetry. The *Segunda parte* is overshadowed by its predecessor, but repays study.[8]

Other notable plays by Guillén de Castro are another powerful epic drama, *El Conde Alarcos*; three *comedias* based on works by Cervantes: *Don Quijote de la Mancha, La fuerza de la sangre,* and *El curioso impertinente*; and a stirring family tragedy, *El amor constante,* which ends with a justification of tyrannicide that is in perfect accordance with the political theories of the Spanish sixteenth-century thinkers, although the political dramatists of the later seventeenth century prudently declined to propose regicide as a legitimate way out of a nation's political problems.[9] Guillén de Castro, on the whole, offers strong *dramatismo* and psychological and emotional conflicts, but he also had his lighter side. He could write delightfully witty *comedias de capa y espada*, like *El Narciso en su opinión* and *Los mal casados de Valencia*.

Diego Jiménez de Enciso (1585-1634?) was another *ingenio* who excelled at powerfully dramatic subjects. His most famous play in his own times was *Los Medicis de Florencia*, which Pérez de Montalbán said, in his *Para todos* (1632), 'ha sido pauta y ejemplar para todas las comedias grandes'. This is a superb and dignified tragedy on the treacherous and cowardly killing of Alessandro de Medici by his cousin Lorenzo. Another very good drama by Enciso is *El príncipe don Carlos*, one of the first attempts to dramatise the tragedy of Philip II's mentally deranged son, his attempt to join a rebellion in Flanders against his father and the Spanish Crown, the King's necessary decision to have him locked up in his apartment, and his death there in 1568. Many critics consider this play to be Enciso's masterpiece. It is a masterfully conceived drama, particularly strong in its contrasts of characterisation, and a fine example of the application of the Aristotelian principle of the superiority of universal or poetic truth to historical truth. At the end, when everyone believes Don Carlos to be dead, he is miraculously revived by St James of Alcalá, sees a vision of his father's descendants down to the first marriage of Philip IV, and, calling for the King, humbly swears that he has repented of his ways and will amend his life in future. *El príncipe don Carlos* illustrates particularly well Bances Candamo's statement that 'la historia nos expone los sucesos de la vida como son, la comedia nos los exorna como debían ser, añadiéndole a la verdad de la experiencia mucha más perfección para la enseñanza'.[10] Enciso's drama on Don Carlos and his father is, in fact, the finest of the many plays which were later written in various countries of Europe on their relationship. *El príncipe don Carlos* is for dignity and refinement of characterisation better than Schiller's *Don Carlos* and only surpassed by Verdi's opera.[11]

Another noteworthy talent of this period was that of Lope de Vega's protégé and biographer, Dr Juan Pérez de Montalbán (1602-38). Nowadays, Montalbán is best known for the *Fama póstuma* and the miscellany of prose, poetry, and plays after the manner of Boccaccio's *Decameron*, the *Para todos*, which was published in 1632 and thereafter repeatedly reprinted, being one of the most popular Spanish books of the seventeenth century, in Spain and in other countries.[12] Montalbán's life was a tragic one. In his thirties, to the distress of his friends and admirers, he suffered a mental decay which reduced him to a state of childishness. By 1637, when the *Segunda parte* of Montalbán's *comedias* was published, he must have been too ill to supervise its preparation for the press: three of the plays in the book do not appear to be his.[13] The plays by Montalbán best known today are those which Mesonero Romanos reprinted in the nineteenth century.[14] Montalbán wrote three plays about Philip II, the best, and one of the best of all his dramatic works, being *El segundo Séneca de España, y príncipe don Carlos,* for which he wrote a second part. One of the liveliest of his *comedias* is a novelesque drama, *No hay vida como la honra,* which appears to have been exceedingly popular in his own times. He also wrote a much-praised play, *De un castigo dos venganzas,* an unusual honour-drama in which the adulterous wife and her lover are killed not by her husband but by her lover's rejected mistress; this *comedia* was perhaps a parody on a play by his former friend, later his enemy, Jerónimo de Villaizán y Garcés.[15] Montalbán also composed, as one might expect of a theologian, good *autos sacramentales.* One of these is the *Auto Escanderbech,* a *refundición a lo divino* of one of his own *comedias de privanza, El príncipe Escanderbey.* Another is his *Auto del Polifemo,* which was attacked, like the *Escanderbech,* by another of his enemies, Quevedo. Quevedo's attacks on the *Auto del Polifemo* were spiteful and unjust: the play is a skilfully contrived allegory which is dramatically and poetically satisfying.[16]

One of Lope's most successful contemporaries, and one of the closest to him in poetic and dramatic spirit, was Luis Vélez de Guevara (1579-1644). Nowadays remembered above all for his satirical novel *El diablo cojuelo,*[17] he was also a fertile dramatist, especially given to historical and heroic themes, treated often with the same satirical spirit which we admire in his novel. His dramatic sense was strong. The most celebrated of his plays, *Reinar después de morir,* is a moving dramatisation of the tragedy and posthumous crowning of Inês de Castro.[18] One of Vélez's most attractive qualities as a dramatist is his healthy exploitation of melodrama, savagery, and violence. One of his most remarkable plays in this vein is his tragedy *La serrana de la Vera,* based on a *comedia* by Lope with the same title. The protagonist of Vélez's drama is Gila, an extraordinary example of an interesting type of character in the Golden Age drama, the *mujer varonil.* Gila is a startlingly strong and muscular peasant feminist who rebels against the idea of marriage because she considers it degrading to her sex. But, eager to rise in the world, she is easily seduced by a Captain who offers to marry her. Abandoned by the seducer, she swears to take vengeance on him, turns bandit, and kills two thousand men before she at last catches up with the Captain, whom she hurls over a cliff. Nevertheless, her arrogant feminism is not allowed to triumph in the end, for Gila is condemned and executed.[19] Other good plays by Luis Vélez are *El Rey en su imaginación, La luna de la sierra, Más pesa el Rey que la sangre, El privado perseguido, El ollero de Ocaña,* and *El diablo está en Cantillana.*

Two less important but nevertheless interesting disciples of Lope de Vega were Luis de Belmonte Bermúdez (1587-1650?) and the unfortunate writer of Jewish descent Felipe Godínez. Belmonte is best remembered for a good religious drama which he probably wrote, *El diablo predicador,* in which Lucifer plays an unusual role. This play is a recasting of an earlier one, entitled *Fray Diablo,* which has been attributed to Lope.[20] Tradition also attributed to Belmonte another play, *La renegada de Valladolid,* the composition of which, in reality, he shared with Moreto and Martínez de Meneses.[21] Godínez, who was at his best in religious dramas, particularly with Old Testament subjects (*Los trabajos de Job, o la paciencia en los trabajos; Judit y Olofernes; Amán y Mardoqueo*), was tried by the Inquisition on a charge of secretly being a practising Jew.[22]

A much more gifted dramatist than either of these was Juan Ruiz de Alarcón y Mendoza (1581?-1639). Born in Mexico and a hunchback, he fitted uneasily into Spanish society, which was both chauvinistic and apt to mock at physical deformities. Highly intelligent, proud, and doubtless often embittered by the jibes of his rivals for literary fame in Madrid, he showed himself in many of his plays to be a sharp critic of Spanish society, particularly amongst the nobility. His plays show a marked seriousness of moral purpose which is not always evident in those of his contemporaries. Many of his *comedias* are thesis-plays directed against social vices. His plays clearly were intended to rouse dormant consciences, but they sometimes fail to please, despite the excellence of their versification. They can be pedantic, and hence fail to 'deleitar aprovechando'. Perhaps the serious-minded Alarcón scorned to delight.

Alarcón's most famous play is *La verdad sospechosa,* which begins with fun which turns black and ends in bitterness. The plot concerns the exploits of a habitual liar and, finally, after an amusing series of complications, his frustration in finding himself obliged to marry a girl he does not love. The most striking thing about this play, especially when we compare it with the much less sharply moralistic comedy, *Le Menteur,* which Corneille made out of it, is the gravity of Alarcón's censure. For Alarcón, to lie is to negate nobility and honour; and we can, when we read *La verdad sospechosa*, begin to appreciate more fully than before the ideal which lay behind the traditional *¡Mentís!* as a cause of dishonour. Infuriated by his son's behaviour, the well-born delinquent's father in the play gives us in a sarcastic and arresting tirade a telling expression of the true principles of honour:

Don Beltrán	¿Sois caballero, García?
Don García	Téngome por hijo vuestro.
Don Beltrán	¿Y basta ser hijo mío
	para ser vos caballero?
Don García	Yo pienso, señor, que sí.
Don Beltrán	¡Qué engañado pensamiento!
	Sólo consiste en obrar
	como caballero, el serlo.
	¿Quién dio principio a las casas
	nobles? Los ilustres hechos
	de sus primeros autores.
	Sin mirar sus nacimientos,
	hazañas de hombres humildes
	honraron sus herederos.
	Luego en obrar mal o bien
	está el ser malo o ser bueno.
	¿Es así?
Don García	Que las hazañas
	den nobleza, no lo niego;
	mas no neguéis que sin ellas
	también la da el nacimiento.
Don Beltrán	Pues si honor puede ganar
	quien nació sin él, ¿no es cierto
	que por el contrario, puede,
	quien con el nació, perdello?
Don García	Es verdad.
Don Beltrán	Luego si vos
	obráis afrentosos hechos,
	aunque seáis hijo mío,
	dejáis de ser caballero.
	Luego si vuestras costumbres
	os infaman en el pueblo,
	no importan paternas armas,
	no sirven altos abuelos.

But García does not learn his lesson, and therefore he is aptly but severely punished, with a life of regret and frustration of his desires.

In *Las paredes oyen* Alarcón castigates slander, one of the perpetual vices of closed societies. This *comedia* has, with reason, been said to contain a certain amount of self-portrait by the author, in the character of Don Juan, a poor but noble hunchback who finally triumphs over his rival in love, Don Mendo, the handsome, rich slanderer, because the lady whom they both desire prefers the truly honourable man to the vicious. In *Los pechos privilegiados* the playwright presents his ideal of what a king's favourite ought to be, loyal to his monarch even in the most difficult of circumstances—an ideal not always realised in the seventeenth century. *La prueba de las promesas,* based on a medieval tale, is a wittily damning portrayal of a man who will not keep his word.

Alarcón's plays are all carefully constructed, and all moral and reflective. Those which do not attack moral turpitude present aristocratic ideals of moral integrity. *Ganar amigos* is a particularly good example of this type of play: in it, offences are pardoned because the offended man realises the unshakeable integrity of his offender. And Alarcón was not always harsh in his judgments. In *No hay mal que por bien no venga,* a slothful man and a man sunk in habitual debt discover that they are really idealists and patriots at heart. Alarcón's was not a lyrical or sentimental nature, and he never raises us to the heights of emotion which we feel in many plays by Lope. But he was a supreme idealist; and his fervent idealism and meticulous dramatic craftsmanship prepare us for the markedly idealistic and carefully wrought plays of the second part of the seventeenth century.

Antonio Mira de Amescua (1574?-1644) was another playwright who pointed towards the later drama, but he did so in very different ways from Alarcón. In most of his *comedias* he was far from being as careful a dramatic craftsman as was the Mexican; indeed, his plot-construction is often very disorderly, though exuberantly abundant in striking situations. Nevertheless Mira, who like many other seventeenth-century dramatists was a churchman and like various others a doctor of theology, began to show a richness of thematic and symbolistic content in many of his plays which indicates a move towards the complex but coherent thematic unity of the best plays of the Calderonian school. The bulk of Mira's dramatic output has not been studied with sufficient perception. Incoherence of action, in an intelligent seventeenth-century dramatist's works (and Mira was certainly highly intelligent), may be deliberate, in order to provoke speculation on the playwright's motive in creating it; and incoherence in action may also be an invitation to seek underlying coherence of theme. Mira also moves towards the style of the Calderonian school in his blending of the often straightforward poetic language of the school of Lope with the more complex, Gongoristic diction which, in the drama, reached its height in the mature plays of Calderón.

Mira's best play, *El esclavo del demonio*, is a fine example of how an exceedingly complicated plot, with an extraordinary richness of varied incidents, can coherently convey a clear series of moral and doctrinal points. Written before 1612, this drama is an important predecessor of later great religious plays, such as Tirso de Molina's *El condenado por desconfiado* and Calderón's *La devoción de la Cruz* and *El mágico prodigioso*. It is a vigorous and impressive Spanish contribution to the legends which comprise the Faust tradition in European literature. Don Gil, the ascetic canon of Coimbra, who preaches to others

> Busca el bien, huye el mal, que es la edad corta,
> y hay muerte y hay infierno, hay Dios y gloria,

falls victim to lust, sleeps with a girl, Lisarda, under the pretence that he is her lover, and rebels against his own asceticism, fleeing with her to the mountains, where they become bandits. In the course of their exploits, Don Gil sees and becomes enamoured of Lisarda's sister, Leonor, and he makes a pact with the Devil to become his slave in exchange for the possession of Leonor. Nevertheless, what Gil embraces is not Leonor but a skeleton! He now becomes terrified of perdition, for at last he truly understands what being the Devil's slave implies for him. But his guardian angel saves him, so that he may preach on his penitence and God's mercy, and Lisarda's soul is also saved.[23]

Amongst other interesting plays by this dramatist, two are particularly important. These are *La próspera fortuna de don Álvaro de Luna*, which was first printed in the *Segunda parte* of Tirso de Molina but has recently been attributed, with convincing reasons, to Mira, and a work which he certainly wrote, *La adversa fortuna de don Álvaro de Luna* (*La segunda de don Álvaro*), a sequel to the former play. These are both fine tragedies and notable examples of the *comedias de privanza* intended as warnings to kings and their favourites.[24] Although he is best known for his religious *comedias* and *autos sacramentales* (*Pedro Telonario, La jura del Príncipe*), for the keenness of his perception of the clash between divine love and the power of the flesh, of the inevitability of the fall of the man who is raised high by fortune, this predominantly serious dramatist was capable of writing light-heartedly, in nimbly delightful comedies like *La Fénix de Salamanca, No hay burlas con las mujeres,* and *La tercera de sí misma.*

As Flecniakoska has shown, the *auto sacramental* developed remarkably in the period up to Lope's death in 1635. It borrowed metrical and dramatic techniques from the *comedia,* it became more polished and more skilled in its allegorical and doctrinal content, more and more effective in the manner in which the argument of each play led logically to the exaltation of the Eucharist in the joyful festival of Corpus Christi.[25] A notable contributor to this development was the religious poet José de Valdivielso (?-1638?), some of whose *autos* are exceedingly fine (e.g. *El hospital de los locos, La amistad en el peligro, El peregrino*).[26] And, in an age as exuberantly creative as this was, it is not surprising that the minor dramatic forms also evolved remarkably. In particular, the *entremés* reached its height with the brilliantly witty dramatist Luis Quiñones de Benavente (?-1651) and was also skilfully cultivated by Quevedo.

NOTES

1. An idea of the number can be got from Cayetano Alberto de la Barrera y Leirado, *Catálogo bibliográfico y biográfico del teatro antiguo español desde sus orígenes hasta mediados del siglo XVIII* (Madrid, 1860; reprinted London, 1968; Madrid, 1969).

2. Albert E. Sloman, *The Dramatic Craftsmanship of Calderón. His Use of Earlier Plays* (Oxford, 1958), pp. 278-9.

3. See Moir, 'The Classical Tradition...', 193-208, and E. C. Riley, 'The Dramatic Theories of Don J. A. G. de S.', *HR,* XIX (1951), 183-203.

4. See *Preceptiva,* pp. 182-7, 191-200, and Moir, 'The Classical Tradition...', 199-200.

5. Luis de Morales Polo, *Epítome de los hechos y dichos del emperador Trajano* (Valladolid, 1654), 61r, in M. Menéndez Pelayo, *Historia de las ideas estéticas en España,* II (Santander, 1947), 316n.

6. This is clearly demonstrated in the unpublished doctoral dissertation by Sister Mary Austin Cauvin, O.P., *The 'Comedia de privanza' in the Seventeenth Century* (University of Pennsylvania, 1957).

7. See Francisco Tomás Valiente, *Los validos en la monarquía española del siglo XVII (estudio institucional)* (Madrid, 1963).

8. On Castro's poetic techniques, see E. Juliá Martínez, 'La métrica en las producciones dramáticas de G. de C.', *AUMad,* III (1934), 62-71.

9. On this play, see José María Roca Franquesa, 'Un dramaturgo de la Edad de Oro: G. de C.: Notas a un sector de su teatro', *RFE,* XXVIII (1944), 378-427.

10. op. cit., p. 82. See also above, p. 55 and p. 71 note 27.

11. On Enciso, see Cotarelo y Mori, 'Don D. J. de E. y su teatro', *BRAE,* I (1914), 209-48, 385-415, 510-50.

12. See Victor Dixon, 'J. P. de M.'s *Para todos*', *HR*, XXXII (1964), 36-59. The book contains a fascinating series of comments on contemporary playwrights, entitled *Memoria de los que escriben comedias en Castilla solamente*.

13. See Dixon, 'J. P. de M.'s *Segundo tomo de las comedias*', *HR*, XXIX (1961), 91-109. One of the wrongly included plays is Lope's *El sufrimiento premiado* (see above, pp. 44, 53). The best study on Montalbán is Dixon's unpublished thesis, *The Life and Works of J. P. de M., with Special Reference to his Plays* (Cambridge, 1959-60). See also George W. Bacon, 'The *comedias* of Dr. J. P. de M.', *RH*, XVII (1907), 46-65, and 'The Life and Dramatic Works of Dr. J. P. de M.', *RH*, XXVI (1912), 1-474.

14. *BAE*, LV, 477-604.

15. See Dixon, 'J. P. de M.'s *Para todos*'. For Villaizán, see Dixon, 'Apuntes sobre la vida y obra de J. de V. y G.', *Hisp*, núm. 13 (1961), 5-22.

16. See Glaser, 'Quevedo versus P. de M.: the *Auto del Polifemo* and the Odyssean Tradition in Golden-Age Spain', *HR*, XXVIII (1960), 103-20.

17. See Jones, op. cit., pp. 196-7.

18. See above, pp. 29-30.

19. On this play, see Melveena McKendrick, 'The *bandolera* of Golden-Age Drama: a Symbol of Feminist Revolt', *BHS*, XLVI (1969), 1-20. On Luis Vélez in general, see Cotarelo y Mori, 'L. V. de G. y sus obras dramáticas', *BRAE*, III (1916), 621-52; IV (1917), 137-71, 269-308, 414-44; F. E. Spencer and R. Schevill, *The Dramatic Works of L. V. de G.* (Berkeley, 1937).

20. See introduction to Léo Rouanet's French version, *Le Diable Prédicateur* (Paris and Toulouse, 1901); Morley and Bruerton, *Cronología*, pp. 468-9.

21. See Juliá Martínez, '*La renegada de Valladolid*', *BRAE*, XVI (1929), 672-9. The play is a dramatisation of a chap-book; see E. M. Wilson, 'Samuel Pepys's Spanish Chap-books', *TCBS*, II, 3 (1965), No. 23/163, 237-8.

22. On Belmonte, see W. A. Kincaid, 'Life and Works of L. de B. B. (1587?-1650?)', *RH*, LXXIV (1928), 1-260. On Godínez, Adolfo de Castro, 'Noticias de la vida del Dr. Felipe Godínez', *MRAE*, VIII (1902), 277-83; Menéndez Pelayo, *Historia de los heterodoxos españoles*, IV (Santander, 1947), 323; Cecil Roth, *A History of the Marranos* (New York, 1959; reprint of 1932 ed.), pp. 383, 397.

23. On this play, see Ángel Valbuena's prologue to his edition of it in CC 70 (Madrid, 1943); Melveena McKendrick, art. cit.

24. See Margaret Wilson, '*La próspera fortuna de don Álvaro de Luna*: an Outstanding Work by M. de A.', *BHS*, XXXIII (1956), 25-36. On Mira, see also Cotarelo y Mori, 'M. de A. y su teatro', *BRAE*, XVII (1930), 467-505, 611-58; XVIII (1931), 7-90; Claude E. Anibal, *Mira de Amescua* (an edition of *El arpa de David* and other notes) (Columbus, Ohio, 1925); Flecniakoska, '*La jura del príncipe*, auto sacramental de M. de A., et l'histoire contemporaine', *BH*, LI (1949), 39-44.

25. See Flecniakoska, *La formation de l' 'auto'*, pp. 429-49.

26. See Wardropper, *Introducción al teatro religioso*, pp. 293-320.

Chapter 5

TIRSO DE MOLINA

ONE GREAT DISCIPLE OF LOPE DE VEGA deserves a chapter to himself. This is Fray Gabriel Téllez (1581?-1648), who wrote under the pseudonym of Tirso de Molina. The theory that he was the illegitimate son of the duque de Osuna has been proposed, but it has been rejected by most serious scholars.[1] Tirso entered, about 1600, the Order of Mercy, an institution founded with the purpose of ransoming Christian captives from the Muslims. After his novitiate, he became a friar of the order, was thoroughly trained in theology, and gradually was entrusted with positions of increasing responsibility by the Mercedarians. In 1616 he was sent by his order across the sea to Santo Domingo on an official visit. Two years later he was back in Spain, applying for the title of *Presentado* (qualified theologian aspiring to become a Master) on the strength, amongst other things, of having given several courses of theology in Santo Domingo. He lived for a time in Toledo and, about 1621, moved back to his birthplace, Madrid, where he published his celebrated book *Cigarrales de Toledo* (prose, poems, plays). In 1625 a Junta de Reformación de las Costumbres, which had been set up under the administration of the conde-duque de Olivares, discussed 'el escándalo que causa un fraile mercenario que se llama maestro Téllez, por otro nombre Tirso, con comedias que hace profanas y de malos incentivos y ejemplos', and the committee recommended to Philip IV that Tirso be sent to a remote house of his order and forbidden to write *comedias* and profane verse. It is probable that this recommendation was never put into force. The following year the Mercedarians made Tirso prior of their friary at Trujillo in Estremadura, very far from Madrid. He stayed in Trujillo until 1629, perhaps moved from there to Toledo, and in 1631 completed the composition of a book which was clearly an intentional parody *a lo divino* of the *Cigarrales de Toledo* and a type of answer to the accusations of the Junta. This new book, entitled *Deleitar aprovechando*, was a collection of strictly religious works: pious stories, three *autos sacramentales*, and devotional

86

poetry. It was published in 1635, three years after Tirso had been promoted to the position of official chronicler of the Order of Mercy and *definidor* of the order in the province of Castile, a post which obliged him to accompany the principal of the order on missions concerned with the discipline of its members and their houses. Thus dignified, Tirso returned to Madrid in 1634 and in the next two years, with the aid of a nephew, he published four volumes of his plays. He was attacked, or believed he was attacked, by an enemy within his own order in 1640, when Fray Marcos Salmerón, official visitor to the Mercedarian friary in Madrid, ordered that none of its inhabitants should keep in his cell any book of profane plays or poetry and that no member 'escriba versos algunos de coplas, en forma de sátira o cartas, aunque sean en prosa, contra el gobierno público ni contra otras personas'. Tirso, who apparently did not keep to the letter of these laws, was temporarily banished to Soria but eventually allowed to return to Madrid. In 1645 he was appointed prior of the order's friary at Soria, in 1647 he moved to Almazán, in the same province, and there he died in the following year.[2]

Tirso was a sensitive lyrical and dramatic poet, with a naturalness of style akin to that of Lope de Vega.[3] He was also a brilliant playwright. Certain critics have, judging the matter by canons of realism and naturalism, considered him to be the greatest of all the Spanish dramatists of the Golden Age. This is debatable: but he was certainly one of the three most important playwrights of the seventeenth century in Spain, a fertile talent surpassed in quality only by Lope de Vega and Calderón. He did not have Lope's spontaneous creative genius; Lope *was* a genius, Tirso was not. But Tirso excelled Lope in his trained and subtle intellect, an intellectual discipline of a sort that Lope never achieved. In rather different ways from those of Mira de Amescua and Alarcón, he formed a bridge between the early *comedia nueva* and the intricately developed drama of Calderón and his school. In his dramatic techniques, Tirso tended to construct his plots rather more carefully than Lope, emphasising the plays' structure and combining sub-plot with main plot, or double plots of equal importance, in a skilfully controlled and meaningful manner. He also tended to move away from the type of play, very common in Lope, in which there is no single central character but a group of several salient figures of roughly similar dramatic importance, towards the Calderonian type of play which usually revolves round one protagonist, or at most two, with the other agonists in the background. Tirso had a great gift for witty satire, and he used it freely. Nevertheless, as Paterson has observed, satire plays only a small part in Tirso's theatre; rather it reinforces a deeper theme that runs right through his plays: the opposition between artificial or inadequate habits of mind, and real integrity.[4]

These words, which are shrewd, may suggest to the reader that there is a close resemblance between Tirso's plays and those of Alarcón. In certain ways there is indeed such a resemblance. But there is also a great difference between the drama of Tirso and that of Alarcón—the warmth of humanity and the uncondescending understanding of human frailty which pervade Tirso's theatre but are not so often evident in the Mexican's *comedias*. Wisdom, subtlety of mind, and sympathetic comprehension of humanity are the greatest qualities of Tirso as a dramatist.

Tirso is most widely known for two truly magnificent plays, *El burlador de Sevilla* and *El condenado por desconfiado*, his authorship of both of which has been denied by some critics. Together with most *tirsistas*, however, we believe both of them to be his. In their themes, in their action, and in their poetic and dramatic style they fit perfectly into the body of Tirso's drama.

El burlador de Sevilla is the main source of a great international literary tradition, that of the myth of Don Juan, which has produced many, often extraordinarily different, works of good quality from seventeenth-century Spain to the England of our own times.[5] Yet *El burlador de Sevilla* does not appear to be the first play which was written on Don Juan. *El burlador* was printed in the seventeenth century as a work of Tirso but does not figure in any of the books he himself published; it was included in a volume entitled *Doce comedias nuevas de Lope de Vega y otros autores* (Barcelona, 1630). But there also appeared in print in the same century an undated edition of a play entitled *Tan largo me lo fiáis* and attributed to Calderón, a drama which is a version of the same theme as *El burlador* and more than half of whose lines are identical with lines of *El burlador*. Scholars have long been preoccupied by the very close relationship between *El burlador* and *Tan largo* and the problems which this relationship and the disparities between the two *comedias* pose. *Tan largo* is, because of its style, clearly not by Calderón, although it has recently been re-printed as his. But, then, whose play is it? Whose is *El burlador*? And which was the earlier play? Sloman has meticulously compared their texts and come to the conclusions that, both *El burlador* and *Tan largo* being defective texts in many ways (and especially in their versification), both are versions, *Tan largo* the earlier and *El burlador* the later and more skilful, of an original which has not been preserved.[6]

El burlador de Sevilla concerns the outrages perpetrated by the arrogant and unscrupulous Don Juan Tenorio, son of the King of Spain's favourite and nephew of the Spanish Ambassador to Naples. At the Court of Naples Don Juan, pretending in the darkness to be the lover and intended husband of the Duchess Isabela, fornicates with her. When she discovers that he is not her lover, Isabela screams and the King and courtiers come to her aid, but Don Juan's uncle helps his nephew to escape and thinks that he has made him promise to go to Sicily or Milan. Instead Don Juan sets off for Spain. On the way he and his servant Catalinón are shipwrecked. Catalinón's struggles to swim almost drown Don Juan, who has been trying to save him, and when they are cast up on the strand a fisher-girl, Tisbea, begins to fall in love with the unconscious nobleman. Tisbea is an interesting character, in a way a female counterpart to Don Juan. Before she saw him she scorned all the fishermen who sought her hand; she boasted that she was not subject to the power of love and triumphed in her freedom to make men unhappy. She is, however, easily seduced, with a false promise of marriage, by Don Juan, who, as he violated the sanctity of the Court of Naples, violates the hospitality which Tisbea gives him and, after sleeping with her, makes off. When she first saw him striving to save Catalinón, Tisbea had said of Don Juan that he was like Aeneas carrying Anchises in a sea which had been turned into Troy. When she fell in love with him she feared he would be like the Trojan horse. Now, deserted by her seducer, she laments that her burning hut is like Troy in flames, the symbol of the destruction of the citadel of her honour and the torture of her mind, and also an image suggesting the hellfire which Don Juan will in the end suffer. In Seville, Don Juan pretends, under cover of darkness, to be his dissolute friend, the Marqués de la Mota, and thus he seduces Doña Ana de Ulloa, the lady whom Mota loves. As he escapes from this exploit, Don Juan kills Doña Ana's father, Don Gonzalo. Then he seduces a second plebeian woman, Aminta, after her wedding to a peasant and on what should have been her wedding-night. As in the case of Tisbea, Don Juan deceives Aminta by a false promise of marriage. Again he flees. But he sees the stone statue of Don Gonzalo on his tomb, pulls its beard, and invites it to supper. To his surprise, the statue attends the supper and, after it, invites its host to sup with it in its chapel. Don Juan accepts this invitation and keeps his promise to go. In the chapel, after a grim meal of scorpions, vipers, and gall, the statue grasps Don Juan's hand and, as he screams for confession, sinks with him down to Hell. The play ends when the King of Spain re-establishes order in society by marrying off Don Juan's victims in appropriate pairs.

In order to appreciate *El burlador de Sevilla* properly, one must put out of one's head (as an imaginative reading of the play will do inevitably) any romanticised notions of a really likeable or enviable Don Juan which later versions of the legend, in literature or popular psychology, may have suggested to us. Tirso's Don Juan Tenorio is not admirable. Tirso did not try to present him to his audiences as likeable, apart from the one incident in which Don Juan strives to rescue his Catalinón from drowning. Tirso's Don Juan is never, apart from that incident, really brave. His acceptance of the statue's invitation to supper and his going to keep the invitation must have been construed by the sensible members of Spanish audiences of the seventeenth century as acts not of courage but of crass rashness. Nor is it wise to be misled by Catalinón's statement that Don Juan is an honourable man in all things except where women are concerned. Tirso's Don Juan is not, within the terms of the action of *El burlador*, even the 'occasionally honourable' man that a modern critic has called him.[7] He uses 'mental reservations' which (though they may have been acceptable to certain of Tirso's contemporary ecclesiastical casuists) are presented in the play as despicable, in order to avoid keeping his word; being normally a coward, he keeps it only to the statue, and that action shows him to be a fool. The 'likeable' Don Juan was probably not born, in fact, until the early eighteenth century, when Antonio de Zamora recast *El burlador* into a play called *No hay plazo que no se cumpla ni deuda que no se pague, y convidado de piedra*. Tirso spares no sentimentality on *his* Don Juan; he looks on him, and on the other characters of the play, ironically and with detachment. Tirso's Don Juan is a fool who, perhaps because he lives in a world of fools, will not take to heart the warnings which are repeatedly given to him by other people who, however stupid themselves, are the mouthpieces of an essentially merciful God. Don Juan, who gambles ('¿Tan largo me lo fiáis?') on his youth and his prospects of a long life in which to mend his ways, suddenly finds out, too late, that life may be very short. *El burlador* is, fundamentally, a religious play whose 'message' is: 'Repent now! For the Day of Judgment may already be at hand!'

But there is much more to the play than that. Don Juan is not simply the blind sinner who will not repent; he is also a diabolical wrecker. Much of the tension in this very smartly paced play derives from the tussles between Don Juan the destroyer and the forces for order and harmony (the King of Spain; Don Juan's father). *El burlador* is a play in which the fabric of human society is shown to be both flimsy and soiled. Don Juan does not dishonour women out of sheer sexual desire but for the delight of dishonouring; and, as we have said, honour in the eyes of his contemporaries was one of the great binding forces in society. Like the Comendador in *Fuenteovejuna*, Don Juan in *El burlador* is a representative of the Devil; like Fernán Gómez, he is surrounded, in the poetry of the play, by devil-symbolism. God triumphs and God's living representatives on earth make a sort of harmony out of the resultant *débris*; but they only pair off fools encumbered with guilt and shame. Don Gonzalo, who is dead, is the only character who has shown real integrity of character in all circumstances. The play, in fact, exposes the frailty of human society at various levels. Tirso does not (and carefully does not) lead us to feel deeply enough about any character of *El burlador de Sevilla* for the play to be called a great personal tragedy; but the drama is certainly a great and moving social tragedy.[8]

El condenado por desconfiado is a different kind of play, though thematically closely linked to *El burlador*. *El condenado* was published by Tirso in his *Segunda parte* (Madrid, 1635). In his dedication to this volume, he declared that four plays in it were not his; such a statement may well have been a means of self-defence—we have no doubt that *El condenado* was his own work.

At the beginning of this play, Paulo is living the religious hermit's life, far from human society, which he considers to be the gateway to Hell. His aim in fasting and praying is to save his own soul, and he rashly begs God to tell him whether he will go to Heaven or to Hell. Seeing that Paulo is doubting in his faith and sinning by pride, the Devil decides to tempt him and assumes the guise of an angel. Then, pretending to be an emissary from God, he tells Paulo that he will meet the same end as a famous, bold man called Enrico, who lives in Naples. Assuming that this man will be a saint, Paulo goes to Naples to see him. He is horrified when he finds that Enrico is an arrogant, sacrilegious criminal, although Enrico's mention of his affection and care for his old father, at the end of a tirade in which he boasts of the many atrocities he has committed, goes unnoticed by the hermit. Paulo, convinced that Enrico will go to Hell and that therefore he himself must be damned, decides to merit damnation by becoming a bandit, worse than Enrico if he can be, in order to avenge himself on God. As the play proceeds, both Paulo and Enrico commit terrible crimes. God sends a shepherd-lad to convince Paulo that he ought to repent, but again he doubts. When, wearing his hermit's garb, he fails to make Enrico (who believes himself about to be killed) confess and be shriven, Paulo releases him and will not accept his advice that he himself should repent. Enrico is executed for his crimes; but before he is killed his father persuades him to repent and confess his sins, and his soul is saved. But not even another intervention by the divinely inspired shepherd-boy and the sudden vision of Enrico's soul in glory turn Paulo from his life of crime. He is killed, unrepentant, by a posse of peasants and his soul goes to Hell. In one sense the Devil's prophecy turns out to be true; in another it has been shown to be false.

The intellectual background to *El condenado por desconfiado* was a heated and subtle theological controversy, known as *De Auxiliis*, waged between the Molinists (the Jesuit followers of Luis de Molina) and the Banezians (the Dominican followers of Domingo Báñez) over the nature of Divine Grace, the ways in which it can assist a man to salvation, and the extent to which a man can of his own free will co-operate with God in attaining salvation. Banezians accused Molinists of attributing too much power to the free-will of man and of tending, thus, towards the Pelagian heresy, which held that man might attain salvation without the help of Divine Grace. Molinists argued that the Banezians tended towards the Calvinistic heresy, according to which God himself predestined some souls to Heaven and some to Hell. The controversy started in 1588; in 1607 it was officially banned by Pope Paul V, but in fact it went on well into the seventeenth century, both in Spain and in France. *De Auxiliis* left deep preoccupations in the minds of many. The disputing theologians themselves no doubt were immune to its dangers, but the unsubtle layman might swing either towards an over-confident expectation of salvation and a consequent neglect of the essentials of the Christian life, or towards morbid fatalism and despair.

But, although the *De Auxiliis* controversy forms the background to *El condenado por desconfiado*, the play is not concerned with theoretical speculation on Divine Grace and human free-will. It is, rather, a powerfully moving dramatic poem intended to direct the layman away from the snares of morbid preoccupation with impenetrable mysteries towards sound Christian practice. It is, above all, a play about practical Christian life and death.

El condenado por desconfiado has two protagonists and two intertwined plots of equal thematic importance. Though some critics have been shocked by the apparent unexpectedness of the ends which the hermit and the criminal meet, the damnation of an initially holy man and the salvation of a criminal are clearly intended to provoke reflection on the nature of true devotion and of the ways of God towards man. From the very first scene one is led to suspect that the ostentatiously pious Paulo is not all that he ought to be, and later to realise that there is something in Enrico more important than his criminality. The play is a masterly and subtle demonstration of a favourite theme of Golden Age literature, that appearances deceive.

El condenado por desconfiado is not just about the disastrous effects of lack of Faith, or lack of Hope; it is, rather, a demonstration of the necessity of all the three theological virtues–Faith, Hope, and Charity. By Faith the intellect is led to assent firmly to the truths of Revelation; Hope gives confidence in Divine assistance to attain life everlasting; by Charity we are united to God through love of him and love of our fellow-men. Faith and Hope, both to a certain degree imperfect, are vivified by Charity, for St Paul said, 'And now abideth faith, hope, charity, these three; but the greatest of these is charity' (I Cor., 13, xiii). In *El condenado por desconfiado* we see how Paulo fails in the practice of all the three great theological virtues and is damned. We also see how, in Enrico, an embryonic and imperfect practice of one aspect of Charity eventually burgeons and fertilises his crude Faith and Hope to bring about, with God's help, the salvation of his soul.

It is arguable that the central theme of the profoundly moral drama of the Golden Age is the power of man's free-will to overcome all obstacles in life, however great. *El condenado por desconfiado* also skilfully emphasises the crucial importance of free-will in man's approach to death. But the ideas of the play are not confined to the problem of salvation. In fact it presents three sets of ideas, moral, psychological, and theological, which are closely knit together. It teaches that it is wrong to judge other men by appearances; that a bold, positive attitude to life is more fruitful than cowardice, which leads nowhere but to frustration of one's desires; that a belief in absolute and irremediable predestination which does not take good works into account can lead to fatalistic pessimism and despair; that God is a Being on whose mercy we can rely if we choose actively to co-operate with him and approach him in true humility; that the basic virtue of all is Charity.

El condenado por desconfiado is a subtle and widely ranging sermon in verse. It is also a masterpiece of drama. Its dramatic power derives mostly from the playwright's imaginative use of surprise in his parallel plots, and even more from his remarkably fine characterisation of Paulo and Enrico, who are contrasted with consummate skill. Rarely have two better foils been presented on the Spanish stage; it is in the comparison between Paulo, the cold, proud mistrustful intellectual, and Enrico, the simple, arrogant, but spontaneous criminal who is capable of love, that the true greatness of the play lies.[9]

Perhaps the most striking group of *comedias* by Tirso are his Old Testament plays. On these he worked with a craft which is, in general, notably more subtle than Lope's in his treatment of similar themes. As a trained theologian, Tirso selected his source-materials with great care, normally keeping, in his main plots, close to the biblical stories which were his primary sources but also significantly modifying details, for greater dramatic and thematic effectiveness, often in accordance with interpretations of these stories by Jewish and Christian exegetes. The best of Tirso's biblical plays tend, in consequence, to have more doctrinal value and more point to them than Lope's. The most impressive of all Tirso's plays of this type is *La venganza de Tamar*, a powerful dramatisation of the manner in which King David's eldest son, Amnon, falls in love with his half-sister Tamar, rapes her, and is punished for his incestuous crime by being stabbed to death at a banquet by the servants of his half-brother, the envious and ambitious Absalom, who is eager to inherit the throne. Simple and straightforward in its dramatic structure, the play is deeply moving, not only because of its most memorable feature, the brilliant characterisation of the neurotic, indecisive, melancholic Amón and his gradual involvement in a sordid affair over which he lets himself lose control, but also because of the drama's sad, disenchanted revelations of guilt and sordid motives in other members of his family and his father's dilemma and grief. *La venganza de Tamar* is not a simple moral play in which good triumphs over evil. It is much more complex than that in its moral implications. As Paterson has shown, in a subtle and sensitive analysis of the *comedia* and the ideas which it suggests, '*La venganza de Tamar* is a drama about guilt, justice and mercy'.[10] The play raises disturbing questions of perennial importance. Another fine Old Testament play by Tirso is *La mejor espigadera*, a cunning dramatisation of the Book of Ruth, probably intended not just as a naïve, pleasant, and idyllic representation of Ruth's conversion, but to illustrate a clash between *pietas* and *impietas* in the broadest senses of these terms.[11] Like *El condenado por desconfiado*, this play concerns the three theological virtues, and in particular the supreme virtue of Charity. Less distinguished than either of these two dramas, but none the less a very good and tense work, is *La mujer que manda en casa*, in which Tirso put on the stage the story of the licentious Jezebel, the trials and martyrdom of the 'Christian Stoic' Naboth who steadfastly avoids her snares, and the queen's terrible death.[12]

Some critics exaggerate Tirso's genuine gift for creating strong female characters in his plays, and attribute to him a special insight into female psychology. A typically exaggerated statement on this subject, which nevertheless seems to point towards the truth, was made in the nineteenth century by Durán:

> Lo cierto es que los hombres de Tirso son siempre tímidos, débiles y juguetes del bello sexo, en tanto que caracteriza a las mujeres como resueltas, intrigantes y fogosas en todas las pasiones que se funden en el orgullo y la vanidad. Parece a primera vista que su intento ha sido, contrastar la frialdad e irresolución de los unos con la vehemencia y aun obstinación que atribuyó a las otras en el arte de seguir una intriga, sin perdonar medio alguno por impropio que sea.[13]

It cannot reasonably be maintained that Naboth is weak and irresolute in *La mujer que manda en casa*, or that Don Juan in *El burlador* or Enrico in *El condenado* are so. And not all Tirso's female characters are strong in personality and character. Nevertheless, there are plays in which Tirso plays ironically with contrasts of character and attitudes of the sexes, giving to each sex the moral and psychological characteristics expected in the other. Instead of representing a triumph of the naturalness of characterisation which critics have always rightly praised in Tirso, such transferences of stock characteristics appear generally to be a conscious artistic technique employed by the dramatist in order to make, more forcefully than he could otherwise do, points of moral, social, and political criticism.

An interesting example of this technique is his most famous play on a Spanish historical subject, *La prudencia en la mujer*, which concerns the efforts of Queen María, widow of Sancho IV of Castile and León, to preserve the throne for her son Ferdinand, in a time of chaos, rebellion, and treachery; to educate the child to wisdom as a monarch; and, when he comes of age, to set him back on the path of justice and duty from which traitors have drawn him away. Much of the effectiveness of this play depends on the trick which its title suggests. The drama is, in fact, a clever play on the stupidity of the ancient and persistent anti-feminist prejudice which holds that woman, the daughter of Eve, is weak, inconstant, foolish, and lacking in the cardinal virtue of prudence. In this play, Doña María is a paragon of prudence, even when she would seem to modern eyes to take somewhat rash, imprudent risks. In contrast, the men who oppose her, her foils, the great nobles who expect her to be a fool and who strive to win her hand, to take over the throne, and later to denigrate her character, stand out clearly as weaklings and imprudent, short-sighted fools themselves. The Queen's prudence is, of course, divinely inspired; she is the viceroy of God in the state, and credibly an analogue, in her protective function, of the Virgin Mary. In a fascinating study of this play, Ruth Lee Kennedy has argued that it was composed between 1621 and 1623, shortly after Philip IV's accession to the throne at the age of sixteen, and that in this *comedia* Tirso 'was penning a *de regimine principum* in dramatic form', a series of warnings to the young king of Spain and his advisers about the principles of good and just government and the perils which inevitably confront all monarchs and are especially dangerous for those who will not apply themselves to cultivate, as they rule, the long and keen vision of prudence.[14]

Another good chronicle-play by Tirso which presents an extraordinary woman in contrast to weaker men is *Antona Garcia*, the action of which takes place in the Guerra de la Beltraneja between Ferdinand and Isabella and the pretender Doña Juana. The simple but warlike country-girl who is the heroine of this play is a prodigy of beauty, strength, and valour who, in her remarkable exploits in defence of the Catholic Monarchs, scarcely takes any time off in order to give birth, in the course of the third *jornada*, first to one girl and a little later to another. This is a highly entertaining and amusing drama of adventure, but it also has moral point to it. The song which is sung at Antona's wedding in the First Act,

> Más valéis vos, Antona,
> que la corte, toda,

prepares the audience for sharp contrasts between the honesty, integrity, and loyalty of the girl and the hollowness of characters of higher degree and status.

With his naturalness, compassion, and gaiety, Tirso excelled at humorous drama, not only as comic relief in his serious plays but also in numerous witty comedies. One of the best of his *comedias de capa y espada* is *Don Gil de las calzas verdes*, in which Doña Juana, having been abandoned for another lady by her lover Don Martín, decides to set about the business of winning him back by disguising herself as a man, Don Gil, and making sure that her rival, Doña Inés, falls in love with her in this guise and out of love with Don Martín.[15] Another celebrated play of the same type is *Marta la piadosa*, in which the clever Marta, in order to avoid being forced to marry an old man instead of the youth she loves, pretends to become deeply religious and to take a vow of chastity, although she has her lover admitted to her father's house in the guise of a poor, sick student who can teach her Latin. Not everyone will enjoy this play lightheartedly, for *Marta la piadosa* is tart, acrid comedy; it points, amidst its humour, at the unpleasantness of hypocrisy and deception. A much lighter play, and a much funnier one, is *Por el sótano y el torno*. Tirso also wrote good and subtle comedies which involve characters of higher rank than the *comedias de capa y espada*. In *El vergonzoso en palacio* a shepherd-lad, Mireno, feels an instinctive urge to lead a noble life and, by a happy accident, is arrested while wearing the clothes of a Duke's secretary. In the ducal household he calls himself Don Dionís, and the Duke's daughter, who falls in love with him, persuades her father to free him and make him her secretary. By a series of tricks and wiles, she gradually convinces the disarmingly timid and diffident youth that she is in love with him. All turns out well in the end, for it is found that, unlike the secretary in Lope's *El perro del hortelano*, the young man is really the son of a great nobleman and therefore a suitable husband for his mistress. Another good play of similar nature is *El melancólico*, which concerns a country youth's transformation into the ruler of Brittany and his attempts to have the peasant girl whom he loves accepted at Court. Again, the ending is happy, but the satirical content of the play is greater than that of *El vergonzoso*.[16]

Tirso wrote also some good *autos sacramentales* for Corpus Christi. The most delightful of these is *El colmenero divino*, a delicately lyrical allegorical fantasy in which Christ is represented as the beekeeper who comes down into the valley to woo the bee (the soul of man) in opposition to his rival, the drone, who represents the power of the flesh. Another well-conceived *auto* by Tirso is *Los hermanos parecidos*, an ingenious interweaving of the story of the Fall of Adam and Eve and the death of Christ, neatly and effectively linking the ideas of original sin and redemption.

NOTES

1. It was proposed by Doña Blanca de los Ríos, to whom we owe the standard edition of the dramatist's plays (3 vols., Madrid, 1947-58). Her interpretations and dates are highly questionable. Her claim about Tirso's

parentage was based on her interpretation of an indecipherable scrawl on the baptismal certificate of an illegitimate child, Gabriel, born in Madrid in 1584, who may not have been Tirso at all.

2. On the details of his life, see Alexandre Cioranescu, 'La biographie de T. de M. Points de repère et points de vue', *BH*, LXIV (1962), 157-89; Tirso de Molina, *La venganza de Tamar*, ed. A. K. G. Paterson (Cambridge, 1969), pp. 1-4.

3. See Tirso de Molina, *Poesías líricas*, ed. Ernesto Jareño, CCa 17 (Madrid, 1969).

4. *La venganza de Tamar*, ed. cit., p. 8.

5. On the tradition, see, in particular, Georges Gendarme de Bévotte, *La légende de Don Juan*, 2 vols. (Paris, 1911); Leo Weinstein, *The Metamorphoses of Don Juan* (Stanford, Calif., 1959); and the fascinating number of *La Table Ronde* (Nº 119, November 1957) dedicated to *Don Juan: thème de l'art universel*; E. W. Hesse's bibliography 'Influencia del tema de Don Juan', in *Tirso de Molina. Ensayos sobre la biografía y la obra del P.M.F.G.T. por Revista Estudios* (Madrid, 1949), pp. 850-89.

6. Albert E. Sloman, 'The Two Versions of *El burlador de Sevilla*', *BHS*, XLII (1965), 18-33. *Tan largo me lo fiáis* is now most conveniently read in the edition by Xavier A. Fernández (Madrid, 1967), but in this edition it is attributed to Calderón; see a review by Sloman in *BHS*, XLVI (1969), 164-7.

7. By Wardropper in '*El burlador de Sevilla*: A Tragedy of Errors', *PQ*, XXXVI (1957), 61-7.

8. See Daniel Rogers, 'Fearful Symmetry: The Ending of *El burlador de Sevilla*', *BHS*, XLI (1964), 141-59, and C. B. Morris, 'Metaphor in *El burlador de Sevilla*', *RR*, LV (1964), 248-55. See also Parker, *The Approach to the Spanish Drama*, pp. 12-14; A Marni, 'Did Tirso employ Counterpassion in his *Burlador de Sevilla*?', *HR*, XX (1952), 123-33.

9. On the long intellectual tradition behind the play's immediate sources, see Menéndez Pidal, '*El condenado por desconfiado*', in his *Estudios literarios*, Austral 28 (Buenos Aires, 1938, etc.), pp. 11-85. See also T. E. May, '*El condenado por desconfiado*', *BHS*, XXXV (1958), 138-56; Ch. V. Aubrun, 'La *comedia* doctrinale et ses histoires de brigands. *El condenado por desconfiado*', *BH*, LIX (1957), 137-51; Carlos A. Pérez, 'Verosimilitud psicológica de *El condenado por desconfiado*', *Hisp*, núm. 27 (1966), 1-21; A. A. Parker, 'Santos y bandoleros en el teatro español del Siglo de Oro', *Arbor*, XIII (1949), 395-416.

10. ed. cit., p. 22. Calderón took over Act III of Tirso's play almost intact to form the second *jornada* of his less moving *refundición* of the story, *Los cabellos de Absalón*, which carries on to the death of Absalom. See Albert E. Sloman, *The Dramatic Craftsmanship of Calderón* (Oxford, 1958), pp. 94-127.

11. See Glaser, '*La mejor espigadera* de T. de M.', *LR*, XIV (1960), 199-218.

12. See Glaser, 'T. de M.'s *La mujer que manda en casa*', *AIUN*, Sez. Rom., II (1960), 25-42.

13. Agustín Durán, *Talia española* (Madrid, 1834); see *BAE*, V, xi.

14. See Ruth Lee Kennedy, '*La prudencia en la mujer* and the Ambient that Brought it Forth', *PMLA*, LXIII (1948), 1131-90.

15. See Everett W. Hesse, *Análisis e interpretación de la comedia* (Madrid, 1968), pp. 43-51.

16. On *El melancólico*, see Paterson's introduction to his edition of *La venganza de Tamar*, pp. 10-11.

Chapter 6

CALDERÓN

DON PEDRO CALDERÓN DE LA BARCA was born in Madrid on 17 January 1600. His father held a good government post, and his mother's family was respectable. He had two brothers: Diego, the elder, later became a lawyer; José, the youngest of the three, was to prove himself a brave and competent army officer. Their maternal grandmother endowed a family chaplaincy for their benefit, and Pedro was brought up with the plan that he should succeed to it after he came of age. Their mother died in 1610. Their father married again, but the stepmother had little affection for the three boys. In 1615 the father died, after making an uncharitable will that threatened Diego with disinheritance should he continue to court a certain young woman and commanded Pedro to follow the course set out for him.[1] Lawsuits with the stepmother made this will of little effect; the boys were brought up by one of their mother's brothers.

Pedro received an excellent education at the Jesuit Colegio Imperial and then went to Salamanca to study canon law. He got into a serious scrape for non-payment of rent and damages, which involved him in excommunication (the rent was owed to a convent) and imprisonment in the university prison. We do not know the outcome of the proceedings against him. He did not, apparently, take a university degree. In 1621 the three brothers were involved in a murder and took sanctuary in the Austrian embassy. They had to compensate the victim's relatives, and their only means of doing so was by the sale of their dead father's office, which Diego would otherwise have inherited. In the same year Pedro entered the household of Don Bernardino Fernández de Velasco, the constable of Castile.

Poetical pieces by Pedro began to appear in print in 1620. His earliest datable plays are of 1623. He was praised by Lope de Vega and became a friend of Lope's protégé Dr Juan Pérez de Montalbán. His relations with Lope were broken when, in 1629, one of his brothers was treacherously stabbed by an actor, who sought sanctuary in the

Trinitarian convent in which Lope's daughter was a nun. Pedro and the police followed the criminal into the convent, where, the preacher Hortensio Paravicino (himself a Trinitarian also) alleged in a sermon, they manhandled the nuns. Calderón imprudently introduced into his great play *El príncipe constante* a mild burlesque of Fray Hortensio's oratory. Cardinal Trejo y Paniagua, then President of the Council of Castile, mildly reproved him for attacking Paravicino by name and showed that the sermon had grossly exaggerated the earlier offence. Calderón was not blamed for entering the convent; the would-be assassin—not he—was guilty of violating the sanctuary of the nuns.

He now began to earn fame as a playwright. The early masterpieces followed one another through the 1630s. His early plays were for the *corrales*, though they were often repeated at Court. When the palace of the Buen Retiro was completed he wrote plays specially to suit the new theatrical properties available only there. He did not, apparently, neglect the *corrales* during this decade, but the association with the court theatre was to last until his death. Philip IV recognised his gifts by initiating proceedings for his election as a Knight of St James; he entered the order in 1637. Two volumes of his plays (twelve in each) were first printed in 1636 and 1637 respectively.

In 1640 the Catalans revolted against the central government, and Calderón fulfilled his obligations to the order by serving bravely in the war in the campaigns of 1640-41 and in 1642.[2] Ill-health compelled him to retire from the forces in that year. He resided for some time in Toledo and served in the household of the duque de Alba. National disasters, combined with the sense of guilt of the king, brought about restrictions of performance and finally the closure of the theatres during the periods October 1644 to Easter 1645 and from 1646 to 1649 or 1650. The possibility that such closures might become permanent, the fall of Spain as a great power, the deaths of the queen, Isabel of France, and of the heir to the throne, Don Baltasar Carlos, the death of his elder brother in 1647 and of his younger one, hacked to pieces at the bridge of Camarasa, in 1645, made Calderón return to the original plan mapped out for him. He took up his grandmother's chaplaincy and sang his first Mass in October 1651.

At this point he had seriously considered the abandonment of writing for the theatre. The anti-theatrical campaign of the Jesuits and of other ecclesiastics during the forties must have seemed a serious problem to a newly-ordained priest. But on the one hand he was asked to produce *autos sacramentales* for the celebration of Corpus Christi and to devise new court shows for the palace, on the other hand an application by him for a post suitable to his new condition was refused by an ecclesiastic, 'que juzgó incompatibles el sacerdocio, con la poesía'. He wrote a finely phrased letter to the Patriarch of the Indies about his dilemma.[3] We do not know how the Patriarch replied, but from 1651 onward Calderón wrote Corpus *autos* for the city of Madrid and plays for the royal palace. He ceased to write directly for the *corrales*.

In 1653 Calderón became—thanks to Philip IV—one of the chaplains of the Chapel of the *Reyes Nuevos* (i.e. the Trastamaran kings) in the Cathedral at Toledo. Eventually, because of ill-health and the necessity of attending rehearsals, he moved back to Madrid, where he remained until his death. He continued to write two *autos* a year for the city and *comedias de tramoyas* for the palace, except during the periods when stage-plays or *autos* were forbidden. He enjoyed the favour of Philip IV, of the queen, Mariana of Austria, of Charles II of Spain, of Don John Joseph of Austria. His secular swan-song was a chivalresque drama to celebrate the arrival of Charles's French queen, Marie-Louise, in Madrid in 1681. He completed one *auto* and half another one for performance in that year. He died on 25 May 1681.

Calderón wrote more than 120 *comedias* and over seventy *autos sacramentales*. He collaborated with other known dramatists in a further thirteen or so plays. The number of his *loas* (dramatic prologues) to full-length plays and to *autos sacramentales* remains, for the present, undetermined; nor do we know how many comic *entremeses* he also wrote. His dramatic productivity, though less astounding than Lope's, remains considerable. He was a gentleman, who called himself Don Pedro Calderón Riaño or Calderón de la Barca before he came of age; but he depended on the theatre for his living and wrote with the assurance of a professional. He wrote half a dozen or so poems that are worth a place in the history of Spanish seventeenth-century poetry and are of some merit in themselves.

Even in the earliest plays there is a considerable competence of a technical sort. He was of course learning from his elders: Lope, Tirso de Molina, Ruiz de Alarcón, Mira de Amescua, Luis Vélez de Guevara. At first his relations with Lope were more than cordial, but the affair of the Trinitarian nuns broke their friendship. He paid a moving tribute to Tirso when he approved the *Quinta parte* of that dramatist's plays in 1636: 'hay en ellas [las comedias de Tirso] mucha erudición, y ejemplar dotrina por la moralidad que tienen, encerrada en su honesto y apacible entretenimiento; efectos todos del ingenio de su Autor, que con tantas muestras de ciencia, virtud y religión *ha dado a aprender a los que más deseamos imitarle*'.[4] He collaborated once with Mira and once with Luis Vélez. His closest links during his early years were with his own contemporaries: Montalbán, Rojas, Antonio Coello. And he collaborated more often with them: five times with Coello, four with Rojas, and three with Pérez de Montalbán. Praises of Calderón's works in the early thirties can be found—he was especially lauded for his ability to use stage effects and machinery—but he was not till much later regarded as a supreme dramatist. Lope, Vélez, even Montalbán, were more highly esteemed than he was. Lope died in 1635, Montalbán in 1638, Vélez in 1644; though from 1629 until the forties Calderón's masterpieces continued to appear, his reputation as the great playwright of the reign of Philip IV did not become established until after his return from the Catalan war.

His studies at the Jesuit Colegio Imperial at Madrid undoubtedly gave him many skills needed by a dramatist. There he was taught Latin and rhetoric, read widely in past authors, and shown how to combine arguments with elegant figures of speech in order to cultivate the arts of persuasion and at the same time to examine and comprehend the traditional psychology of neo-scholasticism. He learned both how to argue and how to define. His later legal studies at Salamanca no doubt continued the process,[5] though these years were, as we have seen, troubled. The peculiar features of Calderonian verse: those close-knit speeches, with elaborate analogies, continued metaphors, conceits, and rhetorical colours, probably originated in the Jesuits' classrooms and the works he studied there. Their school plays and public recitations must also have aroused his imagination and creative talents. We cannot be surprised at his enthusiastic collaboration in the poetic competitions for the beatification and canonisation of St Isidro (1620 and 1622) and in that of the five saints in 1622.

Of course he must often have gone to the public theatres while he was still a lad, and the influence on him of the dramatists already mentioned would have begun then. His ordinary reading must have been almost equally influential. Góngora's great *culto* poems were circulating in manuscript in Madrid and in Salamanca before 1620. They were to leave many traces on the descriptive passages in his plays. The nine parts of the *Romancero general* appeared in a collected edition in the year of his birth; they were reprinted—sometimes with additions—during his boyhood. Other anthologies were printed or reprinted or circulated in manuscript during the same period, to say nothing of the appearance in Madrid of volume after volume of poems by Lope and by other famous names. The songs by other writers so frequently sung on the stage in Calderón's plays and *autos* often come from such collections.[6] And we must not forget the fact that they had a different kind of circulation by professional and amateur musicians.

Among the prose-works printed in Madrid during these years were some of the most famous works of Cervantes. There are many recollections of Cervantes in Calderón's plays, though unfortunately his play *Los disparates de don Quijote* has not survived.[7] At first sight Cervantes's broad view of life and his large tolerance seem quite apart from Calderón's formal constructions and orthodox morality. But the two novels of *El curioso impertinente* and *El celoso estremeño* seem to have impressed the young dramatist, who perhaps saw in them a reflection of his own situation. Cervantes had shown the disastrous consequences of the subjection of human beings to the domineering will of two unwise husbands; Calderón was likewise dominated by the plans of a tyrannical father who intended that his second son should not choose the life he wanted to lead. Calderón's explorations of the father-son relationship (*La devoción de la Cruz—La vida es sueño*) have something in common with Cervantes's stories of marital dishonour.[8]

When Calderón came of age in 1621 he refused to become a priest. He stopped signing his name D. Pedro Calderón Riaño (the surname of the grandmother who had endowed the chaplaincy) and called himself D. Pedro Calderón de la Barca. But no one can doubt the religious faith of the boy who had belonged to the confraternity of the Anunciata at the Colegio Imperial, or of the man who wrote and dramatised a savagely ascetic *romance* on St Ignatius's penances at Manresa (1622) and who was later to write three or four of the finest religious plays in Spanish, as well as to become the greatest of all writers of *autos sacramentales*. The Jesuit upbringing had bitten very deep. Several poems show the influence of the Ignatian system of meditation; he also wrote plays about St Francis Borja (Borgia) and about the Moorish convert Baltasar de Loyola. The fact that his early life was sometimes lawless does not mean that he did not read or study, nor does it mean that his religion at that time was merely conventional.

The wild oats have sometimes been exaggerated by modern critics, who have not taken notice of the fact that the statements of a prejudiced accuser were not those of an impartial judge; we should follow Trejo, not Paravicino, to comprehend the Trinitarian affair. But we do find some reflections of a lawless attitude in some of the early plays. *Luis Pérez el gallego* (1629?) is one in which the poet sympathises with an outlaw hero and his humiliation of a New Christian villain. In it we can find sentiments like these:

Viéndome, pues más culpado
yo que Don Alonso estaba,
pretendí que me valiese
antes el salto de mata
que ruego de buenos.

Llegad conmigo: veréis
del modo que he de vivir,
tomando lo que me den,
sin hacer agravio a nadie,
que soy ladrón muy de bien.

The play is lively and amusing. In *El purgatorio de San Patricio*—
based on one of Montalbán's novels, published in 1627—the villain-
hero is finally converted by the appearance of his own ghost and thereafter leads an ascetic life after travelling through the famous cave on
Lough Derg, where he sees visions of Hell and purgatory. Nevertheless,
though Ludovico Enio is shown to be a wicked man, he relates his
crimes with enormous gusto and piously remarks 'que Dios le tenga en
el cielo' of each of the victims whom he had killed. The play, crude but
lively, contains a very beautiful scene when Ludovico, now converted,
meets Polonia, whom he had murdered, but whose life had been miraculously restored to her. Sternly they both refuse to allow their past
emotions to interfere as she guides her murderer to his redemption.
Lawlessness is beginning to be critically surveyed in this early play.

These and the other early plays were written for the public theatres,
though from time to time they were acted also in the palace for the
benefit of the young Philip IV. They are readable, though the author
has not yet discovered his full powers. They include a play about the
contemporary wars in Flanders: *El sitio de Bredá* (1625), a genre
Calderón was never to attempt again. Perhaps the best of them—if it
is really as early as some critics think—is *El astrólogo fingido*, which
moves quickly, is full of Madrilian local allusions, and is well put
together. It contains a direct imitation of the Clavileño episode in
Don Quixote, Part II. The influence of Tirso is strong here and in
other early plays.

The first great masterpiece, *El príncipe constante*, was performed in
1629. It is based on the story of the historical prince Ferdinand of
Portugal, who died in Algiers, a captive of the Moors, of whom
Calderón made a Christian martyr who chose abject slavery and death
rather than allow himself to be exchanged for the city of Ceuta and

the loss of souls to Christ. The play has been much discussed by English, American, and German critics; there is also an excellent monograph on how Calderón shaped the story from history and from an earlier play, probably by Tárrega. The play contrasts the hero with his own brave but irresolute brother (the historical Henry the Navigator), with the King of Fez, his general Muley, and with Fénix, the Moorish princess. The series of contrasts culminates in a painful death-scene: Fernando, dying on a dunghill, defies the King and reduces Fénix's pity to nothingness. Earlier he has outshone his brother in military determination and Muley in the observance of the rules of loyalty. The famous scene in which the Constant Prince refuses to allow the exchange with Ceuta ('porque es de Dios y no es mía), his sonnet that challenges Fénix's beauty with death, his dying speech of defiance of the King and acceptance of death, Muley's description of the sea-battle, rightly praised by Professor Gombrich,[9] show that the poetic texture of the parts in no way betrays the superb construction of the whole. In the last scenes the hero's spirit leads the Portuguese army to victory, so that he can receive Christian burial and Fénix can marry Muley. One critic has seen this merely as a kind of epilogue, in which the miracle provides the main feature. Entwistle reminded him that in this scene Fernando utters a sentence that shows a deeper truth than its mere occasion provides:

> En el horror de la noche,
> por sendas que nadie sabe,
> te guié.

The saintly hero knew the unknown paths through the horror of the night of his living death.

Also written in 1629 were Calderón's two most famous cloak-and-sword plays: *La dama duende* and *Casa con dos puertas mala es de guardar*. He wrote many others later, some of them (e.g. *No siempre lo peor es cierto, Mañanas de abril y mayo, No hay burlas con el amor*) as good as, if less famous than, the two just mentioned.[10] These comedies are the continuation of Lope's and Tirso's plays of love and jealousy, only they are now more stylised, more complicated, more ingenious. They were primarily devised as civilised entertainment—to amuse rather more cultivated audiences than those usual in the *corrales*, but so lively are they that even the illiterate must have enjoyed them too. In these *comedias* the gentlemen are gentlemen, the ladies ladies. Men of honour court women of quality. The men uphold the code of honour; the ladies are chaste. Two or more pairs of lovers take part. Complications occur because of mistakes of identity caused by speeches in the dark, borrowed shawls, or other trivial enough mistakes. As the behaviour of an unmarried woman was considered to affect the honour of her male parent or guardian, one of these gentlemen can appear both as a guardian of one lady and the suitor of another. Friendships between men and between ladies often make the tangles still more intricate. So the rash impulse of one of either sex will not only affect his own affair but those of others as well. Rashness in speech and action, lack of knowledge, jumping to conclusions, failures to see that appearance does not always conform to reality, all these mistakes involve everyone in difficulties, in duels, in lovers' quarrels, and in broken friendships. But eventually the wiser or more prudent pair help the less wise to the usual denouement: declarations of marriage before witnesses and the satisfaction of the guardian's honour by the removal of the lady from his keeping to that of her husband, who henceforth will regard himself as responsible for her.

These plays, then, though they are intended as entertainment, did not merely serve to 'amuse an idle moment in their day'. They were based on certain strict conventions of manners and upheld them: be polite, keep your word, protect the helpless, help your friends, and so forth. They also show, '*sine periculo vitae*',[11] that mistakes in conduct and in the interpretation of the circumstances in which we are placed, can, and do, have disagreeable consequences. At times the expression of the difficulties of the cloak-and-sword world parallels the more serious ones to be found in graver dramas. Insight and prudence are valuable qualities that help men and women in their difficulties. Rashness, impulses, hunches, are dangerous traps for the unwary. These plays almost deserve the title of entertaining moral allegories.

Some social criticism occasionally shows itself in these comedies. Calderón, perhaps with the memory of Ruiz de Alarcón's *figurones* in mind, sometimes incorporated a similar person into the play. In *Mañanas de abril y mayo* (1634?) Don Hipólito boasts of his abilities as a lover: 'Yo tengo notable estrella con mujeres'; at the end of the play he is left unmarried! In *No hay burlas con el amor* Doña Beatriz is a pedantically Gongoristic lady; she demands in these terms that her sister show her a letter:

> Con vulgar disculpa
> me has obstinado dos veces;
> ese manchado papel,
> en quien cifró líneas breves

cálamo ansariano, dando
cornerino vaso débil
el etíope licor,
ver tengo.

But at the end of the play she has learned prudence and earned her reward for it.

Another variation in theme transferred the setting from a city to the palace. Besides the difficulties outlined above, the hero finds himself with conflicts of love and loyalty to his prince, as well as the prevailing struggle of love with honour. These plays are less enjoyable than the others, largely because palaces have become more remote from us than cities are. Dámaso Alonso's impatience with *Amigo, amante y leal* is shared by others.[12] One of the more readable of these plays is *La banda y la flor*. In many of these plays, comedies of the cloak and sword, comedies set in palaces (*comedias palaciegas*), Calderón expressed his belief in the work of time to reveal the truth and to heal broken relationships and other difficulties. One such play has the title *Dar tiempo al tiempo*: give Time time to take its course and all may yet be well. The proverbial titles of many of these plays and their very basis—the world is a confusing labyrinth—as well as the virtues they instill (prudence and trust) bear some relation to the moral system of the Christian faith in which their author had been brought up.

The thirties were to show Calderón's other gifts. During that decade many of his best-known plays were first performed, and had he died in 1641 he would have had little less posthumous fame. The new palace of the Buen Retiro, with its brilliant stage-designer Cosme Lotti (later to be replaced by Baccio del Bianco), provided new resources for a writer skilful enough to make use of them. Probably Calderón often still wrote in the first place for the actor-managers of the *corrales*, but the two spectacle-plays *El mayor encanto Amor* (early version performed in 1635)[13] and *Los tres mayores prodigios* (1636) were the first specimens of mythological palace-plays such as he was to continue to write almost up to his death. The earliest datable *auto*, *El nuevo palacio del Retiro* (1634), gives a symbolic aspect to the new palace; but by this time other *autos*, including *El gran teatro del mundo* and *La cena de Baltasar*, must already have been written and performed.

In a survey such as this, space cannot be given to all the interesting plays that Calderón wrote. Two religious masterpieces must be mentioned. *La devoción de la Cruz* concerns a critically surveyed bad man named Eusebio, who kills the brother of a woman named Julia and abducts her from the convent in which her father Curcio has placed her. Eusebio finds that she has a birth-mark in the form of a cross and deserts her, for he also bears a similar birth-mark. They are in fact brother and sister. He becomes a bandit, and she, unable to re-enter the convent, takes also to this life. Curcio, the leader of the forces of law and order, pursues them both and kills Eusebio. But Eusebio's devotion to the Cross was such that his life is now miraculously pre-served in order that he may be shriven before his death. This situation has horrified Protestant and agnostic critics, to whom the miracle appears superstitious, but Eusebio's appeal to God through the Cross after he had been wounded is as moving as the words of the Good Thief Dimas, and his repentance is shown to have been genuine. Pro-fessor Parker has brilliantly shown that in fact the play also depicts the tragedy of Curcio, whose rigid sense of honour made him kill his wife and lose his son Eusebio.[14] The son's violence and the daughter's rebel-lion are consequences of Curcio's own harshness. This interpretation adds a new dimension to a play full of stirring situations and moving poetry.

El Mágico prodigioso is Calderón's greatest religious play. It was originally composed for the Corpus festivities at Yepes (province of Toledo) in 1637. There are two different versions of it: that printed in 1663 and that of an autograph manuscript;[15] the former seems the more mature. Part of the text has disappeared: we never learn Justina's origins, though we expect to. The play has been much discussed in relation to the Faust story; we shall consider it without reference either to Marlowe or to Goethe. Cipriano, a pagan philosopher, loves Justina, a Christian virgin. His approaches are rebuffed, and in agony he offers his soul if he can win her. The Devil accepts the offer, and the compact is made. Cipriano forgets his philosophy and is taught magic; the Devil tries to tempt Justina, who is constant in her purity. The Devil, therefore, is driven to conjure up a wraith disguised as Justina in order to deceive Cipriano; he embraces her, and she turns to a skeleton in his arms:

> Así, Cipriano, son
> todas las glorias del mundo.

Earlier he had been puzzled by the passage in Pliny's *Natural History* (II, v) where there is a definition of the true God. The Devil, by his failure to stand up to Cipriano's recovered powers of logic, is driven to admit that the true God is the Christian God. Cipriano is converted, and in company with Justina, accepts martyrdom and salvation.

God is the protagonist of this play, the unseen actor, the true Wonder-working Magician. Justina's prayers move Him to save her honour and to rescue Cipriano from damnation by turning her appearance into a skeleton. Such is the heart of the play. In its details Calderón produced some of his best dramatic writing: the first conversation of Cipriano with the Devil on the mountain, the *décimas* in which Cipriano praises her beauty, Justina's temptation (translated into English by Shelley), and the terse, eloquent lines in which she overcomes it. There is also a telling contrast between the world of faith, religion, magic, and diabolic compacts and the low world of the two *graciosos*, who share the favours of the same woman on alternate days, and, as the martyrs go to their deaths, cannot comprehend the serene happiness of Justina and her former lover. The play throughout is rich in its texture; its sensational miracle is not merely a brilliant stage-effect but the central metaphor of the worthlessness of worldly glories.

Two of Calderón's tragedies of honour or of wife-murder also belong to this decade. *El médico de su honra* was performed in June 1635; it was a rewritten and replanned version of a play formerly attributed to Lope, but more probably is by another hand.[16] In most of Calderón's works honour (or reputation) is regarded as a positive virtue; this play—though traditionally it has been interpreted in the opposite sense—contrasts an extreme case of the honour code (a scrupulously honourable man has his innocent wife bled to death) with Christian principles. Don Gutierre believes that his wife, Doña Mencía, has betrayed him with Don Enrique (later Henry II of the house of Trastámara). Earlier Don Gutierre had scorned Leonor, because he thought that her maid's lover was her lover. Though the murder is premeditated and carefully planned, he is as rash in his judgments as Mencía is in her actions. The scene is set in the reign of Pedro the Cruel (1350-66), and there are many subtle parallels between the just but cruel King and the honourable but cruel husband. Calderón has deliberately distanced the events by putting them into their medieval setting. Marital honour, in itself good, is, without prudence, cruel and unjust. The play exemplifies the theory of secret vengeance for a secret outrage; if the revenge of stained honour is public, the avenger remains dishonoured because his fellows know that he once had it and had lost it. Here Calderón shows the whole working of the code in all its savagery; in the most telling scene Mencía's bloodless corpse provides a horrible contrast with the Crucifix that dominates the stage. The imagery of surgery in the play is consistent with its climax and aftermath. Pedro's death at Montiel is foreshadowed in eight lines of a *romance*, and Gutierre is strongly linked with his king.

A secreto agravio secreta venganza, first performed in the palace in June 1636, also deals with the theme of its title: the secret vengeance for a secret outrage. It is perhaps best seen as a study of the implications of the code of honour in itself. We are shown how Don Lope de Almeida learns the importance of a secret vengeance from a less prudent friend. Lope's wife is guilty in thought, and her former lover is moved almost as much by the desire to ruin Don Lope's honour as by his love for her. Again Calderón chose a setting in the past: in Portugal (where women were more subjected to their husbands than in Castile) during the reign of Sebastian (1557-78). Don Lope's fate is linked with that of Sebastian, who perished in the battle of Alcazar-quivir. The play has been interpreted as an allegory of prudence in a world obsessed by the code of honour. It is brilliantly written, brilliantly planned.

Calderón's finest play in this decade is undoubtedly *La vida es sueño*, written in 1635, printed the following year. The story of the Sleeper Awakened is given a new setting. Segismundo, son of the astrologer-king Basilio, is brought up like a caged animal in a country tower, because the horoscope cast by his father foretold nothing but disasters. One day Basilio has him drugged and transferred to the palace, where he wakes up to find himself regarded as a prince by all around him; his unruly nature shows itself when he reviles his father, makes violent love to two women, tries to kill Clotaldo, his former tutor, and throws a troublesome servant out of the window. Basilio, convinced that Segismundo is unredeemable, has him drugged again and returned to the tower. There Clotaldo convinces him that his experience in the palace was only a dream.

The Poles learn that their lawful prince will not reign over them, and the soldiers release Segismundo, who leads the rebels against his father. His experience of the dream of life has convinced him that he must now act cautiously, and—as a consequence of meeting for a third time the woman (Rosaura) whom he had seen before outside the tower and inside the palace—he comes to realise that he was in fact awake in both places. His caution turns to real prudence as he leads his army to victory; after defeating Basilio's forces he restores his father to the throne. Order has come out of chaos.

This play has impressed deeply all those who have read it without

parti pris. Nevertheless, it has often been misunderstood. The title does
not mean that all life is a dream but that worldly values have only a
dreamlike reality; in the palace Segismundo 'dreams' that he can act
as he pleases, but he learns caution and then prudence after he awakes.
Until comparatively recently the relation of the sub-plot with the main
plot was not perceived. Even the argument that Segismundo reforms
himself too quickly can also be refuted. The dream of life affects others
besides Segismundo: Basilio, a Polish prince, the *gracioso*—all have
their dreams and painful awakenings. Clotaldo and Rosaura, by their
devotion to unworldly values (loyalty and honour), escape the disillusion gone through by the others.[17]

Segismundo's two soliloquies (on the loss of his liberty and on the
dream of life) are justly famous. Some less-quoted words from that in
the Third Act are no less memorable:

> ¿Qué pasado bien no es sueño?
> ¿Quién tuvo dichas heróicas
> que entre sí no diga, cuando
> las revuelve en su memoria:
> 'sin duda que fue soñado
> cuanto ví'?

A play called *El alcalde de Zalamea* is known to have been acted at
Court on 12 May 1636. Whether this was Calderón's play or its
source—attributed to Lope, but very doubtfully his—remains disputable. The argument that Calderón's play must be based on his
army experiences during the years 1640-42 is also disputable. *El
alcalde* belongs to the family of Lope's *Peribáñez*, etc., a drama of
rustic honour threatened—in this case destroyed—by a gentleman.
Troops are billeted in Zalamea. A wealthy farmer named Pedro
Crespo entertains first an army captain and later his general, Don Lope
de Figueroa. As the troops leave the town the Captain abducts Pedro's
daughter and rapes her. Pedro captures the Captain and pleads with
him to marry Isabel, but the Captain refuses to marry a peasant girl.
Crespo, now mayor of Zalamea, has him garrotted and faces an indig-
nant Don Lope, furious at the loss of one of his officers. The arrival of
Philip II interrupts the conflict of wills: Pedro Crespo is made perpetual mayor of Zalamea, his son replaces the Captain as Don Lope's
officer, poor Isabel gladly retires to a convent.

The extraordinary vigour of this drama has made it Calderón's
second most famous play. Crespo and Don Lope parallel one another
in their manliness, in friendship as in enmity. The progress of the

Captain's lustful curiosity (like that of Loaysa in Cervantes's *El celoso extremeño*), the military ardour of Crespo's son Juan, the emptiness of the local *hidalgo* Don Mendo, the prudence of the sergeant, the lawlessness of the soldier Rebolledo and his woman Chispa, all are depicted with wonderful spirit. Every scene is excellent in itself and fits into the plan of the whole. Crespo's vengeance on the Captain defied legal niceties but was humanly justified, as Philip the Prudent saw. The play combines the rich humanity we associate with Lope at his best with the superb technique of Calderón.

Calderón, before his ordination, wrote many other plays that are almost of equal merit to those we have already examined. They can only be mentioned here, for lack of space prevents their receiving the criticism they deserve. Many of them rival all but the finest of the plays we have so far looked at. *Amar después de la muerte*, which deals with the revolt of the Granada *moriscos* in 1569, contains one of Calderón's most dramatic scenes. *La cisma de Ingalaterra*, the story of Henry VIII, Catherine of Aragon, Anne Boleyn, and Mary Tudor, twists history to conform with the general truths of poetry. *El José de las mujeres*, the story of St Eugenia, has some of the merit of *El Mágico*. *La niña de Gómez Arias*, a *refacimento* of a play by Luis Vélez, is a moving story of how a selfish soldier sells to the Moors the woman he has seduced. *No hay cosa como callar* (1638-39), the most serious of the *comedias de capa y espada*, is based on a situation like that of Cervantes's *La fuerza de la sangre*. *Las tres justicias en una* explores again the father-son relation. *El pintor de su deshonra*—in some ways the most profound of the wife-murder tragedies—is too complex to summarise. It explores the common responsibility in the final denouement of all those who take part in this tragedy.[18]

Calderón wrote few plays during the forties. His service in the Catalan war and the closing of the theatres during the second half of that decade necessarily restricted his output. The restrictions gradually lessened as Philip's second wife Mariana slowly approached Madrid. Probably he wrote two or three comedies before he took Holy Orders in 1651. Contrary to his own decision at the time of his ordination, pressure from high quarters induced him to continue to write for the court theatre. He now wrote exclusively for a stage with a proscenium and curtain, not for the old open stage of the *corrales*. These plays involved the use of elaborate scenery and music; they are more stylised, less realistic, and less obviously poetical than the earlier plays. Nevertheless, they are well worth study for their own sakes; the idea, frequently expressed by nineteenth-century critics, that they depended exclusively on the work of Lotti and his followers is quite false. We have a set of stage-designs for *La fiera, el rayo y la piedra* (first produced in 1652) used at a later performance in 1690; they show both the considerable resources of the new stage-designers and the formal stances of the actors. They help us materially to visualise the conditions of performance as we read the plays themselves.

Four semi-historical plays provide a link with what had gone before. *Darlo todo y no dar nada* (performed in December 1651) treats of Alexander the Great, Diogenes, and Apelles and exemplifies some of Calderón's artistic preoccupations.[19] *Las armas de la hermosura* (probably of 1652) uses the story of Coriolanus to symbolise the reconciliation of Castile and Catalonia after the fall of Barcelona on 13 October of that year. The two parts of *La hija del aire* (1653?) reach again towards the level of the great plays of the thirties; the history of Semiramis and Ninus gave an opportunity for the study of ambition and rashness.[20] *En la vida todo es verdad y todo mentira* (1658-59)—the title is that of the autograph manuscript; printed texts read *En esta vida . . .*—earned some praise as a *drama filosófico* from Menéndez Pelayo; it contains some very fine scenes and a startling projection of the future into the present.[21] These plays have had some recognition, though they are not very frequently read today.

The mythological dramas of this period are equally remarkable. They have been little studied, and much remains in them to be explained. We can mention only a few of them. *Eco y Narciso* (1661) is in part a study of a mother-son relation and the son's timidity; it contains a scene of great lyric interest in which the singing of *letras* bewilders the poor hero. *La estatua de Prometeo* has strangely Christian overtones; Prometheus is rescued at the end from the Caucasian rock. *Apolo y Climene* and *El hijo del Sol, Faetón,* concern respectively the birth and death of Phaeton; he perishes through his ambition to prove his divine origin. *Fieras afemina Amor* (1669-70) shows a coarse and brutal Hercules (like the drunken one by Rubens), who, in his anxiety to be heroically self-sufficient, is humiliated by Venus and Cupid to Iole, whom he had thought to enslave.[22] The history of Spanish opera—if we except an unsuccessful attempt by Lope—begins with *La púrpura de la rosa* (1660), the story of Venus and Adonis. The music for *Celos aun del aire matan,* Act I (1660?), and for considerable portions of other plays survives.[23] In all these plays music, poetry, and stagecraft composed a unique whole. There are more or less allegorical hints in their action and in single scenes.

They are a kind of secular *autos*, which hint at philosophical or religious truths without specifically declaring them.[24]

The *auto sacramental* itself was a play in honour of the Eucharist, subsidised by the Madrid municipality and performed in the open air on the Feast of Corpus Christi. The scenery was built on carts, before which a stage was erected; most of the action takes place on this stage, though given figures could and did speak from the structures on the carts. Up to 1645 (and perhaps a couple of years later) four *autos* were given in Madrid at Corpus; from 1648 onwards there were only two. From 1648 onwards four carts, not two as previously, took part in each *auto*. Up to 1648 a number of authors wrote *autos* accepted for performance; from 1649 Calderón was their exclusive author.[25] The later *autos* were longer, more elaborately staged, and with much greater complication and subtlety. They are also more difficult to understand fully. Not surprisingly Calderón's early *autos* are nowadays more widely read than the later ones.

These plays treat allegorically the central mysteries of Christianity. The abstract is made concrete. They deal with the Fall and Redemption of mankind, the superiority of Catholicism to paganism, Judaism, and modern heresies; they culminate in the worship of the Blessed Sacrament. The subject-matter of the allegory is profoundly human, and non-Catholic readers need find no difficulty in being rewarded for their 'willing suspension of disbelief', provided they are prepared also to try to comprehend as they read. The allegories come sometimes from the Bible, from classical legend, from Calderón's own *comedias*, from history, or from contemporary events. The allegorical interpretation of Scripture was a commonplace in seventeenth-century Spain; classical legends were sometimes regarded as imperfect manifestations of Christian doctrine; the will of God worked through history and contemporary events. The influence of emblem literature and the continued metaphors of *conceptista* poetry were also assimilable to this type of drama. All could be illustrated or clarified by appropriate scenery, music, choreography, and staging. The arts collaborated here, as they were to do in the mythological plays at the royal palace. Again the reader must visualise as he reads.

The two best-known *autos* are early and relatively simple. *El gran teatro del mundo* surveys the social scene: the king, the rich man, the farmer, the beggar, a child, Beauty, Discretion (i.e. religion). Each is given his (or her) clothes, acts the part assigned, and then makes an exit to an appropriate reward or punishment. The king, the farmer, and

Beauty are obsessed with their roles but are saved by their good deeds and by their good end. The child (unbaptised) goes to limbo. Only the rich man is damned. The other *auto* is *La cena de Baltasar*; it uses the story of Belshazzar's feast as an allegory; Baltasar means 'hidden treasure', Daniel 'God's judgment'. In a sense the persons are all part of Baltasar: Daniel his conscience, his wives his vices (vanity and idolatry), Pensamiento his thoughts. Daniel keeps Death in check until Baltasar has exhausted all opportunities to repent. He profanes the sacred vessels, the writing appears on the wall, Death strikes him down. These two plays are extremely effective drama; the one shows a humane attitude towards class relations, the other depicts death as the final end to moral disorder. Neither relies on music or on elaborate staging.

The second, definitive, version of the *auto* of *La vida es sueño* was acted in 1673. Segismundo becomes Mankind, Basilio the Trinity (Power, Wisdom, Love), the courtiers the four elements. The comparison with the *comedia* shows how radically Calderón transformed his material. The *auto*, in itself, is good, but other later ones are more outstanding. *No hay más Fortuna que Dios* (1652 or 1653) resembles *El gran teatro* in theme, but it is a more mature work. The various persons regard the world as the source of happiness until Beauty falls into a pit and a skeleton emerges to take her place. Disillusion enables the others to see evil for what it is, and salvation awaits them as the play ends. *Los encantos de la culpa* (1649) interprets in a Christian sense the story of Ulysses and Circe, which Calderón had used earlier in his mythological play *El mayor encanto Amor*. Ulysses is Mankind, his sailors are his senses, the pilot his understanding, and Circe is 'la Culpa'. The ship represents the Church. The play follows closely earlier interpretations of the myth, such as that given in the *Filosofía secreta* (1585) of Pérez de Moya. The material, then, of this *auto* was familiar, at least to the instructed; Calderón welded it together, and by means of a lyric by Antonio Hurtado de Mendoza brilliantly executed its main temptation-scene. This could take place only when Ulysses had sent the pilot back to the ship; the pilot's return challenges Circe's enchantments; Ulysses goes back to his task, while Circe is left cursing from the ruins of her burning palace.

A tu prójimo como a ti (1657?) transfers to the stage a traditional interpretation of the parable of the Good Samaritan. The traveller is Mankind, the thieves the three enemies of man (the World, the Flesh, and the Devil), the Levite Natural Law, the priest that of Moses, the Samaritan Jesus Christ. The priest and the Levite pass by fallen man on the other side of the road because they cannot redeem him; the

Samaritan can, and does, after Man, aided by his Desire (who earlier
had helped the robbers), has expressed his contrition and the wish to
amend his life. After the highway robbery there is a series of beautiful
parallels as night is lit by the morning star and then turns to day. The
Levite precedes the priest, the priest the Samaritan; Job's complaints
lead on to the singing of the *Magnificat*; St John the Baptist and the
Virgin Mary give place to the Samaritan; Melchisedek's bread is borne
by the Levite, manna by the priest—these foreshadow the final
Eucharistic discovery at the end of the play; at intervals a continuous
divine dawn-song mingles with the action. The enemies are routed.
Man, redeemed, is housed with St Peter.

Many other *autos* might be mentioned here. Among the mythological
allegories *El divino Orfeo* and *El verdadero dios Pan*; among the
historical, *La devoción de la Misa* and *La segunda esposa*; among the
purely doctrinal, *A Dios por razón de estado*. Although there are family
likenesses between many of them and occasionally self-repetition, their
merit remains consistently high, unless the reader demands a type of
drama Calderón never meant to write. In 1634 a Jesuit wrote of *El
nuevo palacio del Retiro*:

> He visto con admiración este auto . . . Está en la doctrina ajustado,
> por la disposición tan dulce de los versos, tan elegante en los con-
> ceptos, tan agudo en el asunto, tan peregrino y tan felizmente con-
> seguido en el intento . . . de donde me prometo grandes aplausos en los
> interesados que nunca me parecerá que llegue a ser los que merece.

In the eighteenth century Calderón's *autos* continued to be performed
until the genre was suppressed by government decree in 1765. Spaniards
appreciated their greatness.

The *loas* of Calderón, many of them for his *autos*, raise problems
of attribution and of distribution. Not all the existing *loas* that accompany *autos* were his work, and some of them were clearly intended for
other *autos* than those to which they have become attached. They are
as a rule—the genuine ones—elegant and appropriate, though they
seldom reach great heights of merit. Many problems of attribution and
so forth remain unsolved. Some of the *entremeses* attributed to
Calderón are also of uncertain authorship, but the best of the genuine
ones are unjustly neglected. The *Mojiganga de la muerte* (or more
properly *de las visiones*) is the best: actors dressed for an *auto* awake
a drunken man lying by the roadside; he is astounded to hear an angel
swear, to see the Devil cross himself, and to watch the soul enjoy a long

drink from the wineskin. *El pésame de la viuda* is a very funny burlesque of mourning extravagances and visits of condolence. *El dragoncillo* is a stylised retelling in verse of Cervantes's *La cueva de Salamanca*.

The non-dramatic works are also worth a little more than some critics realise. Some of his *aprobaciones* to other men's works are routine exercises, but that written to Cristóbal Lozano's *Soledades de la vida* (1658) is important for the comprehension of Calderón's own intentions as a writer. His *Deposición a favor de los profesores de la pintura* has, thanks to Curtius, had some recognition for its importance in the history of seventeenth-century art-theory. It contains some beautiful prose. Fine too is the prose of the letter to the Patriarch which we have already mentioned.

Many of Calderón's poems were academy pieces of little importance or occasional poems that merely fulfilled their immediate purpose: a compliment to a book by a friend or a possible patron, a competition-piece in honour of a saint, a conventional lament for a death. His longer efforts, though, sometimes transcend their mere occasion. The *romance* about the penance of St Ignatius at Manresa—with its semi-dramatic setting—was a competition submission, but it remains powerful and moving. The tercets on the death of the Infante Carlos (1632) incorporate a celebrated line from a sonnet by that prince and contain some profound lines. The Panegyric to the Admiral of Castile after the relief of Fuenterrabía (1638) has some dignity. Finest of all is his poem *Psalle et sile* on the inscription on the choir-screen at Toledo; based on the Ignatian scheme of meditation, the poem provides an apology for religious poetry and inculcates the duties of members of the priesthood. Two other poems deserve mention: an ascetic *romance* beginning 'Ahora, Señor, ahora . . .' which first appeared in the much-reprinted anthology entitled *Avisos para la muerte* (Madrid, 1635) and was later published in a greatly expanded version in the eighteenth century. The other is a set of *décimas* on death—an impressive work, but direct proof of Calderón's authorship is not yet available. Other poems ascribed to Calderón have proved to be other men's work: the *romance* that begins: 'Curiosísima señora . . .' is by Carlos Alberto de Cepeda y Guzmán; two others ('¿No me conocéis serranos?' and 'Salid ¡oh Clori divina!') are attributable to García de Porras according to Don Juan Manuel Blecua, who has, however, redressed the balance by printing the *Elegía a doña María Zapata* (1628), an authentic and meritorious poem certainly Calderón's.

NOTES

1. Narciso Alonso Cortés, 'Algunos datos relativos a don P.C.', *RFE*, I (1915), 41-51.

2. E. M. Wilson, 'Un memorial perdido de don Pedro Calderón'—to appear in the Festschrift in honour of Professor William L. Fichter.

3. E. M. Wilson, 'Calderón y el Patriarca', to appear in the Festschrift in honour of Professor Hans Flasche.

4. E. M. Wilson, 'Seven *aprobaciones* by D. P. C. de la B.', *Studia Philologica—Homenaje ofrecido a Dámaso Alonso*, III (Madrid, 1963), 605-18.

5. Heliodoro Rojas de la Vega, *Juicio crítico de las obras de C. de la B. bajo el punto de vista jurídico* (Valladolid, 1883); José María de Cossío, 'Racionalismo del arte dramático de Calderón', *Notas y estudios de crítica literaria—siglo XVII* (Madrid, 1939), pp. 73-109; W. J. Entwistle, 'Controversy in the dramas of Calderón', *RF*, LX (1947), 631-6; 'La controversia en los autos de Calderón', *NRFH*, II (1948), 223-38.

6. E. M. Wilson and J. Sage, *Poesías líricas en las obras dramáticas de Calderón*. . . . (London, 1964).

7. Shergold, *History*, pp. 288-9 note 6.

8. A. A. Parker, 'The father-son conflict in the drama of Calderón', *FMLS*, II (1966), 288-9.

9. E. H. Gombrich, *Art and Illusion* (London, 1962), pp. 223-5.

10. Wardropper, 'Calderón's comedy and his serious view of life', *Hispanic Studies in Honor of Nicholson B. Adams* (Chapel Hill, 1966), pp. 179-93; J. E. Varey, '*Casa con dos puertas*: Towards a definition of Calderón's view of comedy'—to appear shortly; some help may also be found in Menéndez y Pelayo, *Calderón y su teatro* (Madrid, 1881), Ch. VII; Ángel Valbuena Prat, *Calderón* (Madrid, 1941), Ch. X; and in Ángel Valbuena Briones's prefaces to the different comedies in the Aguilar edition.

11. From the *Prohemio* to the *Propalladia* of Bartolomé de Torres Naharro —a quotation from Badius.

12. Dámaso Alonso and Carlos Bousoño, *Seis calas en la expresión literaria española* (Madrid, 1951), pp. 152-9. The whole chapter, entitled 'La correlación en la estructura del teatro calderoniano', is a most useful contribution to Calderonian studies.

13. Shergold, 'The first performance of Calderón's *El mayor encanto Amor*', *BHS*, XXXV (1958), 24-7.

14. W. J. Entwistle, 'Calderón's *La devoción de la Cruz*', *BH*, L (1948), 472-82; Parker, *The Approach to the Spanish Drama*, 17-22; 'The father-son conflict . . .', 105-6.

15. The autograph was printed by A. Morel-Fatio (Heilbronn, 1877). A. A. Parker and Melveena McKendrick are at present engaged on an edition of both texts.

16. The best edition of this play is by C. A. Jones (Oxford, 1961). For its relation to its predecessor see A. E. Sloman, *The Dramatic Craftsmanship*, Ch. II. For the source play Morley and Bruerton, op. cit., pp. 311-12. For a remote source, E. M. Wilson, *Some aspects of Spanish literary history* (Oxford, 1967), Appendix B.

17. See the essays by Wilson, Sloman, Whitby, and Hesse in Wardropper, *Critical Essays on the Theatre of Calderón* (New York, 1965); Michele Federico Sciacca, 'Verdad y sueño en *LVES* de Calderón', *Clavileño*, 2 (1950), 1-9; P. N. Dunn, 'The horoscope motif in *LVES*', *Atlante*, I, 187-201; Wardropper, ' "Apenas llega cuando llega a penas" ', *MP*, LVII (1959-60), 225-32.

For a different interpretation see H. B. Hall, 'Segismundo and the rebel soldier', *BHS*, XLV (1968), 189-200; 'Poetic justice in *LVES*: a further comment', *BHS*, XLVI (1969), 128-31; and a reply by A. A. Parker, ibid., 120-7. R. Pring-Mill, 'Los calderonistas de habla inglesa y *LVES*: métodos del análisis temático-estructural,' *Litterae Hispanae et Lusitanae* (Munich, 1968), 369-413. For another kind of approach see Lionel Abel, *Metatheatre—A new View of Dramatic Form* ... (1963), pp. 59-72.

18. In addition to studies listed in the Bibliography see also E. M. Wilson, 'Hacia una interpretación de *EPDSD*', *Ábaco*, 3 (Madrid, 1970).

19. Eunice Joyner Gates, 'Calderón's interest in art', *PQ*, XL (1961), 53-67.

20. Gwynne Edwards has published an edition of these two plays. See also his articles: 'Calderón's *LHDA* in the light of his sources', *BHS*, XLIII (1966), 177-96; 'Calderón's *LHDA* and the classical type of tragedy', ibid., XLIV (1967), 161-94.

21. D. W. Cruickshank is preparing an edition of the autograph manuscript of this play. See also Menéndez y Pelayo, *Calderón y su teatro*, pp. 243-64; D. Alonso and C. Bousoño, op. cit., pp. 124-31.

22. E. M. Wilson is preparing a study of this play.

23. Gilbert Chase, *The Music of Spain* (New York and London, 1959), Ch. VI.

24. Ángel Valbuena Prat has frequently pointed out Calderón's debt to the mythographers Juan Pérez de Moya, *Filosofía secreta* (Madrid, 1585) and Fray Baltasar de Vitoria, *Teatro de los dioses de la gentilidad* (Salamanca, 1620).

25. The fundamental work on the *autos* is A. A. Parker, *The Allegorical Drama of Calderón* (Oxford, 1943). For other works, see Bibliography, pp. 155-61.

Chapter 7

THE SCHOOL OF CALDERÓN UP TO 1700

THE SECOND GREAT SCHOOL OF DRAMATISTS of the seventeenth century in Spain was that which drew its principal inspiration from the works of Calderón, who continued to be revered and imitated as the supreme model by Spanish dramatists until the eighteenth century was well advanced. As in the case of the school of Lope, it is necessary to make certain reservations about the extent to which the Calderonian school derived its techniques from the master. Calderón's art evolved alongside that of many dramatists whom we call his disciples, and doubtless he learned points of technique from some of them as well as from his predecessors and contemporaries who wrote in the manner of Lope de Vega. Yet Calderón's brilliance as a dramatic poet and a constructor of polished plots was so great and was so generally acclaimed by the populace and by the critics, that for dramatists who wished to have their plays performed and applauded in the *corrales* and in the court theatres there was little incentive to do anything but imitate his way of writing. When Calderón became so famous that in the later part of his career no *autos sacramentales* but his were performed for the annual celebrations of Corpus Christi in Madrid, because the populace would accept and approve of no others, *ingenios* had no alternative but to imitate his dramatic and poetic style, in their secular and religious dramas. The *poetas* of the period after Lope's death in 1635 did well to imitate the manner of Calderón, partly because it was effective and popular, partly because it disciplined them, and enabled them to write elegant and well-formed plays, which yet gave plenty of freedom for originality. In our approach to the drama of the Calderonian school, it would be a mistake to assume that, because a playwright's text, at first sight, reads 'just like Calderón', the writer is slavishly following Calderón's recipe. They imitated an admired master, but without servility. It is perhaps rather more difficult for us nowadays to distinguish between the stylistic idiosyncrasies of the various Calderonian playwrights than between those of the playwrights

of Lope's school. Nevertheless, when we study the Calderonians carefully, each *ingenio*'s personal characteristics stand out clearly. At a
glance, the dramatic output of the Calderonians might seem repetitive,
monotonous, and over-precise. In reality there is little monotony in
their plays; there is, instead, variety, marked originality (except in the
potboilers), and often considerable subtlety. These dramatists supplied
the great bulk of the repertoire of the Spanish *corrales*, ousting all but
the most magnificent of the plays of Lope and his school, from the
middle of the seventeenth century to the middle of the eighteenth.
The best of these plays are very good. Because of the modern prefer-
ence for the more obviously original and spontaneous drama of Lope's
school and the idea that a play which is a rewriting of an earlier one is
less worthy of study than the primitive play, remarkably few good
studies of the work of the Calderonians, apart from Moreto and Rojas
Zorrilla, have been published. One of the most important tasks which
Hispanists are at last beginning to take seriously is the revaluation of
the drama of the Calderonian school.

Various general features tend to distinguish the Calderonians from
the playwrights of the school of Lope. One such important feature is
the Calderonians' use of richly rhetorical *culterano* imagery and expres-
sive devices in their dramatic poetry, especially in descriptive and
emotional speeches. Góngora was the main source of this style;
Calderón and the most sensitive dramatists of his time carefully took
over, experimented with, and adapted certain of Góngora's and other
poets' techniques to form a sonorous, ornate, and balanced type of
dramatic poetry. At its worst, the imagery of the Calderonians'
dramatic verse can be pompous, hollow, and almost purposelessly
repetitive. At its best, it can express concisely and quickly to the
practised mind a series of often cleverly linked mental and emotional
experiences. Within this poetic system, even the very commonplace
image (e.g. 'cítara de pluma' = bird) may acquire a new and striking
value in the particular poetic and dramatic context in which it occurs.
In the best work of the Calderonians the verse is carefully integrated
into the dramatic and thematic whole of the play. Very skilfully
wrought chains of related images and ideas running throughout the
play are commoner in the work of the Calderonians than in the drama
of Lope's school. The best Calderonians produced complete thematic
as well as poetic unity in their plays.

In the drama of the Calderonians, all the individual elements of a
play tended in fact to be subordinated meticulously to, and determined
by, the total impact which the playwright intended his work to have

upon the audience. These writers' art of plot-construction was usually much more careful and polished than that of the spontaneous playwrights of the early seventeenth century. The causes of this tightening-up of dramatic structure are not hard to detect. The debates on free versus neo-classical dramatic theory at the beginning of the century must have induced practising dramatists to think seriously about the art of good playmaking. The publication of key treatises on dramatic art which emphasised the necessity of careful play-construction (for example, López Pinciano's *Philosophía antigua poética* [1596], Lope de Vega's *Arte nuevo* [1609], Francisco Cascales's *Tablas poéticas* [1617], and Jusepe Antonio González de Salas's *Nueva idea de la tragedia antigua* [1635]) must have had profound effects on the thinking of sensitive playwrights. Also, the two great classical works on playwriting were themselves available in Spanish translation: the first printed Castilian version of Horace's *Ars poetica* was published in Madrid as early as 1591, and a Spanish rendering of Aristotle's *Poetics* was printed there in 1626.[1] In addition, as the seventeenth century advanced, playwrights seem to have tended to write more frequently for the court stages than for the *corrales*. The court theatres came to be, by the middle of the century, the really vital centres of dramatic activity in Madrid; ambitious dramatists sought social and often political preferment by composing their best plays not for the populace but for the educated audiences of the Court. Plays performed at Court—if their scenery was not too complicated—were often shown later in the public theatres. This tendency did not apply in all cases; many *ingenios* wrote plays for the *corrales*. But the court drama became so important that the canons of the dramatic taste of highly critical courtiers tended to prevail, in later seventeenth-century playwriting, over popular taste and indeed to influence and change popular taste, because the good Madrid *ingenios* were writing primarily with an eye to court performances and also because some performances in the larger court theatres were open to the general public. The international culture of court circles was bound to encourage careful playmaking, and the taste for such playmaking was, in the circumstances, bound to become generalised in Madrid society. Bances Candamo saw this when he commented in 1689 or 1690 that 'El mismo gusto de la gente fue adelantando cada día la lima en la censura' in the course of the seventeenth century.[2] The change in popular dramatic taste and critical discernment was most powerfully determined by the pervasive influence of court taste in the capital.

Nowadays, after the vitality and the spontaneity of early seventeenth-century Spanish drama, the careful precision of the Calderonians' play-making may prove irritating. It may seem too finical, too carefully and too consciously contrived, too repetitive in its dramatic techniques and devices. Modern scorn for the 'well-made play' may prejudice us when we approach the Calderonian drama. As may the tendency of modern dramatists to write deliberately non-Aristotelian 'experimental drama'. Nevertheless, a careful and perceptive reading and imaginative re-creation of plays of the Calderonian school will make us see that very many of these plays are not only excellent drama but surprisingly subtle poems.

The Calderonians often rewrote earlier plays, sometimes their own but mostly plays by Lope and his school, to satisfy the new aesthetic canons of the theatre and to convey new moral and political ideas to their audiences. Several generations of modern dramatic critics tended to despise such *refundiciones*, which they believed to be plagiarisms. Their attitude displays lack of appreciation of what the seventeenth-century writer considered to be originality. He did not usually aim at writing something 'all out of his own head' but often preferred to remould given material in order to add to it a new purpose and intellectual point as well as a more satisfying form. Much good seventeenth-century writing, in all the genres of literature, consists in intelligent and sensitive glossing on traditional material and themes. The technique of lyrical or dramatic recasting is, in the seventeenth century, usually indeed to a certain degree ironical and in most cases intellectually stimulating. Such were the recasters' intentions, as far as we can judge them. The good literary *refundición* is not just a trite formal remoulding but a redirection of the readers', or listeners', thoughts and emotions. The Greek tragedians after Aeschylus did not scorn to remould earlier plays; neither did Seneca. We should certainly not despise the Calderonians for recasting earlier plays; rather should we examine their motives for doing so and the degree of success with which they did so. Not all the Calderonians' *refundiciones* were good ones. *El mejor representante, San Ginés*, by Cáncer, Rosete, and Antonio Martínez is very poor stuff in comparison with Lope's *Lo fingido verdadero*. Zamora's *No hay plazo que no se cumpla*...is much inferior to *El burlador de Sevilla*. Monteser's burlesque *El caballero de Olmedo* deserves to be read because it is a funny play, but, if we think of Lope's masterpiece when we read the recast version, we cannot help regretting that Monteser ever wrote it. Monroy's *Fuenteovejuna* is a good play, but it is not a patch on Lope's.[3] Calderón's *Los cabellos de Absalón* incorporates a *jornada* of *La venganza de Tamar* but does not match Tirso's tragedy. Nevertheless, if the Calderonian dramatists did not excel at re-creating earlier master-pieces, they often did excel at creating very good plays, and even masterpieces, out of weak early plays.

Another very important feature of the Calderonian school was its greater preoccupation with the classical principle of decorum in the drama than had been the case in the school of Lope. Seventeenth-century Spanish dramatists appear to have had a triple vision of society as they wrote their plays: the vision of the ideals of conduct and morality which each man and woman *ought to* fulfil in his or her social class or role (the vision of decorum, essentially Platonic in its origins); the vision of what each individual in each social class *usually does do, or can usually be expected to be* (the vision of verisimilitude, deriving theoretically from the *Ethics* of Aristotle, II, xii-xviii, and from Horace's *Ars poetica*, 158-78); and the vision of what, in history or in the present, a given individual *really was or is*. In seventeenth-century drama we see society looked upon through all of these visions, but as the century advanced a change of focus took place. Gradually the idealistic, decorous view came to predominate in the drama over the views of verisimilitude and of realism. This tendency is shown clearly, and rather absurdly exaggerated, in a passage of the theorist José Pellicer de Tovar Abarca's *Idea de la comedia de Castilla, deducida de las obras cómicas del doctor Juan Pérez de Montalbán* (1639):

> Hay sucesos en las historias y casos en la invención incapaces de la publicidad del teatro. Tales son las tiranías, sediciones de vasallos contra Príncipes, que no deben proponerse a los ojos de ningún siglo. Ni menos inventar ejemplos de poderosos libres que, fiados en la Majestad, se atreven absolutos a la violencia y a los insultos, violando su gravedad a vueltas de sus torpezas.[4]

Had Pellicer's advice been followed to the letter, much good Calder-onian drama would not have been written at all. But one can detect in his words his and several other generations' concern over the problem of the advisability or permissibility of 'showing bad examples' on the stage. The Church and the increasingly powerful censorship had undoubtedly a great effect in the development of the decorous drama. The principle of decorum in the theatre is most rigorously defined by Bances Candamo, in the last years of the century:

> Precepto es de la comedia inviolable que ninguno de los personajes tenga acción desairada, ni poco correspondiente a lo que significa.[5]

In other words, each dramatic character must fulfil, and must *never* betray, the ideal of the social role in which he or she is cast. If this definition had been strictly observed in every play of the mid- and late seventeenth century, no tragedies on the misdemeanours of nobles, kings, and emperors would have been composed, but such plays continued to be written. Ruth Lee Kennedy has stated that the typical protagonist in Moreto's plays is

> the courteous gentleman whose morals are as irreproachable as his manners, regardless of the role he may play. He is loyal to his friends, faithful to his monarch, unswerving in his devotion to his lady.[6]

So are most characters of noble status in the works of the Calderonians. These characters, in a fundamentally didactic drama, showed the spectator how he or she ought to act, not the contrary.

But if, in the typical play of the Calderonian school, all the main characters demonstrate moral integrity, the reader may wonder how dramatic tension was created and how the audiences' interest was maintained. The answer is that most of these dramas are puzzle-plays. They show the complexity of the moral dilemmas which in this world may face any man of integrity. They show noble characters confronted by conflicting loyalties and apparently mutually exclusive obligations. The tension and the interest of such plays lie, in the main, in the problem of their solution. These dramas were evidently intended not to move their audiences deeply but rather to make them think. In this way, most plays of the Calderonian school are more intellectual than emotional in their effect. Rather than involving the spectator in fear and pity, they aroused his admiration and made him exercise his wits. Problematic drama of this sort was not unknown or even uncommon in the work of Lope and his school, but it came to be predominant in the art of the Calderonians. A few play-titles may suffice to illustrate the basic attraction of this type of drama of dilemmas for seventeenth- and early eighteenth-century audiences: *Cumplir dos obligaciones* (Luis Vélez de Guevara); *¿Cuál es mayor perfección, hermosura o discreción?* (Calderón); *No hay ser padre siendo Rey* (Rojas Zorrilla); *¿Cuál enemigo es mayor, el destino o el amor?* (Cañizares); *¿Cuál es afecto mayor, lealtad, o sangre, o amor?* (Bances Candamo).

The greatest of Calderón's disciples was the one who perhaps wrote less Gongorine dramatic verse than any of the others, Agustín de Moreto y Cabaña (1618-69). A son of well-to-do Italian parents, he was born in Madrid, studied logic and physic at Alcalá, took minor orders, held a benefice in Toledo, and later moved back to Madrid, where he lived in the early and mid-1650s, probably as a courtier. The first volume of his plays was published there in 1654. He became a priest and in 1657 was chaplain to Cardinal Moscoso, who appointed him as head of a charitable fraternity in Toledo, where he resided, administering the hospital and caring for the city's poor, until his death.

Gracián called Moreto the 'Spanish Terence', and his best plays are indeed all comedies. He had no great lyrical gift, but he could write sharp, balanced, witty verse with facility and skill. The dialogue of the best of his comedies is sparkling and unaffected. But the quality of his plot-construction is exceptionally good. His plots 'normally fall into great blocks'[7] which are arranged in precise and orderly fashion and with striking economy in the amount of material and number of characters used in them. Each of the 'blocks' tends to end with a striking and important scene, and all the scenes lead logically to the climax of the play. Nothing is superfluous in these dramas; the various plots within each play are carefully interlinked and are thematically interdependent.

Moreto excelled at that elevated type of play which Bances Candamo called the *comedia de fábrica* and defined in the following words, to distinguish it from the humbler *comedia de capa y espada*:

Las [comedias] de fábrica son aquellas que llevan algún particular intento que probar con el suceso, y sus personajes son Reyes, Príncipes, Generales, Duques, etcétera, y personas preeminentes sin nombre determinado y conocido en las historias, cuyo artificio consiste en varios acasos de la fortuna, largas peregrinaciones, duelos de gran fama, altas conquistas, elevados amores y, en fin sucesos extraños, y más altos y peregrinos que aquéllos que suceden en los lances que, poco ha, llamé caseros ... El argumento de aquellas comedias que llamo de fábrica suele ser una competencia por una Princesa entre personas reales, con aquel majestuoso decoro que conviene a los personajes que se introducen, mayormente si son Reyes o Reinas, o damas de palacio, porque, aunque sea del palacio de la China, sólo por el nombre lleva el poeta gran cuidado en poner decorosa la alusión, venerando por imágenes aun las sombras de lo que se puede llamar real.[8]

The finest of all Spanish comedies of this type, which aim at a more refined amusement than the *comedias de capa y espada*, is Moreto's greatest masterpiece, *El desdén con el desdén*. This drama has all the dignity and majesty of the *comedia de fábrica* at its best, and also the smooth, almost ballet-like action on the stage which is a characteristic of good court drama of the Calderonian school. And it is a very funny play. Carlos, Count of Urgel, has been led by curiosity to come to the County of Barcelona to join in the jousts and tournaments which two other great nobles are holding in order to try to win the favour and the hand of Diana, daughter and heiress of the head of state. But Diana, convinced that the passion of love is destructive, is determined never to love or to marry, despite her father's entreaties. Carlos wins her by himself feigning disdain until, in pique at his indifference, Diana falls in love with him. Another good high comedy by Moreto, and apparently a source of *El desdén con el desdén*, is the very similar play *El poder de la amistad*, which also treats of the overcoming of a great lady's disdain.

Moreto's talent for humorous drama was, however, most frequently shown in the *comedia de capa y espada*. His other masterpiece, *El lindo don Diego*, can also be called a *comedia de figurón*, a type of comedy depending mainly, for its effects, on the presentation of an exaggeratedly ridiculous figure who is a personification of a particular vice or flaw of character. Moreto's Don Diego is the best such caricature in the drama of the Golden Age. The play is a brilliant recasting of Guillén de Castro's *El Narciso en su opinión*.[9] When Moreto's drama opens, the young Don Juan is consternated to hear that his older friend, Don Tello, intends to marry his two daughters, Leonor and Inés (whom Don Juan loves), to his two nephews, Don Mendo and Don Diego. Like Molière with his Tartuffe, Moreto carefully delays as long as possible the appearance of Don Diego on stage. The audience is kept in suspense, wondering what Don Diego and his brother will really be like. Don Tello's description of Don Diego in the first scene is ironical:

> Su gala y bizarría
> es cosa de admiración;
> de Burgos es el blasón.

When, after scenes in which Don Juan and Doña Leonor express their desperation and later their determination to prevent Leonor's marriage to Don Diego, this youth is described again, it is by the *gracioso* Mosquito, who bursts into the company of the sisters and Don Juan and tells them first of the gallant, courteous, and sensible Don Mendo and only then, in an amusing monologue, of the narcissistic foppishness of Don Diego, who rises at five in the morning to dress, does not finish this elaborate process till after 2 p.m., and is convinced that diligent attention to his toilette is an act of worship of God as efficacious as going to any of the Masses which he thus misses. At last, in the great visual climax of the first *jornada*, the ludicrously apparelled fop himself is seen, prancing between two mirrors and exasperating his brother with ravings about his imaginary power to make all women fall in love with him. His grotesque appearance and narcissistic obsessions—he even thinks that his looks induce not only women but men to fall in love with him—make Don Diego a magnificent comic character. But, unlike many *comedias de figurón, El lindo don Diego* does not depend for its humour solely on the ridiculousness of its central character. As well as being an excellent comedy of character it is a very good comedy of situation, and the story of how the lovers and their servants play on Don Diego's ambition and work his downfall with the bait of marriage to a false Countess is both amusing and skilfully contrived.

Moreto wrote other good *comedias de capa y espada. No puede ser* (sometimes given the long title of *No puede ser el guardar una mujer*) is, like Calderón's *La dama duende*, an attack on men who carry their obsession with family honour to extremes. Moreto's play sets out to demonstrate that, as one of its characters says,

> cuando la mujer quiere,
> si de su honor no hace aprecio,
> guardarla no puede ser,
> y es disparate emprenderlo.

The brother who locks his sister up to guard her from men is easily outwitted by the lady and her abettors.[10] *El parecido en la corte* is a fine comedy of intrigue skilfully reworked from Tirso's *El castigo del penseque*. Another well-made *comedia de capa y espada*, exceedingly complicated in plot, is *La confusión de un jardín*, drawn from a story by Castillo Solórzano (*La confusión de una noche*).

All the plays by Moreto which we have so far mentioned appear to be perfectly decorous, and the decorum of Moreto's drama as a whole is an aspect which has been emphasised by many modern critics. Nevertheless, it is possible that modern readers are blind to other features of his plays that may be less decorous. In a rapid account of the development of the seventeenth-century drama, Bances Candamo said that

> Don Agustín Moreto fue quien estragó la pureza del teatro, con poco reparadas graciosidades, dejándose arrastrar del vulgar aplauso del pueblo.[11]

It may be that the patent moral integrity of many of Moreto's main characters so dazzles us that, with our imperfect knowledge of seventeenth-century slang and innuendo, we fail to detect a certain scurrility in some of his *graciosos* and jokes. Bances's remarks may possibly express only a purist's finical distaste for writing which is more free than any that he would permit himself to indulge in, but the fact that he singles Moreto out from the Calderonians in order to condemn him on this score must put us on the alert.

Moreto's serious drama is overshadowed by his funny plays, but of the serious ones several are worthy of note. The best of his religious plays is *San Franco de Sena*, which treats the conversion and saintliness of a previously evil and blasphemous young man. Into it Moreto wove material clearly derived from Tirso's *El condenado por desconfiado*.[12] *El defensor de su agravio* and *Primero es la honra* are good examples of tragedy with a happy ending. *Antíoco y Seleuco* also falls into this category. The play treats of the conflicts of loyalty aroused by the love of Antiochus for his father's intended bride, and of Seleuco's heroic decision to let his son marry her; but this decorous drama is disappointing in comparison with Lope de Vega's magnificent *El castigo sin venganza*, to which it is indebted for the structure of its First Act and for the basis of many episodes. Perhaps the most interesting of all Moreto's serious plays is *El licenciado vidriera*, which is adapted in a subtle manner from Cervantes's short story. Both authors present a scholar who goes mad, but whereas Cervantes's Tomás Rodaja really becomes mad, Moreto's Carlos is forced to feign madness in order to overcome other people's ingratitude. As Casa has shown, 'Whereas Cervantes treated the impossibility of showing humanity its shortcomings, Moreto was forced to abandon much of his source material and to limit himself to a consideration of human ingratitude'.[13] The play is, in fact, an effective satire on ingratitude and its effects in society when persons of various social positions, from the head of state downwards, do not fulfil their obligation to give rewards when rewards are due. In this way, *El licenciado vidriera* is, like many other Golden Age plays, a satirical commentary on abuses of the honour-system. Thematically, it is closely related to earlier plays like *Fuenteovejuna* and *El mejor alcalde, el Rey*, as well as to Calderón's ironical honour-plays. *El licenciado vidriera* is, in fact, Moreto's most telling contribution to the main current of social drama in seventeenth-century Spain.

The second most important of the Calderonians was Francisco de Rojas Zorrilla (1607-48). Born in Toledo, the son of a naval officer, he was moved with his family in 1610 to Madrid, where his father became major-domo to a marquess. After his university studies, probably at

Salamanca, Rojas moved back to the capital and became a prolific court dramatist. In 1643 Philip IV nominated him for membership of the Order of Santiago, but Rojas's entry into the order was delayed, for when investigations were held to determine whether he was of pure Christian stock (customary procedure for all candidates for entry into the Military Orders) it was alleged that he had Moorish and Jewish ancestors. The investigations dragged on till late in 1645, when the Council of Orders issued its approval of his candidature and Rojas was at last able to wear the habit of Santiago. He wrote a great variety of plays, from the horrifically tragic to the lightly comic. Recent studies of his work have tended to be concentrated on his serious plays; not nearly enough attention has been given to his comedies, which are, in the main, better.

In serious drama, Rojas wrote two important plays. One of these, *Del Rey abajo ninguno*, otherwise known as *García del Castañar*, is one of the best honour-plays of the Golden Age. Apart from Calderón's *El alcalde de Zalamea*, it is the finest peasant-honour-play produced by the Calderonian school. It also puts forward a notable moral dilemma caused by the fact that, as the king is the primary source of his subjects' honour, he stands outside the normal range of men amongst whom honour-problems may be solved by revenge. The king has a double personality: he is the supreme *persona publica* in the state; and he is also *persona privata*, and, being capable of such acts as rape or seduction, may insult and dishonour private individuals. But he is the king and, if he offends a man's honour, that man cannot take revenge. In Rojas's play, the noble-hearted peasant, García del Castañar (who, in the end, turns out to be of noble stock), mistakes for the King a courtier, Don Mendo, who tries to seduce his wife, the chaste Blanca. García's anguish in his dilemma is eloquently and lyrically presented. So is Blanca's grief when she has to flee to escape being killed by her half-crazed husband. Finally, when García discovers that Mendo is not the King, he kills the courtier and justifies his action before his monarch, because

> No he de permitir me agravie,
> del Rey abajo, ninguno.

Politically, as well as dramatically, this is an excellent play. It might be described as a *culto Peribáñez*, which of all the peasant-plays it most closely resembles. Yet there is in *Del Rey abajo ninguno* much more marked *dramatismo* than in Lope's play, for amongst the seventeenth-century dramatists Rojas was the most given to melodrama.

Rojas's other most significant serious play, *Cada cual lo que le toca*, is more melodramatic; its ending, in which the heroine brandishes her bloody dagger, seems exaggeratedly violent. This sensitively conceived play concerns the problems which face a nobleman, Don Luis, and his wife, Isabel, after he discovers on their wedding night that she is not a virgin. According to Bances Candamo, this play was hissed by the public because it offended their sense of honour and decorum:

> A Don Francisco de Rojas le silbaron la comedia de *Cada cual lo que le toca*, por haberse atrevido a poner en ella un caballero que, casándose, halló violada de otro amor a su esposa.[14]

That this play should have shocked a people obsessed by a narrow and rigid conception of marital honour seems very probable. It is a sensitive thesis-drama which deals seriously with the pharisaism of societies and men who make a fetish of the virginity of brides. Presumably the audience was shocked because Don Luis did not kill his wife that very night and instead continued to live with her. Yet Rojas, who treated their relationship with a delicacy and a sympathetic understanding which are rarely shown in his other plays, expressed in *Cada cual lo que le toca* certain ideas about what really constitutes honour which transcend the social problems of the seventeenth century and are not unimportant in our own times. Doña Isabel herself kills her violator, who, ironically, was her husband's best friend. Don Luis forgives her for all that has happened. The spectacle is over, but the thoughts it raises for the prudent linger on.

None of Rojas's other serious plays is of as high quality as *Del Rey abajo ninguno* and *Cada cual*. He delighted in the macabre; as a dedicated neo-Senecan tragedian, he tended to pile horror upon horror, in violent vengeance dramas. In *Morir pensando matar*, a naïve example of this type of play, he makes King Alboino give his forced bride Rosimunda wine to drink in the skull of her father, whom he has vanquished. Naturally, she swears vengeance, and, with the help of a lover, secretly kills the king. But, in the end, both Rosimunda and her new husband die in horrible agony, having drunk the poison that was intended for one of their enemies. A better tragedy than this, although no masterpiece, is *Lucrecia y Tarquino*, on the rape of Lucretia.[15]

The genre in which Rojas Zorrilla is most frequently pleasing is comedy. His best *comedia de capa y espada* is *Entre bobos anda el juego*, a witty *comedia de figurón* which moves at a lively pace. The *figurón* is Don Lucas del Cigarral, rich, skinny, miserly, and a complete fool (he is magnificently described in the First Act by his servant, the *gracioso* Cabellera). Don Lucas is intended and intends to marry the impoverished Doña Isabel, but she falls in love with his cousin Don Pedro and, after a plot full of darkness scenes and mistaken identities (in the course of which Isabel is wooed by a third gallant), Don Lucas takes what he thinks is vengeance on Pedro and Isabel by 'condemning' them to marry in poverty. Other good *comedias de capa y espada* by Rojas are *Donde hay agravios no hay celos, y amo criado*, in which the roles of master and servant are amusingly reversed; *Lo que son mujeres*, which, because each sex learns what the other sex is like, ends, unusually, with the ladies and their gallants deciding *not* to get married; *Abre el ojo*; and *No hay amigo para amigo*. Effective comedies outside the narrow *capa y espada* range are *Don Diego de noche* and *Obligados y ofendidos y gorrón de Salamanca*.

The eldest of the playwrights of the Calderonian school was probably born before Calderón himself. This was Álvaro Cubillo de Aragón (1596?-1661), who at first wrote in the manner of Lope but later changed over completely to the Calderonian style. In 1654 he published ten plays and other miscellaneous works in a book entitled *El enano de las musas*, and other dramas of his were printed elsewhere. The most famous of his plays is a delicate *comedia de capa y espada*, *Las muñecas de Marcela*, in which the heroine, when she falls in love, is still so young that she holds dialogues with her dolls, which intervene almost as characters in the play. Another good *comedia* by Cubillo is *El señor de las noches buenas*, in which two brothers compete for the hand of the same lady; one of them, the first-born, is a fool, whereas his younger brother, in this veiled satire on the law of primogeniture, is the ideal gentleman. One of Cubillo's best serious plays is his *Tragedia del Duque de Berganza*, on a subject from Portuguese history, similar to that of Lope's *El Duque de Viseo*. Another good play is *Los desagravios de Cristo*, in which, as Glaser has shown, the capture of Jerusalem by Vespasian, Titus, and Domitian and the love-story of Titus and the Jewess Berenice are not really the principal matter of the play but are 'secondary plots, subordinated to the main theme outlined in the title: the Passion of Christ and the punishment of His murderers who, to the very last, show an irreconcilable hatred toward their divine victim'.[16] The main character in the drama, portrayed with great dignity, is Josephus, the famous Jewish general and historian, who, captured by the Romans, informs the ignorant Vespasian of the greatness and innocence of Christ, while himself remaining true to the tenets of the Jewish faith.

A notable Calderonian *ingenio* whose best plays remained very popular well into the eighteenth century was Antonio de Solís y Ribadeneyra (1610-86). Like most Golden Age dramatists, Solís regarded versifying and playwriting as a secondary, part-time activity.[17] He was secretary to the viceroy of Navarre and Valencia, then became one of the royal secretaries to Philip IV and Charles II, and was most famous in his own times as Royal Chronicler of the Indies, a position in which he composed his best-known book, the *Historia de la conquista de Méjico, y progresos de la América septentrional, conocida por el nombre de Nueva España* (Madrid, 1684). He appears to have written his first play, *Amor y obligación*, as early as 1627, and forty years later he took Holy Orders and ceased to write for the theatre.

Like most of the dramatists of his time, Solís wrote some *comedias* in collaboration with other *poetas*. He composed the first *jornada* of a *refundición* of Guarini's *Il pastor fido*, the Second Act of which was written by Antonio Coello and the third by Calderón; also, he wrote the Second Act of a burlesque version of Belmonte Bermúdez's *La renegada de Valladolid*, the First Act of which was by Francisco de Monteser and the third by Diego de Silva. He appears to have composed twelve *comedias* on his own. *Las amazonas* is an interesting heroic drama in which the warlike ladies are remarkably decorous. *Triunfos de amor y fortuna*, an elaborate machine-play on the legends of Endymion and Psyche, was performed at Court in 1658, with sensational scenic effects, to celebrate the birth of Philip IV's ill-fated son, Prince Felipe Prosper.[18] In another mythological play, *Eurídice y Orfeo*, not nearly so complicated in its staging, Solís enlivened an often-treated subject by working into the plot a jealousy-theme between Eurídice and another woman, in a manner that fits neatly into the pattern to which most of this dramatist's works conform. As Eduardo Juliá Martínez has pointed out, there is in almost all Solís's *comedias* a common situation-structure that is also a character-structure.[19] They normally have five main characters: two young men and two young ladies, who at the end are married off in appropriate pairs, plus, in most cases, a third gallant who is a relative of one of the ladies and complicates matters by being another suitor for her hand, although at the end it may be discovered that he is her brother and he withdraws from the lists. Gentleman A loves, and is loved by, lady B. His friend or rival, gentleman C, is also in love with lady B. Lady D is in love with gentleman A, and she and lady B are therefore jealous of each other. Gentleman E provides further complications.

All Solís's most celebrated plays, which are his best *comedias de capa y espada*, are written according to this formula. The liveliest of them, composed with the wit and with the lightness of touch which characterise Solís as a writer in this genre, is *El amor al uso*, a good little satire on the courtship of the moaning, sighing gallants of tradition, whom Solís sees as lacking in self-respect. Other smartly-paced and funny plays of this type are *Un bobo hace ciento*, *Amparar al enemigo*, and *Amor y obligación*. Solís's *El doctor Carlino* is a very funny *comedia de figurón* whose starting-point is Góngora's dramatic fragment of the same title. The *figurón* is a clever rogue who pretends to be a doctor in order to gain a profitable living as a go-between in amorous affairs:

> Alcahuete soy de fama,
> que con cauteloso ardid
> soplo la amorosa llama,
> y ando por ese Madrid
> saltando de rama en rama;
> y es tanta la industria mía
> que si aviso a mi cuidado
> y hablo a mi bellaquería,
> sabré meter un recado
> por el ojo de una tía;
> con ser médico allano
> cuantas casas hay, y gano
> nombre de atinado y bueno,
> sin que el libro de Galeno
> me haya tomado una mano.

This play is, of course, in the tradition of *La Celestina*; it is an ironical though not harsh satire on some of the activities that must have gone on behind the decorous façade of Madrid society. *La gitanilla de Madrid* elaborates amusingly some of the basic details of Cervantes's short story and, in fact, adapts *La gitanilla* to the Solís formula.

Another good Calderonian playwright was Juan de Matos Fragoso (1610?-92), an ingenious constructor of plots and a good Gongorine dramatic poet. The best of his serious plays is *El sabio en su retiro y villano en su rincón, Juan Labrador*, a *refundición* of Lope's famous play, and, surprisingly, not much inferior to Lope's original. Matos develops his plot with skill and originality, and the quality of some of the lyrical passages is high. Particularly moving are Juan Labrador's speeches in praise of the country life. Another play by Matos is particularly interesting in connection with the Golden Age view of theatrical decorum. Its sensational title, *El marido de su madre*, was obviously devised with an eye on the box-office. But the Spanish censors would never, in the mid-seventeenth century, have permitted an Oedipus-play to be performed in the *corrales* (and even in the middle of the eighteenth certain Spanish critics were protesting against what they saw as the immorality and indecorousness of Racine's *Phèdre*). The subject of *El marido de su madre*, however, is not incest. The play concerns St Gregory, Patriarch of Syria. As a young man he marries the woman who is revealed, later on, to be his mother, but when they marry she, for her own reasons, denies him his marital rights and they go on throughout their marriage sleeping in separate bedrooms. When they realise that they are mother and son, the marriage is dissolved. They, and indeed the whole play, are perfectly innocent and decorous in the strictest Spanish interpretation of the concept. Among other interesting plays by Matos Fragoso are the heroic *Lorenzo me llamo, y carbonero de Toledo* and the *comedia de capa y espada, El galán de su mujer*.

A lesser dramatist of this group was Antonio Coello y Ochoa (1611-52). Because of the relative simplicity of his poetic style, he has been said to be an imitator of Lope rather than of Calderón, but his techniques of dramatic construction are mainly Calderonian and he composed plays in collaboration with Calderón, Rojas Zorrilla, and Solís, as well as with *poetas* of the school of Lope. Coello is remembered mainly for one fascinating tragedy, *El Conde de Sex*, which tradition at various times has wrongly attributed to the pen of Philip IV. This is a play, published in 1638, on the supposed love of Queen Elizabeth I of England and her young favourite Robert Devereux, Earl of Essex, and on Essex's tragic death. As one might expect, Queen Elizabeth was hated by many Spaniards both in her own time and throughout the seventeenth century. Spanish writers often presented her not as the Virgin Queen but as a lustful Jezebel. But, following the laws of decorum in the drama, Coello certainly did not present her in his play as corrupt and lascivious. Bances Candamo commented on this drama in 1689 or 1690:

Ninguna Reina ha sido más torpe que Isabela de Inglaterra. Ni era hija legítima de sangre real, ni ha dejado sucesión real, porque los últimos Reyes de Inglaterra, de cuya tragedia acaba de ver la Europa una infeliz catástrofe, son de la Casa Estuarda de Escocia que, siendo la más antigua que tiene cetro en Europa, de poco tiempo a esta parte tuvo a María y Jacobo degollados, a Carlos Segundo peregrino, y a Jacobo Segundo forajido y despojado.

Siendo, pues, cierto que no hay sucesión de Isabela por quien callar, y que ella se humanó con el Duque de Virón, con el de Norfolk, a quien degolló por celos de María Stuard, con el Conde de Essex y con otros muchos, la comedia del *Conde de Essex* la pinta sólo con el afecto, pero tan retirado en la Magestad y tan oculto en la entereza que el Conde muere sin saber el amor de la Reina. Precepto es de la comedia inviolable que ninguno de los personajes tenga acción desairada, ni haga una ruindad ni cosa indecente. Pues ¿cómo se ha de poner una princesa indignamente? Y más cuando la poesía enmienda a la historia, porque ésta pinta los sucesos como son, pero aquélla los pone como debían ser.[20]

Bances had good reason to highlight *El Conde de Sex* when he talked of decorum in the drama and of the superiority of poetic to historical truth. Coello's play is, in its historical circumstances, the most extraordinary example of the use of these principles in the drama of the Golden Age. Queen Elizabeth is presented in *El Conde de Sex* as a model of queenly decorum. She forces herself not to tell the Earl of Essex that she loves him. Because she is a queen, she confides her passion only to the audience, in asides. She is very different from the Queen Elizabeth of Thomas Corneille's *Le Comte d'Essex*, who tells her love not just to a *confidante* (as the Elizabeth of La Calprenède's play of the same title does) but to various courtiers, making no attempt to disguise it. The Spanish Golden Age concept of dramatic decorum was much more strict than the concept observed in the seventeenth-century French theatre. Coello's Elizabeth, being a model queen, stifles her passion, will not permit the Earl to make a declaration of love to her, struggles against her jealousy of the lady whom he then courts, and in the last *jornada*, when he is accused of high treason and is condemned to death, twice tries to save his life. She has a dignity and a majesty which are as great as those of the English dramatist John Banks's Elizabeth in *The Unhappy Favourite or the Earl of Essex* (1681), and, of these two plays, Coello's is the better. In its presentation of clashes of passion against duty and of obligation against obligation, it is one of the best dilemma-dramas of its time, as well as being a good tragedy.[21]

As has been said, the real focal points of creative dramatic activity in the period of the Calderonians were no longer the public *corrales* but the court theatres in Madrid and in the royal palaces outside the capital. Despite Valbuena Prat's publication of the sketches for the scenery of Calderón's *La fiera, el rayo y la piedra*, and despite Pedrell's and Subirá's work on theatrical music of that period,[22] our ideas of the exact nature of the often elaborate performances on the court stages were imprecise and often vague until the publication of Shergold's *A History of the Spanish Stage* . . . , in which four chapters are dedicated to the detailed analysis of dramatic performances at Court up to 1700.[23] The most vivid impression of what an elaborate court performance was really like, however, can be derived from the edition by Varey, Shergold, and Sage of *Los celos hacen estrellas* by Juan Vélez de Guevara (1611-75), son of the more celebrated Luis Vélez.[24] The play is a *zarzuela*, a two-act drama in which spoken and sung passages are mingled. It was performed, with its introductory *loa*, its *entremés*, and *fin de fiesta*, on 22 December 1672, in the Salón Dorado of the old Alcázar of Madrid, to celebrate the birthday of the queen-mother, Mariana of Austria. It is a mediocre play: an amusing but undistinguished routine mythological drama concerning the jealousy of the goddess Juno over Jupiter's infatuation with Isis. The importance of this play does not, nevertheless, depend on its trite intrigue. It lies in the survival of five watercolours and a black-and-white drawing by Francisco Herrera el Mozo which illustrate (in a manner unique in the known history of the Golden Age drama) the stage sets in the Salón Dorado for the play's elaborate first performance, and two-thirds of Juan Hidalgo's musical score, which help to re-create the atmosphere and quality of the elaborate court drama, in which even a mediocre play could be given, in performance, a certain grandeur.

Juan Bautista Diamante (1625-87) wrote *comedias* and *zarzuelas* for the court theatres of Philip IV and Charles II. He also wrote many other dramas which were probably destined primarily for the *corrales*. Many of his *comedias* are recastings (often skilful) of plays by Lope and other early seventeenth-century dramatists. Diamante's most famous play is *El honrador de su padre* (played in 1657), a recasting of Guillén de Castro's *Las mocedades del Cid, Primera parte*, and perhaps also of Corneille's *Le Cid*. Its Third Act is excellent and apparently completely original, having no precedent either in Castro or in Corneille. Another good play by Diamante, much better than certain critics have thought it to be, is *La reina María Estuarda*, on the arrival of Mary Queen of Scots in England, Queen Elizabeth's growing desire to take vengeance on her because of jealousy, and Mary's tragic death. Diamante also rewrote Mira de Amescua's *La judía de Toledo*, in a version so close to the original that it has been described as 'nothing more than a servile plagiarism'.[25] Nevertheless, the play does have power to move us, especially at the end, when we realise that the King has not learned his lesson and is determined to create a blood-bath in Spain to avenge his assassinated mistress. An amusing, and lighter, play by Diamante is *Cuánto mienten los indicios, y ganapán de desdichas*. Amongst his religious dramas, *La Magdalena de Roma* is interesting, as a tale of the conversion of a young courtesan, her subsequent temptation by the Devil in the guise of her favourite lover, who had been killed, and her resistance against the tempter with the aid of divine forces.

Several other seventeenth-century dramatists of the Calderonian school are worthy of mention and of study: Juan de la Hoz y Mota (1622-1714), Francisco de Leiva Ramírez de Arellano (1630?-76?), Antonio Enríquez Gómez (1600-63), 'Fernando de Zárate' (proved by Révah to be a pseudonym of Antonio Enríquez Gómez),[26] Agustín de Salazar y Torres (1642-75), and (as well as the two most celebrated of his prose-works, *Día de fiesta por la mañana* and *Día de fiesta por la tarde*) Juan de Zabaleta (1610?-70?). The old belief that very little literature or drama worth reading was produced in Spain in the second half of the seventeenth century needs re-examination. Because she was the last major poet of the seventeenth century, and also because, as a Mexican who wrote in Mexico, she has attracted the attention of dramatic critics amongst her modern compatriots, the dramatic works of the remarkably talented nun Sor Juana Inés de la Cruz (1648/51-95) have been rescued from the general neglect.[27] Many of her *loas* are delicately contrived and delightful, her *autos sacramentales* (*El divino Narciso; El mártir del Sacramento, San Hermenegildo; El cetro de José*) are by no means despicable, and her *comedia de capa y espada* entitled *Los empeños de una casa* is skilfully written, tense, and amusing.

Some idea of the sound dramatic craftsmanship and the subtlety which can be found in the work of the best of the late seventeenth-century Calderonians can be got from the work of the last important dramatist of the century, Bances Candamo.

Francisco Antonio de Bances y López-Candamo (1662-1704) was an Asturian who, taken as a child to Seville, studied philosophy, law, and canon law at the university there, becoming a Doctor of Canon Law. He was already a poet when he left Seville for Madrid, in search of preferment at Court and better opportunities for his talents than the south could provide.[28] The first recorded performance of one of his plays is of *Por su Rey y por su dama*, a *comedia* which was acted in the Buen Retiro in 1685 to celebrate the birthday of the Holy Roman Emperor. Apparently in 1687, and apparently as a result of the success of his court plays, Bances was granted a distinction which seems to be unique in the history of the seventeenth-century drama: he was appointed official playwright to the king, Charles II, and in this capacity was enjoined to write no plays that were not for the king's festivities. Bances's career as dramatist to Charles II was short. He resigned from his post in 1693 or 1694, probably because of the increasingly audacious attempt at the political indoctrination of the king through his plays. He served for a time as a treasury official in the south, returned briefly to Madrid and made a 'comeback' as a dramatist both in the *corrales* and at Court in 1696 and 1697, then, perhaps because of the obviousness of his attempt to influence the king in his last play, *¿Cuál es afecto mayor, lealtad, o sangre, o amor?*, went back to his life in the provinces as an official of the treasury. His last post was that of Superintendent of the Royal Revenues in San Clemente. While conducting an investigation in the town of Lezuza in 1704, he was suddenly taken ill, perhaps poisoned, and died there.

Bances's most important literary work was his *Teatro de los teatros de los pasados y presentes siglos*.[29] As an exposition of seventeenth-century dramatic theory, the *Teatro de los teatros* is second in importance only to Lope de Vega's *Arte nuevo*, for Bances was the only playwright of the Calderonian school who attempted to write an *Ars dramatica*, and in his treatise he carefully and eloquently expressed the basic principles of the school's dramatic practice and taste. The treatise consists of three incomplete versions. The first of these, written between 1689 and 1690, is a hastily but cleverly composed defence of the Spanish drama of Bances's own times against the attacks directed against the theatre by a Jesuit, Ignacio de Camargo. In this defence the playwright gives a telling account of the development of Spanish drama in the course of the seventeenth century in terms which show his distaste for the artistic crudity and lack of decorum which he observes in early seventeenth-century *comedias*. He gives a clear account of the principles of decorum and of the superiority of poetic to historical or particular truth. He also gives a valuable categorisation of the different types of *comedia*. His fundamental division of *comedias* is between the historical (including *comedias de santo*) and the purely fictitious *comedias amatorias*, which he subdivides into *comedias de fábrica* and *comedias de capa y espada*. His critical remarks on plays by a wide variety of authors are penetrating and shrewd. This fragment of the treatise, along with Father Guerra's *Aprobación* to Calderón's *comedias*, contains the best Spanish dramatic criticism written in the seventeenth century. The second and third versions of

Bances's treatise were written between 1692 and 1694. They represent two stages of an attempt to write a universal history of the drama, from Ancient Greece to Bances's times, and, simultaneously, an exposition of sound dramatic principles, derived from classical and modern theory and from 'el uso y costumbre de nuestros poetas', intended to teach ignorant poets how to write good plays. The second version is chiefly remarkable for Bances's surprisingly frank revelation of the political aims with which he believes the king's plays should be written. The third version contains an eloquent statement of the divine origins and the dignity of poetry and also includes a long account of various types of dramatic performances in classical antiquity.

The *Teatro de los teatros* is an invaluable aid to the understanding of the drama of the Calderonian school as a whole. It also provides an essential key to the most fascinating aspect of Bances's own court drama. He wrote no *comedias de capa y espada*, his *autos sacramentales* are competently written but not outstanding, and what he excelled at was the creation of plays for the king which were not only good Calderonian drama but also didactic rhetoric, sometimes of a very subtle nature. Bances took his post as official dramatist to Charles II very seriously. In the second version of the *Teatro de los teatros* he describes playwriting for kings as a *decir sin decir*, an art of decorously conveying ideas to the monarch without saying them to him openly:

> Son las comedias de los Reyes unas historias vivas que, sin hablar con ellos, les han de instruir con tal respeto que sea su misma razón quien de lo que ve tome las advertencias, y no el ingenio quien se las diga. Para este decir sin decir, ¿quién dudará sea menester gran arte?[30]

The dramatist shows the king stories in action, and these stories must make the king work out for himself their significance for his own activities. And Bances says that he himself has studied everything that can turn the art of entertaining the king into 'arte áulica y política'.[31] We are therefore led to expect that Bances's dramatic art will be fundamentally an art of political persuasion. And, in fact, a careful study of Bances's plays in the context of the events at Court and Charles II's main political problems at the time they were written and performed brings out very clearly their cunning political intentions.[32]

The play by Bances which remained most popular on the public stages throughout the eighteenth century and into the nineteenth, was *Por su Rey y por su dama*. Two versions of this play have been preserved, a primitive one, only in manuscript, and the definitive one, which was repeatedly printed up to the nineteenth century and which was first performed before the king, the queen, and the Court on 15 November 1685. It is an exciting dilemma-play, an adventure-story well dramatised. Its basic subject-matter is historical, the story of the ingenious stratagem by means of which Hernán Tello Portocarrero deceived the French army who were defending the city of Amiens against the Spaniards in 1597. The main political purpose of the play is revealed in a long speech by Portocarrero in the first *jornada*, in which (slightly anachronistically) he praises Spain's handing-over the Netherlands in May 1598 to the sovereignty of the Archduke Albert of Austria and his bride-to-be, Philip II's daughter Isabel Clara Eugenia. In February 1685 Louis XIV of France was gravely worried lest Spain repeat the experiment and hand over the Low Countries to the elector of Bavaria, Max-Emmanuel, and his future wife, Maria-Antonia, daughter of the Emperor Leopold I. Louis sent an ambassador to Charles II to warn him that such a separation of the Netherlands from Spain would be a violation of the Truce of Ratisbon (1684) and would lead to war. In *Por su Rey y por su dama*, Bances seems to urge Charles II to go on with the project of giving up the Low Countries, come what might.[33]

The most fascinating of all Bances's political plays, however, are the trilogy of dramas which he had performed before Charles II between October-November 1692 and January 1693. The first of these, the *comedia* entitled *El esclavo en grillos de oro*, has been, in literary tradition, the most famous of all Bances's plays, and there may be truth in the traditional idea that it was because of the satirical content of this play that Bances received a severe wound in the chest, as a result of which Charles II had the Calle de Alcalá closed to horse-drawn traffic so that his dramatist could convalesce in peace. The plot of *El esclavo en grillos de oro* resembles that of Shakespeare's *Measure for Measure*. It concerns a conspiracy by the Roman senator Ovinius Camillus to have the Emperor Trajan killed and himself put in his place. When he learns of the conspiracy, Trajan condemns the senator not to death but to undertake the government of the Empire. The young man gradually learns that kingship is a form of slavery in golden fetters. At last Ovinius Camillus, at the very moment when the Senate is due to swear allegiance to him, begs to be killed rather than to be made emperor. Trajan pardons him and resumes command of the Empire, appointing as his official heir his own young relative, Hadrian. This play caused a great sensation in Madrid in 1692 because of its political implications, for *El esclavo en grillos de oro* can be shown to be a satire on the

government of the conde de Oropesa (1685-91) intended as a warning
to the king not to restore his fallen favourite to power, a satire on
Charles's own misgovernment since Oropesa's fall, and also a tactful
attempt to persuade the neurotic, impotent, and dull king to nominate
an heir to the Spanish throne.[34]

In the *zarzuela* entitled *Cómo se curan los celos y Orlando furioso*,
a dramatic version of part of Ariosto's poem which was performed at
Court in December 1692, Bances appears to have returned to the theme
of the Spanish Succession. In this play he seems to be mocking at the
disappointment of Louis XIV and of the French pretender Philip of
Anjou (who, eight years later, was in fact to become king of Spain) at
the probability that the infant son of the elector of Bavaria would be
designated Charles II's heir. In *Cómo se curan los celos* the question of
the Spanish Succession is prudently left not over-obvious. But in
January 1693, with *La piedra filosofal*, Bances seems to have become
recklessly bold. In this *comedia* he presents a version of a legend from
Spanish pseudo-history in which Hispán, King of Spain, having no
son to succeed him, proposes to marry his daughter Iberia (who clearly
represents Spain) to a suitable prince, and in which three Princes
(clearly representing Philip of Anjou, the Archduke Charles of Austria,
and the baby son of the elector of Bavaria) compete for her hand![35]
Bances probably overreached himself and this was probably the cause
of his departure from Court to the provinces.

Bances wrote his plays carefully, and most of them are good drama.
In the eighteenth century he was justly praised by that demanding critic
Luzán, 'por su ingenio, su elegante estilo, sus noticias no vulgares y
por el cuidado grande que manifestó en la verisimilitud, decoro y
propiedad de los lances y de las personas'.[36] Careful study of his works
shows techniques of allusion and persuasion which can illuminate the
study of the popular and court drama of the seventeenth century as a
whole (for there is reason to suggest political intent in the dramas
long before Bances's time). It also shows that, with Calderón writing for
the stage up to 1681 and Bances writing in the 1680s and 1690s, there
was no period of total decadence in the seventeenth-century Spanish
theatre, though it is true that fewer new plays seem to have been written
in the second half of the century than in the exuberant first half. On
the whole, the plays of the school of Lope please nowadays more than
those of the school of Calderón, but the work of the Calderonian
epigoni can also give pleasure and evoke admiration of good craftsmanship.

NOTES

1. See Duncan Moir, 'The Classical Tradition...', 195, 200 and notes.
2. op. cit., p. 30.
3. Francisco López Estrada, in *'Fuente Ovejuna' en el teatro de Lope y de Monroy* (Seville, 1965) and in his edition of both plays, *Fuenteovejuna (Dos comedias)*, CCa 10 (Madrid, 1969), argues that Monroy's style belongs to the later period of Lope rather than to the Calderonian type and that Monroy's play is not a *refundición* of Lope's. Both arguments are debatable.
4. Published in *Lágrimas panegíricas a la temprana muerte del gran poeta y teólogo insigne Juan Pérez de Montalbán*, ed. Pedro Grande de Tena (Madrid, 1639), 146r-52v. This version of the *Idea de la comedia* is significantly different from that of the manuscript of 1635 which has been published in *Preceptiva*, pp. 217-27.
5. op. cit., p. 35. For a substantial account of the development of the idea of decorum in Spanish dramatic theory and practice, see the prologue to Moir's edition, pp. lxxiv-lxxxviii. See also Moir, 'The Classical Tradition...', 208-17.
6. *The Dramatic Art of Moreto* (Northampton, Mass., 1931-32) [*Smith College Studies in Modern Languages*, XIII, Nos. 1-4], p. 77.
7. op. cit., p. 44.
8. op. cit., pp. 33-5. The point about the characters not being known historical characters is important. According to traditional Renaissance dramatic theory, historical characters are fitting only for serious plays, tragedies, or tragedies with happy endings; one should not be led to laugh at known historical characters in the drama; therefore the characters who amuse us in the *comedia de fábrica* must not be identifiable as kings, queens, princesses, or great nobles who really did exist. Not all *comedias de fábrica* are funny; many are simply adventure-plays.
9. For the process of the *refundición*, see Frank P. Casa, *The Dramatic Craftsmanship of Moreto* (Cambridge, Mass., 1966), pp. 117-44.
10. On English adaptations of this play see Patricia Mary Seward, *The Influence of the Spanish Drama of the Seventeenth Century on the Restoration Theatre in England, 1660-1700* (unpublished M.Phil. thesis, University of Southampton, 1969), pp. 119-42, 241-68.
11. op. cit., p. 30.
12. See Casa, op. cit., pp. 7-29.
13. ibid., pp. 36-7.
14. op. cit., p. 35.
15. See E. M. Wilson's review of Raymond R. MacCurdy's edition of the play (Albuquerque, 1963) in *Sym*, XVIII (Summer 1964), No. 2, 180-4.
16. Glaser, 'A. C. de A.'s *Los desagravios de Cristo*', *HR*, XXIV (1956), 306-21; for the quotation, 307. See Cotarelo y Mori, 'Dramaticos españoles del siglo XVII: A. C. de A.', *BRAE*, V (1918), 3-23, 241-80.
17. For his poetry, see A. de S., *Varias poesías sagradas y profanas*, ed. Manuela Sánchez Regueira (Madrid, 1968).
18. See Shergold, *History*, pp. 320-4.
19. See A. de S. y R., *Amor y obligación*, ed. Juliá Martínez (Madrid, 1930), pp. xxxvii-xl.
20. op. cit., p. 35. The 'infeliz catástrofe' was the Glorious Revolution of 1689 and the exile of James II. In speaking of the executions, Bances confuses James I with Charles I.
21. On *El Conde de Sex*, see Bances Candamo, op. cit., pp. lxxxvi-lxxxviii

and notes. On Coello's life and works see Cotarelo y Mori, 'Dramáticos españoles del siglo XVII: Don A. C. y O.', *BRAE*, V (1918), 550-600.

22. Ángel Valbuena Prat, 'La escenógrafia de una comedia de Calderón', *Archivo Español de Arte y Arqueología*, No. 16 (1930), 1-16 (some of the drawings are also reproduced in Valbuena's *Literatura dramática* and in Shergold, *History*); Felipe Pedrell, *Teatro lírico español anterior al siglo XIX*, 5 vols. (Corunna, 1897-98); José Subirá's edition of *Celos aun del aire matan. Opera del siglo XVII. Texto de Calderón y música de Juan Hidalgo* (Barcelona, 1933) and his *Historia de la música teatral en España* (Barcelona, 1945).

23. Shergold, *History*, pp. 236-59.

24. The edition (London, 1970) contains a study of the life and works of Juan Vélez.

25. James A. Castañeda in his edition of Lope de Vega's *Las paces de los Reyes y judía de Toledo* (Chapel Hill, 1962), p. 65. On Diamante, see Cotarelo y Mori, 'Don J. B. D. y sus comedias', *BRAE*, III (1916), 272-97, 454-97.

26. I. S. Révah, 'Un pamphlet contre l'Inquisition de A. E. G.', *Revue des Etudes Juives*, 4e Série, I (CXXI) [1962], 81-168.

27. For her poetry, see Jones, op. cit., p. 158.

28. For his poetry, see his *Obras lyricas*, ed. Fernando Gutiérrez (Barcelona, 1949); Juan Manuel Rozas, 'La licitud del teatro y otras cuestiones literarias en B.C., escritor límite', *Seg*, I (1965), núm. 2, 247-73; D. Moir, 'B. C.'s Garcilaso: an Introduction to *El César africano*', to be published in *BHS*.

29. See Moir's edition, which contains an account of Bances's life and career as a dramatist.

30. op. cit., p. 57.

31. ibid., p. 56.

32. D. Moir has in preparation a comprehensive study of Bances's work.

33. D. Moir is preparing an edition of Bances's *Por su Rey y por su dama* and *La piedra filosofal* for CC.

34. For the *decir sin decir* of *El esclavo en grillos de oro*, see the forthcoming edition of this play by D. Moir.

35. See above, note 33.

36. Ignacio de Luzán, *La poética o reglas de la poesía*, ed. Luigi de Filippo (Barcelona, 1956), II, 125. The statement is in both the Saragossa edition and in the posthumous edition of Madrid, 1789.

BIBLIOGRAPHY

Works of Wide Range

(1) *Bibliographical*

Cayetano Alberto de La Barrera y Leirado, *Catálogo bibliográfico y biográfico del teatro antiguo español desde sus orígenes hasta mediados del siglo XVIII* (Madrid, 1860; and reprints of London, 1968, and Madrid, 1969)

Raymond L. Grismer, *Bibliography of the Drama of Spain and Spanish America*, 2 vols. (Minneapolis, n.d.)

Warren T. McCready, *Bibliografía temática de estudios sobre el teatro español antiguo* (Toronto, 1966) [includes studies published between 1850 and 1950]

Bulletin of the Comediantes has, since 1951, included bibliographical notes in each of its numbers. *PMLA* issues an annual bibliography. *The Year's Work in Modern Language Studies* includes each year an indispensable critical bibliography.

José Simón Díaz, *Manual de bibliografía de la literatura española*, 2nd ed. (Barcelona, 1966)

Emilio Cotarelo y Mori, *Bibliografía de las controversias sobre la licitud del teatro en España* (Madrid, 1904) [includes many extracts and complete documents from the disputes]

(2) *General*

N. D. Shergold, *A History of the Spanish Stage from Medieval Times until the End of the Seventeenth Century* (Oxford, 1967)

Hugo Albert Rennert, *The Spanish Stage in the Time of Lope de Vega* (New York, 1909; 2nd ed., 1963)

W. H. Shoemaker, *The Multiple Stage in Spain during the Fifteenth and Sixteenth Centuries* (Princeton, 1935; and, in Spanish translation, in *Estudios escénicos*, núm. 2 [1957], 1-154)

Ángel Valbuena Prat, *Literatura dramática española* (Barcelona, 1930; reprint 1950)

——, *Historia del teatro español* (Barcelona, 1956)

Margaret Wilson, *Spanish Drama of the Golden Age* (Oxford and London, etc., 1969)

J. P. Wickersham Crawford, *Spanish Drama before Lope de Vega* (Philadelphia, 1922; 2nd revised ed. 1937; 3rd revised ed., with Bibliographical Supplement by Warren T. McCready, 1967)

Henri Mérimée, *L'Art dramatique à Valencia* (Toulouse, 1913)

Alfredo Hermenegildo, *Los trágicos españoles del siglo XVI* (Madrid, 1961)

Othón Arróniz, *La influencia italiana en el nacimiento de la comedia española* (Madrid, 1969)

Raymond L. Grismer, *The Influence of Plautus in Spain before Lope de Vega* (New York, 1944)

Dramatic Theory in Spain, ed. H. J. Chaytor (Cambridge, 1925)

Federico Sánchez Escribano and Alberto Porqueras Mayo, *Preceptiva dramática española del renacimiento y el barroco* (Madrid, 1965)

Marcelino Menéndez Pelayo, *Historia de las ideas estéticas en España*, II *(Siglos XVI y XVII)*, Ed. Nacional (Santander, 1947)

Margarete Newels, *Die dramatischen Gattungen in den Poetiken des Siglo de Oro* (Wiesbaden, 1959)

Duncan Moir, 'The Classical Tradition in Spanish Dramatic Theory and Practice in the Seventeenth Century', in *Classical Drama and its Influence*, ed. M. J. Anderson (London, 1965), pp. 191-228

A. A. Parker, *The Approach to the Spanish Drama of the Golden Age*, Diamante VI (London, 1957)

Everett W. Hesse, *Análisis e interpretación de la comedia* (Madrid, 1968)

Noël Salomon, *Recherches sur le thème paysan dans la 'comedia' au temps de Lope de Vega* (Bordeaux, 1965)

Jean-Louis Flecniakoska, *La formation de l' 'auto' religieux en Espagne avant Calderón (1550-1635)* (Paris, 1961)

Bruce W. Wardropper, *Introducción al teatro religioso del siglo de oro*, revised ed. (Salamanca, 1967)

N. D. Shergold and J. E. Varey, *Los autos sacramentales en Madrid en la época de Calderón 1637-1681. Estudios y documentos* (Madrid, 1961)

Colección de entremeses, loas, bailes, jácaras y mojigangas desde fines del siglo XVI, ordenada por Emilio Cotarelo y Mori, 2 vols., NBAE, XVII and XVIII (1911)

Eugenio Asensio, *Itinerario del entremés desde Lope de Rueda a Quiñones de Benavente* (Madrid, 1965)
Ramillete de entremeses y bailes (siglo XVII), ed. Hannah E. Bergman, C Ca, 21 (Madrid, 1970)

Chapter 1

Humberto López Morales, *Tradición y creación en los orígenes del teatro castellano* (Madrid, 1968)
J. Richard Andrews, *Juan del Encina. Prometheus in Search of Prestige* (Berkeley and Los Angeles, 1959)
Juan del Encina, *Églogas completas*, ed. H. López Morales (Madrid, 1968)
——, *Teatro completo*, ed. M. Cañete and F. A. Barbieri (Madrid, 1893; reprint New York, 1969)
——, *El auto del repelón*, ed. Alfredo Álvarez de la Villa (Paris, n.d.)

Lucas Fernández, *Farsas y églogas*, ed. M. Cañete (Madrid, 1867)
——, *Farsas y églogas*, ed. J. Lihani (New York, 1969)

Paul Teyssier, *La langue de Gil Vicente* (Paris, 1959)
Laurence Keates, *The Court Theatre of Gil Vicente* (Lisbon, 1962)
Leif Sletsjöe, *O elemento cénico em Gil Vicente* (Lisbon, 1965)
António José Saraiva, *Gil Vicente e o fim do teatro medieval*, Publicações Europa-América, 2nd ed. (n.p., n.d.)
Gil Vicente, *Obras completas*, ed. Prof. Marques Braga, 6 vols. (Lisbon, 1955-58)
——, *Obras dramáticas castellanas*, ed. T. R. Hart, CC 156 (Madrid, 1962)
——, *Tragicomedia de Don Duardos*, ed. Dámaso Alonso, I, Texto, estudios y notas (Madrid, 1942) [no more volumes were published]
——, *Tragicomedia de Amadís de Gaula*, ed. T. P. Waldron (Manchester, 1959)

Bartolomé de Torres Naharro, *Propalladia and Other Works*, ed. J. E. Gillet, 4 vols. (Bryn Mawr-Philadelphia, 1943-61) [Vol. 4: *Torres Naharro and the Drama of the Renaissance*, transcribed, ed., and completed by Otis H. Green]

Fernán López de Yanguas, *Obras dramáticas*, ed. Fernando González Ollé, CC 162 (Madrid, 1967)

Diego Sánchez de Badajoz, *Recopilación en metro*, ed. Frida Weber de Kurlat (Buenos Aires, 1968)

Teatro español del siglo XVI, Vol. I [all published], ed. Urban Cronan (Madrid, 1913)

Autos, comedias farsas de la Biblioteca Nacional [Nota preliminar de Justo García Morales], 2 vols. (Madrid, 1962-64)

(For editions of anonymous plays and plays by minor dramatists, see the bibliographical sections of J. P. Wickersham Crawford, *Spanish Drama before Lope* ...)

Chapter 2

Colección de autos, farsas y coloquios del siglo XVI, ed. Léo Rouanet, 4 vols. (Macon, 1901)

Lope de Rueda, *Obras*, ed. E. Cotarelo y Mori, 2 vols. (Madrid, 1908)
——, *Teatro*, ed. J. Moreno Villa, CC 59 (Madrid, 1924)
——, *Teatro completo*, ed. A. Cardona de Gibert and D. Garrido Pallardó (Barcelona, etc., 1967)

Juan de Timoneda, *Obras completas*, Vol. I [no more published], ed. M. Menéndez y Pelayo (Valencia, 1911)
——, *Las tres comedias* (Valencia, 1559) (facsimile ed., Madrid, 1936)

Fray Ignacio de Buendía, *Triunfo de llaneza*, ed. E. M. Wilson, Aula Magna 21 (Madrid, 1970)

Hernán Pérez de Oliva, *Teatro*, ed. William Atkinson, *RH*, LXIX (1927), 521-659

Jerónimo Bermúdez, *Nise lastimosa* and *Nise laureada*, in *Tesoro del teatro español*, I, ed. Eugenio de Ochoa (Paris, 1838)

Cecilia Vennard Sargent, *A Study of the Dramatic Works of Cristóbal de Virués* (New York, 1930)

Cristóbal de Virués, plays in *Poetas dramáticos valencianos*, ed. E. Juliá Martínez, I (Madrid, 1929), 25-178

Otis H. Green, *The Life and Works of Lupercio Leonardo de Argensola* (Philadelphia, 1927)
——, *Vida y obras de L. L. de A.* (Saragossa, 1945)

Lupercio Leonardo de Argensola, *Isabela* and *Alejandra* in his *Obras sueltas*, ed. Conde de la Viñaza, I (Madrid, 1889)

A. I. Watson, *Juan de la Cueva and the Portuguese Succession* (London, 1971)
Juan de la Cueva, *Comedias y tragedias*, ed. F. A. de Icaza, 2 vols. (Madrid, 1917)
——, *El infamador, Los siete infantes de Lara y El ejemplar poético*, ed. F. A. de Icaza, CC 60 (Madrid, 1941)

Armando Cotarelo y Valledor, *El teatro de Cervantes* (Madrid, 1915)
Rudolph Schevill and A. Bonilla, *El teatro de Cervantes* (*introducción*), in their edition of his plays, VI (Madrid, 1922), [5]-[187]
Joaquín Casalduero, *Sentido y forma del teatro de Cervantes* (Madrid, 1951; reprint 1966)
Amelia Agostini [Bonelli] de Del Río, *El teatro cómico de Cervantes* (Madrid, 1965: offprint from *BRAE*)
Bruce W. Wardropper, study on the *comedias* of C. in *Suma cervantina*, ed. J. B. Avalle-Arce and E. C. Riley (London, 1971)
Miguel de Cervantes Saavedra, *Comedias y entremeses*, ed. R. Schevill and A. Bonilla, 6 vols. (Madrid, 1915-22)
——, *Entremeses*, ed. Miguel Herrero García, CC 125 (Madrid, 1945)
——, *El cerco de Numancia*, ed. R. Marrast, Anaya 24 (Salamanca and Madrid, 1961)

(For minor dramatists, see the bibliographical sections in J. P. Wickersham Crawford, *Spanish Drama before Lope* . . . and Alfredo Hermenegildo, *Los trágicos españoles* . . .)

Chapter 3

(a) *Bibliographical*
Lope de Vega Studies 1937-1962. A Critical Survey and Annotated Bibliography, general editors J. A. Parker and A. M. Fox (Toronto, 1964)
Raymond L. Grismer, *Bibliography of Lope de Vega*, 2 vols. (Minneapolis, 1965)

(b) *Biographical*
Hugo Albert Rennert, *The Life of Lope de Vega* (Glasgow, 1904, and reprints).

Américo Castro and Hugo Albert Rennert, *Vida de Lope de Vega* (*1562-1635*) (Salamanca, Madrid, etc., 1968)

(c) *Other Books*

Joaquín de Entrambasaguas y Peña, *Estudios sobre L. de V.*, 3 vols. (Madrid, 1946-58)

Arturo Farinelli, *L. de V. en Alemania* (Barcelona, 1936)

Rinaldo Froldi, *L. de V. y la formación de la comedia: en torno a la tradición dramática valenciana y al primer teatro de L.* (Salamanca, Madrid, etc., 1968)

José Francisco Gatti (ed.), *El teatro de L. de V.: artículos y estudios* (Buenos Aires, 1962)

Diego Marín, *La intriga secundaria en el teatro de L. de V.* (Toronto and Mexico, 1958)

——, *Uso y función de la versificación dramática en L. de V.* (Valencia, 1962)

M. Menéndez Pelayo, *Estudios sobre el teatro de L. de V.*, 6 vols., Ed. Nacional (Santander, 1949) [the studies from his ed. of the *Obras* for the Real Academia]

Ramón Menéndez Pidal, *De Cervantes y Lope de Vega*, Austral 120 (Madrid, 1940, and reprints)

José F. Montesinos, *Estudios sobre L. de V.* (Mexico, 1951, and Salamanca, Madrid, etc., 1967)

S. G. Morley and Courtney Bruerton, *The Chronology of L. de V.'s comedias, with a Discussion of Doubtful Attributions, the Whole Based on a Study of his Strophic Versification* (New York, etc., 1940)

——, *Cronología de las comedias de L. de V. Con un examen...*, revised Spanish ed. (Madrid, 1968)

S. G. Morley and R. W. Tyler, *Los nombres de personajes en las comedias de L. de V.: estudio de onamatología*, 2 vols. (Berkeley and Los Angeles, 1961)

Edward Nagy, *L. de V. y 'La Celestina': perspectiva seudocelestinesca en comedias de L.* (Mexico, 1968)

Luis C. Pérez and Federico Sánchez Escribano, *Afirmaciones de L. de V. sobre preceptiva dramática a base de cien comedias* (Madrid, 1961)

R. D. F. Pring-Mill, introduction to his ed. of *L. de V. (Five Plays)* trans. Jill Booty (New York, 1961)

Miguel Romera Navarro, *La preceptiva dramática de L. de V. y otros ensayos sobre el Fénix* (Madrid, 1935)

Noël Salomon, *Recherches sur le thème paysan dans la 'comedia' au temps de L. de V.* (Bordeaux, 1965)

Rudolph Schevill, *The Dramatic Art of L. de V. together with 'La dama boba'* (Berkeley, 1918)

(d) *Editions*

Obras, ed. of the Real Academia Española, 15 vols. (Madrid, 1890-1913) [vol. I contains a biography by C. A. de La Barrera; vols. II-XV texts of plays and studies by M. Menéndez Pelayo; the texts are not always reliable] [To complement the 4 vols. of Lope's *Comedias escogidas* edited for the *Biblioteca de Autores Españoles* by J. E. Hartzenbusch, with unreliable texts, between 1853 and 1860 (*BAE*, XXIV, XXXIV, XLI, LII) and the volume of non-dramatic works ed. by C. Rossell (XXXVIII [1856]), *BAE* has since 1963 been reprinting the Academia *Obras* in tomes numbered from VI onwards; up to 1969, this series had reached Tom. XXVII (*BAE*, vol. CCV)]

Obras (*nueva edición*), ed. of the Real Academia Española, 13 vols. (Madrid, 1916-30) [in reality, a new series, of plays not included in Menéndez Pelayo's, and with studies by E. Cotarelo y Mori and others]

Obras escogidas, ed. F. C. de Robles, vols. I and III: *Teatro* (Madrid, 1946, 1955 and reprints: texts not always reliable)

El acero de Madrid, ed. P. Mazzei (Florence, 1929)

Amar sin saber a quién, ed. Carmen Bravo-Villasante, Anaya 81 (Salamanca, Madrid, etc., 1967)

Barlaán y Josafat, ed. José F. Montesinos (Madrid, 1935)

Las bizarrías de Belisa [see below, under *El villano en su rincón*]

El Brasil restituido, ed. G. de Solenni (New York, 1929)

Las burlas veras, ed. S. L. Millard Rosenberg (Philadelphia, 1912)

El caballero de Olmedo, ed. Inés I. Macdonald (Cambridge, 1934, and reprints)

L. de V.'s 'El castigo del discreto'. Together with a Study of Conjugal Honor in his Theater, ed. William L. Fichter (New York, 1925)

El castigo sin venganza, ed. C. F. A. Van Dam (Groningen, 1929)

——, ed. C. A. Jones (Oxford, etc., 1966)

El conde Fernán González, ed. R. Marcus (Paris, 1963)

El cordobés valeroso Pedro Carbonero, ed. José F. Montesinos (Madrid, 1929)

El cuerdo loco, ed. José F. Montesinos (Madrid, 1922)

La dama boba, ed. Rudolph Schevill, with his *The Dramatic Art of L. de V.* (Berkeley, 1918) [see also under *Fuenteovejuna* and *Peribáñez* ...]

El desdén vengado, ed. M. M. Harlan (New York, 1930)

La desdichada Estefanía, ed. J. H. Arjona (Valencia, 1967)

El duque de Viseo, ed. F. Ruiz Ramón (Madrid, 1966)

La fianza satisfecha, ed. W. M. Whitby and R. R. Anderson (Cambridge, 1971)

La fortuna adversa del infante don Fernando de Portugal (attr.): see A. E. Sloman, *The Sources of Calderón's 'El príncipe constante'* (Oxford, 1950)

Fuenteovejuna, ed. Américo Castro (Madrid, 1935)

——, ed. W. S. Mitchell (London, 1956)

——, *and La dama boba*, ed. E. W. Hesse (New York, 1964)

——, *(dos comedias)* [Lope's and Cristóbal de Monroy's], ed. F. López Estrada, C Ca 10 (Madrid, 1969)

El galán de la membrilla, ed D. Marín and E. Rugg (Madrid, 1962)

El marqués de las Navas, ed. José F. Montesinos (Madrid, 1925)

El mejor alcalde, el Rey, in L. de V., *Comedias I*, 2nd revised ed. by J. Gómez Ocerín and R. M. Tenreiro, CC 39 (Madrid, 1931)

El mejor mozo de España, ed. W. T. McCready, Anaya 75 (Salamanca, 1967)

La moza de cántaro, ed. C. González Echegaray, Anaya (Salamanca, 1968)

La nueva victoria de D. Gonzalo de Córdoba, ed. H. Ziomek (New York, 1962)

Las paces de los reyes y judía de Toledo, ed. J. A. Castañeda (Chapel Hill, 1962)

Peribáñez y el comendador de Ocaña, ed. Ch.-V. Aubrun and J. F. Montesinos (Paris, 1943, and reprints)

——, *y La dama boba*, ed. A. Zamora Vicente, CC 159 (Madrid, 1963)

El perro del hortelano, ed. E. Kohler (Paris, 1951)

Los Ramírez de Arellano, ed. D. Ramírez de Arellano (Madrid, 1954)

El remedio en la desdicha, ed. J. W. Barker (Cambridge, 1931, and reprint 1951)

——, in L. de V., *Comedias I*, 2nd revised ed. by J. Gómez Ocerín and R. M. Tenreiro, CC 39 (Madrid, 1931)

El sufrimiento premiado (attr.), ed. V. Dixon (London, 1967)

El villano en su rincón, ed. A. Zamora Vicente (Madrid, 1961)

El villano en su rincón, y Las bizarrías de Belisa, ed. A. Zamora Vicente, CC 157 (Madrid, 1963)

Chapter 4

Poetas dramáticos valencianos, ed. E. Juliá Martínez, 2 vols. (Madrid, 1929) [includes plays by Tárrega and Gaspar de Aguilar]
Dramáticos contemporáneos a Lope de Vega, ed. R. de Mesonero Romanos, 2 vols. (*BAE,* XLIII and XLV) (Madrid, 1857-58) [include plays by Tárrega, Gaspar de Aguilar, Guillén de Castro, Damián del Poyo, Mira de Amescua, Luis Vélez de Guevara, Godínez, Belmonte Bermúdez, Pérez de Montalbán, and others; the texts are not reliable]

Guillén de Castro y Bellvís, *Obras,* ed. E. Juliá Martínez, 3 vols. (Madrid, 1925-27)
——, *Las mocedades del Cid,* ed. V. Said Armesto, CC 15, 4th ed. (Madrid, 1945)

F. E. Spencer and Rudolph Schevill, *The Dramatic Works of Luis Vélez de Guevara* (Berkeley, 1937)
Luis Vélez de Guevara, *Reinar después de morir y El diablo está en Cantillana,* ed. M. Muñoz Cortés, CC 132 (Madrid, 1948)
——, *El embuste acreditado,* ed. A. G. Reichenberger (Granada, 1956)
——, *La niña de Gómez Arias,* ed. Ramón Rozzell (Granada, 1959)
——, *La serrana de la Vera,* ed. R. Menéndez Pidal and M. Goyri de Menéndez Pidal (Madrid, 1916)
——, *La serrana de la Vera,* ed. E. Rodríguez Cepeda, Aula Magna 9 (Madrid, 1967)

W. Poesse, *Ensayo de una bibliografía de Juan Ruiz de Alarcón y Mendoza* (Valencia, 1964)
Serge Denis, *La langue de J.R. de A.* (Paris, 1943)
Antonio Castro Leal, *J.R. de A., su vida y su obra* (Mexico, 1943)
Alva V. Ebersole, *El ambiente español visto por J. R. de A.* (Valencia, 1959)
Carmen Olga Brenes, *El sentimiento democrático en el teatro de J. R. de A.* (Valencia, 1960)
Ellen Claydon, *J. R. de A., Baroque Dramatist* (Chapel Hill, 1970)
Juan Ruiz de Alarcón, *Obras completas,* ed. A. Millares Carlo, 3 vols. (Mexico, 1957-68)

Juan Ruiz de Alarcón, *Teatro* [*La verdad sospechosa; Las paredes oyen*], ed. A. Reyes, CC 37 (Madrid, 1918)
Juan Ruiz de Alarcón, *Los pechos privilegiados, y Ganar amigos*, ed. A. Millares Carlo, CC 147 (Madrid, 1960)
——, *La prueba de las promesas, y El examen de maridos*, ed. A. Millares Carlo, CC 146 (Madrid, 1960)

Antonio Mira de Amescua, *Teatro I* [*El esclavo del demonio; Pedro Telonario (auto sacramental)*], ed. Á. Valbuena Prat, CC 70 (Madrid, 1928)
——, *Teatro II* [*La Fénix de Salamanca; El ejemplo mayor de la desdicha*], ed. Á. Valbuena Prat, CC 82 (Madrid, 1928)
——, *Adversa fortuna de don Álvaro de Luna*, ed. Luigi de Filippo (Florence, 1960)
——, *La segunda de don Álvaro* [*Adversa fortuna . . .*] ed. N. E. Sánchez-Arce (Mexico, 1960)

Hannah E. Bergman, *Luis Quiñones de Benavente y sus entremeses* (Madrid, 1965)

Chapter 5

(a) *Tirso de Molina. Ensayos sobre la biografía y la obra del P. M. Fray Gabriel Téllez, por Revista Estudios* (Madrid, 1949) [contains an extensive general bibliography by Everett W. Hesse]
Esmeralda Gijón Zapata, *El humor en Tirso de Molina* (Madrid, 1959)
Ángel López, *El cancionero popular en el teatro de T. de M.* (Madrid, 1958)
Ivy L. McClelland, *T. de M.: Studies in Dramatic Realism* (Liverpool, 1948)
Guido Mancini and others, *Studi tirsiani* (Milan, 1958)
Mario Penna, *Don Giovanni e il misterio di Tirso* (Turin, 1958)
Karl Vossler, *Lecciones sobre T. de M.* (Madrid, 1965)

(b) Tirso de Molina, *Obras dramáticas completas*, ed. Blanca de los Ríos de Lampérez, 3 vols. (Madrid, 1946-58, and reprints)
——, *Comedias*, ed. E. Cotarelo y Mori, 2 vols., *NBAE*, 4 and 9 (Madrid, 1906-07)
——, *Obras I* [*El vergonzoso en palacio; El burlador de Sevilla*], ed. Américo Castro, CC 2 (Madrid, 1910)

Tirso de Molina, *Comedias II. El amor médico y Averigüelo Vargas*, ed. A. Zamora Vicente y M.ª J. Canellada de Zamora, CC 131 (Madrid, 1947)

——, *Antona García*, ed. Margaret Wilson (Manchester, 1957)

——, *El burlador de Sevilla*, ed. J. E. Varey and N. D. Shergold (Cambridge, 1952)

——, ——, ed. G. E. Wade (New York, 1969)

——, *El burlador de Sevilla and La prudencia en la mujer*, ed. R. R. MacCurdy (New York, 1965)

——, *El condenado por desconfiado*, ed. Américo Castro (Madrid, 1919)

——, ——, ed. A. González Palencia, Ebro 1 (Saragossa, 1939)

——, *Por el sótano y el torno*, ed. A. Zamora Vicente (Buenos Aires, 1949)

——, *La prudencia en la mujer*, ed. W. McFadden (Liverpool, 1933)

——, ——, ed. A. Huntington Bushee and L. Lavery Stafford (Mexico, 1948)

——, *La venganza de Tamar*, ed. A. K. G. Paterson (Cambridge, 1969)

Chapter 6

Biography

Cristóbal Pérez Pastor, *Documentos para la biografía de D. Pedro Calderón de la Barca*, I [all published] (Madrid, 1905)

Emilio Cotarelo y Mori, *Ensayo sobre la vida y obras de D. Pedro Calderón de la Barca*, I [all published] (Madrid, 1924)

Narciso Alonso Cortés, 'Algunos datos relativos a don Pedro Calderón', *RFE*, I (1915), 41-51

José Simón Díaz, *Historia del Colegio Imperial de Madrid*, 2 vols. (Madrid, 1952-59)

Florencio Marcos Rodríguez, 'Un pleito de D. Pedro Calderón de la Barca', *RABM*, LXVII (1959), 717-31

Edward M. Wilson, 'Fray Hortensio Paravicino's protest against *El Príncipe constante*', *Ibérida, Revista Filológica* (Rio de Janeiro), No. 6, 245-66; 'Un memorial perdido de don Pedro Calderón'—to appear in the Festschrift in honour of Professor William L. Fichter; 'Calderón y el Patriarca'—to appear in the Festschrift in honour of Professor Hans Flasche

E. Juliá Martínez, 'Calderón en Toledo', *RFE*, XXV (1941), 182-204

General Works

Marcelino Menéndez y Pelayo, *Calderón y su teatro* (Madrid, 1881) (Old-fashioned approach)

A. A. Parker, 'The father-son conflict in the drama of Calderón, *FMLS*, II (1966), 288-99

B. W. Wardropper, *Critical Essays on the Theatre of Calderón* (New York, 1965) (Essays by various hands on general questions and on particular plays)

Ángel Valbuena Prat, *Calderón* (Madrid, 1941)

Dámaso Alonso, *Seis calas en la expresión literaria española* (Madrid, 1951), Ch. IV

A. E. Sloman, *The Dramatic Craftsmanship of Calderón* (Oxford, 1958)

A. A. Parker, 'Metáfora y símbolo en la interpretación de Calderón', *Actas I* (Oxford, 1964)

Edward M. Wilson, 'La poesía dramática de don Pedro Calderón de la Barca', *Litterae Hispanae et Lusitanae—Festschrift zum fünfzig-jährigen Bestehen des Ibero-Amerikanischen Forschungsinstituts der Universität Hamburg* (Munich, 1968)

——, 'The four elements in the imagery of Calderón', *MLR*, XXXI (1936), 34-47

——, with J. Sage, *Poesías líricas en las obras dramaticas de Calderón —citas y glosas* (London, 1964)

Editions

The four volumes in the *Biblioteca de Autores Españoles* (VII, IX, XII, XIV), edited by Juan Eugenio Hartzenbusch, are badly printed and unreliable; their pagination in different reprints remains the same, so they are useful to refer to.

The *Aguilar* edition in three volumes, by Ángel Valbuena Briones and Ángel Valbuena Prat, has rather better texts; it does not contain the plays written in collaboration.

The following editions of single plays and *autos* are to be commended:

El sitio de Bredá, ed. Johanna R. Shrek (The Hague, 1957)
El príncipe constante, ed. A. A. Parker (Cambridge, 1968)
Casa con dos puertas mala es de guardar, ed. G. T. Northup, in *Three Plays by Calderón* (Boston, etc., 1926) [mildly expurgated]

El Mágico prodigioso to appear shortly, ed. A. A. Parker & Melveena McKendrick

La vida es sueño, ed. Milton A. Buchanan (Toronto, 1910)

——, ed. E. W. Hesse (New York, 1961)

——, ed. A. E. Sloman (Manchester, 1961)

El alcalde de Zalamea, ed. M. Krenkel (Leipzig, 1887)

——, ed. R. Marrast (Paris, 1959)

——, ed. P. N. Dunn (Oxford, 1966)

La hija del aire (dos partes), edited by Gwynne Edwards (London, 1970)

En la vida todo es verdad y todo mentira, to appear shortly edited by D. W. Cruickshank

No hay más Fortuna que Dios, ed. A. A. Parker (Manchester, 1949, 1962)

El pleito matrimonial del cuerpo y el alma, ed. Manfred Engelbert (Hamburg, 1969)

Obras menores (*Siglos XVII y XVIII*), ed. A. Pérez Gómez (Cieza, 1969)

Psalle et sile, ed. Leopoldo Trenor (Valencia, 1930-39)

Autos

A. A. Parker, *The Allegorical Drama of Calderón* (Oxford, 1943)

Á. Valbuena Prat, 'Los autos de Calderón: clasificación y análisis', *RH*, LXI (1924)

Eugenio Frutos, *La filosofía de Calderón en sus autos sacramentales* (Saragossa, 1952)

N. D. Shergold and J. E. Varey, *Los autos sacramentales en Madrid en la época de Calderón, 1637-1681* (Madrid, 1961)

Single works and groups of works
El príncipe constante

Edward M. Wilson and W. J. Entwistle, 'Calderón's *Príncipe constante*: two appreciations', *MLR*, XXXIV (1939), 207-22

B. W. Wardropper, 'Christian and Moor in Calderón's *EPC*', *MLR*, LIII (1958), 512-20

Carlos Ortigoza Vieyra, *Los móviles de la comedia: EPC* (Mexico, 1957)

A. E. Sloman, *The sources of Calderón's EPC* (Oxford, 1950)

Comedias de capa y espada

B. W. Wardropper, 'Calderón's comedy and his serious view of life', *Studies in Honor of Nicholson B. Adams* (Chapel Hill, 1966), pp. 179-93

La devoción de la Cruz

W. J. Entwistle, 'Calderón's *EDDLC*', *BH*, L (1948), 472-82

A. A. Parker, 'Santos y bandoleros en el teatro español del Siglo de Oro', *Arbor*, Nos. 43-4 (1949)

El Mágico prodigioso

W. J. Entwistle, 'Justina's temptation: an approach to the understanding of Calderón', *MLR*, XL (1945), 180-9

T. E. May, 'The symbolism of *EMP*', *RR*, LIV (1963), 95-112

A. A. Parker, 'The role of the *graciosos* in *EMP*', *Litterae Hispanae et Lusitanae* . . .

El médico de su honra

B. W. Wardropper, 'Poetry and drama in Calderón's *EMDSH*', *RR*, XLIX (1958), 3-11

D. W. Cruickshank, 'Calderón's King Pedro: just or unjust?', *Spanische Forschungen der Görresgesellschaft: Gesammelte Aufsätze zur Kulturgeschichte Spaniens*, XXV (1970), 113-32

A secreto agravio secreta venganza

Edward M. Wilson, 'La discreción de don Lope de Almeida', *Clavileño*, 9 (1951), 1-10

La vida es sueño

Arturo Farinelli, *La vita è un sogno*, 2 vols. (Turin, 1916)

For English criticisms of this play see:

R. Pring-Mill, 'Los calderonistas de habla inglesa y *LVES*', *Litterae Hispanae et Lusitanae* . . .

Lionel Abel, *Metatheatre—A New View of Dramatic Form* (New York, 1963), pp. 59-72

El alcalde de Zalamea

A. E. Sloman, 'Scene division in *EADZ*', *HR*, XIX (1951), 66-71

C. A. Jones, '*Honor* in *EADZ*', *MLR*, L (1955), 444-9

La cisma de Ingalaterra

A. A. Parker, 'Henry VIII in Shakespeare and Calderón', *MLR*, XLIII (1948), 327-52

El pintor de su deshonra

A. A. Parker, 'Towards a definition of Calderonian tragedy', *BHS*, XXXIX (1962), 222-37

A. K. G. Paterson, 'The comic and tragic melancholy of Juan Roca: a study of Calderón's *EPDSD*', *FMLS*, V (1969), 244-61

Las armas de la hermosura

A. A. Parker, 'History and poetry: the Coriolanus theme in Calderón', *Hispanic Studies in Honour of I. González Llubera* (Oxford, 1959), pp. 211-24

La hija del aire, I and II

G. Edwards, 'Calderón's *LHDA* in the light of his sources', *BHS*, XLIII (1966), 177-96

——, 'Calderón's *LHDA* and the classical type of tragedy', *BHS*, XLIV (1967), 161-94

Mythological plays

W. G. Chapman, 'Las comedias mitológicas de Calderón', *RdeL*, V (1954), 35-67

Eco y Narciso

Ch. V. Aubrun, Preface to his edition of this play (Paris, 1961)

E. W. Hesse, 'The terrible mother image in Calderón's *EyN*', *RN,* I (1959-60), 133-6

——, 'Estructura e interpretación de una comedia de Calderón', *BBMP*, XXXIV (1963), 57-72

La estatua de Prometeo

Ch. V. Aubrun, Preface to his edition of this play (Paris, 1961)

Los encantos de la culpa

Hans Flasche, 'Die Struktur des Auto Sacramental *LEDLC* von Calderón', *Arbeits Gemeinschaft für Forschung des Landes Nordrhein-Westfalen*, CL (1968)

Entremeses

Kenneth R. Scholberg, 'Las obras cortas de Calderón', *Clavileño*, 25 (1954), 13-19

Non-dramatic works

Edward M. Wilson, 'A key to Calderón's *Psalle et sile*', *Hispanic Studies in honour of I. González Llubera* (Oxford, 1959), 429-40

Edward M. Wilson, 'Seven *aprobaciones* by Don Pedro Calderón de la Barca', *Studia Philologica—Homenaje ofrecido a Dámaso Alonso,* III (Madrid, 1963), 605-18

Edward M. Wilson, 'Calderón y Fuenterrabía: el *Panegírico al Almirante de Castilla*', *BRAE*, XLIX (1969), 253-78

The early editions of Calderón

Calderón's texts are often defective because of the lack of adequate study of the seventeenth-century editions and manuscripts. The following studies are recommended to those who are curious about such questions. They represent only the preliminary stages of the investigation.

Miguel de Toro y Gisbert, '¿Conocemos el texto verdadero de las comedias de Calderón?', *BRAE*, V (1918), 401-21, 531-49; VI (1919), 1-12, 307-31.

H. C. Heaton, 'On the *Segunda parte* of Calderón', *HR*, V (1937), 209-37

E. W. Hesse, *Vera Tassis' Text of Calderón's Plays* (Mexico, 1941)

——, 'The two versions of *El laurel de Apolo*', *HR*, XIV (1946), 213-34

——, 'The first and second editions of Calderón's *Cuarta parte*', *HR*, XVI (1948), 209-37

——, 'The publication of Calderón's plays in the seventeenth century', *PQ*, XXVII (1948), 37-51

Edward M. Wilson, 'The two editions of Calderón's *Primera parte* of 1640', *The Library* (1959), 175-91

——, 'On the Pando editions of Calderón's *autos*', *HR*, XXVII (1959), 324-44

——, 'Further notes on the Pando editions of Calderón's *autos*', *HR*, XXX (1962), 296-303

——, 'Calderón's *Primera parte de autos sacramentales* and Don Pedro de Pando y Mier', *BHS*, XXXVI (1960), 16-28

——, 'Notas sobre algunos manuscritos calderonianos en Madrid y en Toledo', *RABM*, LXVIII (1960), 477-87

Edward M. Wilson, 'La edición príncipe de *Fieras afemina Amor* de don Pedro Calderón', *RBAM*, XXIV (70), (1961) 7-28
——, 'On the *Tercera parte* of Calderón—1664', *Studies in Bibliography*, XV (1962), 223-30
D. W. Cruickshank, 'Calderón's Handwriting', *MLR*, LXV (1970), 66-77
——, 'The Printing of Calderón's *Tercera parte*', *Studies in Bibliography*, XXIII (1970), 230-51
——, 'Calderón's *Primera* and *Tercera partes*: the Reprints of "1640" and "1664"', *The Library* (1970), 105-19.

Chapter 7

Dramáticos posteriores a Lope de Vega, ed. R. de Mesonero Romanos, 2 vols. (*BAE*, XLVII and XLIX) (Madrid, 1858-59 and reprints) [include plays by Solís, Cubillo de Aragón, Matos Fragoso, Leiva Ramírez de Arellano, Enríquez Gómez, 'Fernando de Zárate', Juan Vélez de Guevara, Diamante, Monroy y Silva, Monteser, Juan de la Hoz y Mota, Salazar y Torres, Sor Juana Inés de la Cruz, Bances Candamo, and others; the texts are not always reliable]

Ruth Lee Kennedy, *The Dramatic Art of Moreto* (Northampton, Mass., 1931-32) [*Smith College Studies in Modern Languages,* vol. XIII, Nos. 1-4]
Frank P. Casa, *The Dramatic Craftsmanship of Moreto* (Cambridge, Mass., 1966)
Agustín Moreto y Cabaña, *Comedias escogidas,* ed. Luis Fernández-Guerra y Orbe, *BAE,* XXXIX (Madrid, 1856; reprint 1950) [texts not always reliable]
——, *Teatro* [*El lindo don Diego; El desdén con el desdén*], ed. Narciso Alonso Cortés, CC 32 (Madrid, 1916)
——, *El poder de la amistad,* ed. D. E. Dedrick (Valencia, 1968)

Raymond R. MacCurdy, *Francisco de Rojas Zorrilla: bibliografía crítica* (Madrid, 1965) [*Cuadernos bibliográficos,* XVIII]
——, *Francisco de Rojas Zorrilla and the Tragedy* (Albuquerque, 1958)
Francisco de Rojas Zorrilla, *Comedias escogidas,* ed. R. de Mesonero Romanos, *BAE,* LV (Madrid, 1861)
——, *Teatro* [*Del Rey abajo ninguno; Entre bobos anda el juego*], 3rd revised ed. by F. Ruiz Morcuende, CC 35 (Madrid, 1944)

Francisco de Rojas Zorrilla, *II: Morir pensando matar y La vida en al ataúd,* ed. R. R. Maccurdy, CC 153 (Madrid, 1961)
——, *Cada qual lo que le toca y La viña de Nabot,* ed. Américo Castro (Madrid, 1917)
——, *Donde ay agravios no ay celos,* ed. B. Wittmann (Geneva and Paris, 1962)
——, *Lucrecia y Tarquino,* ed R. R. MacCurdy (Albuquerque, 1963)
——, *Obligados y ofendidos y gorrón de Salamanca,* ed. R. R. Mac-Curdy, Anaya 26 (Salamanca, 1963)

Álvaro Cubillo de Aragón, *Las muñecas de Marcela; El señor de Noches Buenas,* ed. Á. Valbuena Prat (Madrid, 1928)

Daniel E. Martell, *The Dramas of D. Antonio Solís y Rivadeneyra* (Philadelphia, 1902)
Antonio Solís y Rivadeneyra, *Amor y obligación,* ed. E. Juliá Martínez (Madrid, 1930)

Antonio Coello y Ochoa, *El conde de Sex, o dar la vida por su dama,* in *Dramáticos contemporáneos de Lope de Vega,* II, ed. R. Mesonero Romanos, *BAE,* XLV (Madrid, 1858), 403-20

Juan Vélez de Guevara, *Los celos hacen estrellas,* ed. J. E. Varey y N. D. Shergold, con una ed. y estudio de la música por J. Sage (London, 1970)

Sor Juana Inés de la Cruz, *Obras completas,* ed. A. Méndez Plancarte, vols. III *(Autos y loas)* and IV *(Comedias, sainetes y prosa)* (Mexico and Buenos Aires, 1955, 1957)

Francisco Cuervo-Arango y González-Carvajal, *Don Francisco Antonio de Bances y López-Candamo. Estudio bio-bibliográfico y crítico* (Madrid, 1916)
Francisco Bances Candamo, *Theatro de los theatros de los passados y presentes siglos,* ed. D. W. Moir (London, 1970)
——, *El esclavo en grillos de oro. Estudio sobre teatro político palaciego y ed. de D. W. Moir* [at press]

INDEX

INDEX